Landscapes: the Arts, Aesth

Volume 30

This series aims to provide conceptual and empirical research in arts education, (including music, visual arts, drama, dance, media, and poetry), in a variety of areas related to the post-modern paradigm shift. The changing cultural, historical, and political contexts of arts education are recognized to be central to learning, experience, knowledge. The books in this series present theories and methodological approaches used in arts education research as well as related disciplines - including philosophy, sociology, anthropology and psychology of arts education. The series editor invites you to contact her with plans and ideas for books that would fit in the series. For more information on how to submit a proposal, please write to Associate Editor, Lay Peng, Ang. E-mail: laypeng.ang@springer.com

All proposals and manuscripts submitted to the Series will be subject to external peer review.

More information about this series at http://www.springer.com/series/6199

Kari Holdhus • Regina Murphy
Magne I. Espeland
Editors

Music Education as Craft

Reframing Theories and Practices

 Springer

Editors
Kari Holdhus 🆔
Department of Arts Education
Western Norway University of Applied
Sciences
Stord, Norway

Regina Murphy 🆔
School of Arts Education and Movement,
DCU Institute of Education
Dublin City University
Dublin, Ireland

Magne I. Espeland 🆔
Western Norway University of Applied
Sciences
Stord, Norway

ISSN 1573-4528   ISSN 2214-0069   (electronic)
Landscapes: the Arts, Aesthetics, and Education
ISBN 978-3-030-67706-0   ISBN 978-3-030-67704-6   (eBook)
https://doi.org/10.1007/978-3-030-67704-6

This Springer imprint is published by the registered company Springer Nature Switzerland AG
The registered company address is: Gewerbestrasse 11, 6330 Cham, Switzerland

Preface

When a colleague is fortunate enough to experience a long professional life in the service of music education, it often opens up a special page for reflection on the landscape of a life's work and the significance of its contribution. It is not surprising, then, that several colleagues in music education were instinctively drawn to the idea of creating a Festschrift for their Norwegian colleague, Magne Espeland, in honour of his career as a music educator, researcher, and national and international influencer in music education. In addition to his close colleagues, a quick glance through his comprehensive work created the impression of Magne as a true academic cosmopolite. Any Festschrift, therefore, would have to be international, and not confined to contexts within Norway or Scandinavia per se. At first, the idea of bestowing the honour as something of a surprise, to be revealed on a given date, seemed to be the standard procedure. But on reflection of Magne's expansive and inclusive style, it was clear that a more meaningful approach would involve Magne himself in the crafting of this work: hence, the emergence of a title and editors.

There followed then, an invitation to this book's contributors, where Magne wrote:

Lately, I find myself increasingly wondering whether it is possible to describe something we more or less generally and specifically could discuss as "the 'craft' of Music Education", and where such a "craft" might be heading in the future. Interpretations of the word "craft" are many, but quite similar meanings are found across a number of origins and cultures in Western Societies. An old English and continental use was associated with power, physical strength, might, skill. The old Norse word was "kraptr", meaning strength and virtue. Later the meaning of "craft" has also expanded to include something skilfully built and made.

Music education today has many meanings, many underpinning theories, and many practices. In my professional career, the focus of my interest has primarily been on music education for all, rather than the few. This means that my invitation to focus on the future "craft" of music education is primarily concerned with the future potential of this discipline for school music, for children and young people, and the amateur adult. However, just as in other art disciplines, there are obvious connections between the education of all and the few.

The long question I ask, and which such an anthology could contribute an answer to, is as follows: How should the diverse and long traditions of music education "crafts" respond to a rapidly changing environment in society and education? How could music education conceived of as "craft" contribute to creative and sustainable solutions to societal and educational challenges created by multiculturalism, globalisation, technology and accountability? And what kind of music education skills, virtues, and rationale (kraptrs) need to be changed, modified, developed, invented, dismissed or kept? How, and for what reasons and to what ends?

So, here it is—the result of numerous discussions, questions, interactions and reflections. To us, the concept of "craft" has grown throughout the process, becoming deeper and more unifying over time, while remaining polyphonic enough to relate to its proponents and disciplines. The process of honing "the craft" has been developed collectively by authors, editors and reviewers, resulting in an emergent but iterative process that is captured in the chapters presented here. It should be noted, however, that the diversity of the chapters and the comprehensive elucidations of "craft" are intended since we have applied few caveats to interpretations. Likewise, we have afforded an open approach to concepts central to (music) education, such as "knowledge", "learning", "teaching" and others. Some of the chapters thus contain elements that may be viewed as contradictory to each other in their interpretation and utilisation of concepts. For example, a number of authors reference Aristotle's concept of "intellectual virtues" as forms of knowledge, while others categorise Aristotelian virtues differently, depending on the author's intentions. As a principle, we have chosen not to unify or standardise conceptual interpretations of such kind.

It is our hope, however, that the book and its chapters will enable further dialogue, debate, discussion and interpretations of what crafts in music education are and should be. To this end, we encourage music educators outside the global North especially to join the discussion of what the "craft" in music education is, and ought to be, in the context of globalisation, sustainability and social justice throughout the world in the Covid-19 era and beyond.

Stord, Norway   Kari Holdhus

Dublin, Ireland   Regina Murphy

Stord, Norway   Magne I. Espeland
October 2020

Contents

Part I   Opening

**Craftsmanship in Academia: Skilled Improvisation
in Research, Teaching, and Leadership**   3
Liora Bresler

**Conceptualising Music Education as "Craft":
Responses to an Invitation**   13
Kari Holdhus and Regina Murphy

Part II   "Music Education" as a Sustainable Craft in Society

The Craft of Music Teaching in a Changing Society   27
Geir Johansen

**Crafting Music Education for All? The Composite Knowledge
Base of Music Education in Times of Cultural Diversity
and Social Polarisation**   39
Petter Dyndahl and Siw Graabræk Nielsen

**Music Education in England as a Political Act:
Reflections on a Craft Under Pressure**   51
Martin Fautley

Educating Music Teachers for the Future: The Crafts of Change   63
Catharina Christophersen

Part III   Music Education Practices Reframed

**The Craft of Music Teaching in a Changing Society:
Singing as Meaning, Education, and Craft – Reflections
on Lithuanian Singing Practices**   77
Rūta Girdzijauskienė

Artistic Citizenship and the Crafting of Mutual Musical Care   89
Brynjulf Stige

Music Listening: An Evolution of Craft   105
Jody L. Kerchner

The Craft of (Re-)Presenting Musical Works.   117
Randi Margrethe Eidsaa

**Developing Craftsmanship in Music Education
in a Palestinian Refugee Camp and Lebanese Schools**   133
Signe Kalsnes

**A Creative Global Science Classroom:
Crafting the Global Science Opera**   151
Kathryn Urbaniak, Vivek Venkatesh, and Oded Ben-Horin

**The Craft of Teaching Musical Improvisation
Improvisationally: Towards a Theoretical Framework**.   165
Nick Sorensen

Phronesis **in Music Education**   181
Tiri Bergesen Schei

**Approaching Vulnerability Through Contemporary Music:
The Gelland Approach**   191
Erkki Huovinen

The *Kraptr* **of Aging Folk Musicians: Mental Practice for the Future**   207
Eva Sæther

Music Education as Craft: Reframing a Rationale   219
Magne I. Espeland

About the Editors

Kari Holdhus is Professor of Music Education at the Western Norway University of Applied Sciences. Her research interests include relational pedagogy, dialogic musical encounters, creative teaching and learning as well as pedagogical improvisation. She completed her PhD in 2014 with the title: *Star experiences or gym hall aesthetics? A study of musicians' quality conceptions in visiting school concerts*, in which she explicitly studied communication processes between musicians, teachers and pupils in visiting music practices and musical partnerships. From 2017 to 2020, Kari held the role of project lead on an innovative project that focused on professional guest concerts in Norwegian schools, titled *School and concert, from transmission to dialogue* (DiSko), funded by the Norwegian Research Council. DiSko aimed at developing alternative and more relationally oriented forms of music visits in schools, by initiating and emphasising dialogic encounters between musicians, teachers and pupils, thus fostering pupils' agency and creativity. The project methodology was Educational Design Research, a design based research method which is both researcher-initiated and researcher-led, while also employing participatory and exploratory techniques. Kari has also served as co-researcher in the project, *Improvisation in Teacher Education*. This work explored how pedagogical improvisation could be used and developed as a major vehicle for all kinds of teachers, teacher educators and preservice teachers in their approach to classroom work. Kari's most recent research involves a collaboration with other researchers titled *Music teacher education for the future*. The purpose of this research is to explore ways of developing music teacher education in a number of ways, including through mapping and discussing students' approaches to their future lives as public music educators. As a teacher, Kari emphasises research-based approaches, which means that her teaching and supervision is often based on recent research deemed relevant for student discussion and critique. Conversely, many of the research projects that Kari engages with focus on practical applications to educational contexts.

Regina Murphy is Associate Professor and Head of the School of Arts Education and Movement at the Institute of Education, Dublin City University. As a teacher educator at undergraduate, postgraduate and doctoral levels, she is concerned with the interplay between teacher knowledge, teacher identity, inquiry and critical reflection, and its expression through a range of subject matter. Recently, she initiated the reconceptualisation of music education within the 4-year BEd programme towards a specialist pathway on socially inclusive music education for primary teachers. Her most recent research focuses on the development of social inclusion and social justice in music education. She is also concerned with expressions of, and assessment of creativity in e-portfolios, especially in music education contexts. In 2019, she led a study on creativity and inclusion in showcase musical events in schools funded by the Creative Ireland programme, an all-of-government, interagency culture and wellbeing programme that inspires and transforms people, places and communities through creativity. Regina also leads a team of researchers at DCU on the evaluation of Creative Schools (2018–2022), the flagship initiative of the Creative Ireland programme, commissioned by the Arts Council. Throughout her practice and research endeavours, she seeks to explore transformational and empowering experiences that foster teacher and pupil agency towards informed, inspired, creative and inclusive educational experiences. Previous roles have included primary teacher in Ireland, England and New Zealand, and Education Officer for music education at primary level with the National Council for Curriculum and Assessment in the development of the 1999 curriculum. Regina served as an elected board member for the International Society for Music Education (ISME) from 2008 to 2012. In 2016, she hosted the ISME Commission Seminar: Music in Schools and Teacher Education (MISTEC) at St Patrick's Campus, DCU. At national level, she co-founded the Society for Music Education in Ireland in 2010 and since then has served as committee member in various roles and in hosting several national conferences.

Magne I. Espeland is Professor of Music and Education at Western Norway University of Applied Sciences (WNUAS). His areas of specialisation include curriculum development and innovation in music and arts education, educational design studies, quantitative and qualitative research methodologies for education, masters and PhD supervision, and research project leadership. He currently leads the Center of Creativities, Arts and Science in Education (CASE), which is home to research and development projects at the intersection of arts, science and creative education at WNUAS. Recently he has worked as an advisor and research evaluator for the Swedish Research Council, and is currently conducting similar work for the Portuguese Research Council. He was one of the founders of the Grieg Research School in Interdisciplinary Music Studies, a multi-institutional cooperation among institutions in Western Norway. Nationally, he has chaired and served on a number of Ministerial Committees from 1994 onwards, such as the new national curricula in music (1997), music teacher education (2010), and the national Ministerial Expert Committee on art and culture in education (2014). Internationally, Magne has had a long relationship with the International Society for Music Education (ISME) where he was a commissioner and commission chair for the Music in Schools and Teacher Education Commission (MISTEC). He also served on the ISME board. In 2002, he chaired *Samspel,* the 25th ISME World Conference and Music Festival in Bergen. Magne is a well-known as a clinician, researcher and speaker in numerous contexts, and has given keynote addresses in many countries and at various conferences, such as RIME in the UK, SMEI in Ireland, and EAS in Lithuania. He has researched and published in a variety of fields within music education and beyond, spanning music listening, music composition, creative pedagogies, pedagogical improvisation and relational pedagogy. Since 1994, he has presented numerous academic research papers at major international conferences, e.g., AERA, BERA, ECER, RIME, ISME, EAPRIL and EAS.

About the Contributors

Oded Ben-Horin is Head of the Arts Education Department at Western Norway University of Applied Sciences. He coordinates the Global Science Opera, and is a co-developer of that concept. Oded's research focuses on trans-disciplinary, creative and improvisational educational settings in which inquiry in both art and science occurs simultaneously. He has coordinated several European projects during which those settings were implemented and evaluated.

Liora Bresler is Professor Emerita at the College of Education at the University of Illinois at Champaign. A co-founder and co-editor of the *International Journal for Arts and Education* (1999–2010), Bresler has served as an editor for the book series: *Landscapes: Aesthetics, Arts and Education* (Springer) (2004-present). She has given 145 keynotes and invited talks in five continents and thirty- five countries. Her work has been translated into Spanish, French, German, Lithuanian, Hebrew, Chinese, and Korean.

Catharina Christophersen is professor of music education at Western Norway University of Applied Sciences, where she leads the research project *Music Teacher Education for the Future* (*FUTURED 2019–2022*). Previously she led the research programme, *Arts, Creativites, and Cultural Practices.* She regularly presents in international research conferences, and has published in international journals as well as edited volumes and books. Her research includes studies of creative partnerships, music in schools, music teacher education, game-based music learning, and social justice in music education.

Petter Dyndahl is professor of musicology, music education and general education at the Inland Norway University of Applied Sciences. He has published research results in a wide range of disciplines, including music education, sociology of education and culture, cultural studies, popular music studies, music technology and media pedagogy. In recent years, professor Dyndahl has been project manager for

the research projects *Musical gentrification and socio-cultural diversities* (2013–2017), and *DYNAMUS – The social dynamics of musical upbringing and
schooling in the Norwegian welfare state* (2018–2022). Both projects have been
funded by The Research Council of Norway.

Randi Margrethe Eidsaa is associate professor of music didactics at the University
of Agder, Norway. In 2015 she completed her doctoral study on creative concert
productions for professional musicians and children. Eidsaa teaches musicology,
music pedagogy, concert production and composition. She has produced several
artistic performances together with music students, children and professional performers. From 2015 to 2019 she was in charge of the concert and research project
Musical Dialogues in Conflict Areas, a collaboration with musicians from Armenia,
Bosnia-Herzegovina, Israel and Palestine. She is a member and co-leader of the
research group *Art and conflict,* and her latest publication is "Narratives from
Sarajevo. We didn't let the music die" in Böhnish and Eidsaa (2019) *Art and
Conflict: Theatre, Music and Visual Arts in Context.* She is currently involved in a
pilot project focusing on entrepreneurship and interdisciplinary collaboration in
higher music performance education.

Martin Fautley is Professor of Education at Birmingham City University in the
UK. After many years as a classroom music teacher, he then undertook full-time
doctoral research in the education and music faculties at Cambridge University,
investigating teaching, learning, and assessment of classroom music making. He
has authored ten books, including *Assessment in Music Education*, published by
Oxford University Press, and has written and published over sixty journal articles,
book chapters, and academic research papers on various aspects of music teaching
and learning. He is co-editor of the *British Journal of Music Education.*

Rūta Girdzijauskienė is Professor of Lithuanian Academy of Music and Theatre,
and president of the Lithuanian Music Teachers' Association. She is a board member of the *European Association for Music in Schools (EAS), European Network for
Music Educators and Researchers of Young Children* (EuNET MERYC). The list of
her publications includes two monographs, ten teacher handbooks, more than 80
research studies and practice-based articles. She is co-author of Lithuanian music
education programs and music textbooks. Her research interests lie in the fields of
early childhood music education, musical creativity, vocal pedagogy and teacher
education.

Erkki Huovinen is Professor of Music Education at the Royal College of Music in
Stockholm, Sweden. He originally studied musicology, philosophy, and classical
languages at the University of Turku, Finland, receiving his doctorate in musicology
in 2002 on a topic regarding the perception of tonality. Since then, Huovinen's
research has spanned the psychology of music (e.g., musical imagery, music reading), music education (e.g., creativity, improvisation, composition) and the philosophy of music.

Geir Johansen is professor emeritus of music education and music didactics at the Norwegian Academy of Music, holding a PhD in music education. He has contributed widely at international conferences and in international research journals. His research interests are directed towards all sides of the sociology of music education, theoretical as well as empirical, including curriculum implementation, educational quality, identity, professions and professionalism, talent education, hidden curricula, and conservatoires in society. Johansen teaches and supervises on the Master's and PhD level, and serves as a PhD defence opponent in Norway and abroad. He is co-editor of the Routledge handbook on the Sociology of Music Education.

Signe Kalsnes is Professor in Music Outreach and Music Education at the Norwegian Academy of Music. She is head of a music education programme and teaches music pedagogy. Her fields of interests are aesthetic subjects and art subjects in basic education and teacher education, teacher education and professional development, artist or teacher professional dilemmas that students face in their music and art education, music and arts education for children and young people, and educational policy within school and teacher education. Kalsnes has published books, book chapters and articles in these areas.

Jody L. Kerchner is Professor of Music Education at the Oberlin College & Conservatory of Music (USA), where she is the Director of the Pedagogy/Advocacy/Community Education program. She is also founder and conductor of the Oberlin Music at Grafton (OMAG) Prison Choir. Her research interests include children's multisensory responses during music listening, choral music education, empathetic leadership, teacher identity development, reflective thinking, and prison arts programs. She is a member of the ISME Board.

Siw Graabræk Nielsen is professor of music education at the Norwegian Academy of Music, where she also serves as co-director for the Centre for Educational Research in Music (CERM). She has published research results in music education, psychology of music education and sociology of music education. Professor Nielsen has participated as a senior researcher in the research projects *Musical gentrification and socio-cultural diversities* (2013–2017), and *DYNAMUS – The social dynamics of musical upbringing and schooling in the Norwegian welfare state* (2018–2022). Both projects have been funded by The Research Council of Norway.

Eva Sæther is Professor of Music Education, with Educational Sciences as her profile at Malmö Academy of Music (MAM), Lund University and Docent at University of the Arts, Helsinki. She has developed a research profile that focuses on intercultural perspectives on musical learning and creativity(ies) and has published widely in international journals and books. Her international engagement includes serving as board member in the International Society for Music Education

(ISME) and as commissioner in the Music in Schools and Teacher Education Commission (MISTEC). Since 2017 she is heading the research education in music education at MAM.

Tiri Bergesen Schei is Professor (Dr Art) in Music Education at Western Norway University of Applied Sciences (HVL), Centre for Arts, Culture and Communication. Schei coordinates the master's programme in music education. She is currently responsible for the research education course *Theory of Science, Ethics and Academic Text Work* in the PhD-programme Bildung and Pedagogical Practices at HVL. Tiri also leads the research programme, *Arts, Creativites, and Cultural Practices*. Core fields of interest are topics related to identity formation and vocal expression, the relationship between the audible body and the phenomenology of being heard. Schei chairs the research group Voice InFormation. She also does research in kindergarten education.

Nick Sorensen is a Visiting Research Fellow at Bath Spa University, UK having previously been Assistant Dean and Associate Professor at their Institute for Education. His research is concerned with understanding improvisation as a mode of creativity and is grounded in his practice as a jazz saxophonist. He applies this knowledge within artistic and educational contexts to encourage expertise and democratic collaborative practice. His performance work explores interdisciplinary and transcultural partnerships. He is a Senior Fellow of the Higher Education Academy and a Fellow of the Royal Society of the Arts.

Brynjulf Stige is professor in Music Therapy, University of Bergen (UiB); founding leader of POLYFON Knowledge Cluster for Music Therapy; previously the founding leader of GAMUT – The Grieg Academy Music Therapy Research Centre, UiB & NORCE, Norway. Stige has founded two international peer-reviewed journals, *Nordic Journal of Music Therapy* and *Voices: A World Forum for Music Therapy*. He has published extensively on music therapy theory and on musical participation, culture, and community. International books include. *Where Music Helps* (2010, with Ansdell, Elefant, and Pavlicevic), *Invitation to Community Music Therapy* (2012, with Aarø) and *Music Therapy: An Art beyond Words* (2014, with Bunt).

Kathryn Urbaniak is program manager of Project Someone (Social Media Education Every Day) at Concordia University, Montreal. She is an experienced learning experience designer, instructor, and researcher with degrees in Educational Technology, Information Technology, and Business.

Vivek Venkatesh is a filmmaker, musician and applied learning scientist. His independently co-produced cinemas include *Blekkmetal* (2016), *Where in the hell is the Lavender House? The Longmont Potion Castle Story* (2019) and *Enslaved 25*. He co-curates and plays in the internationally renowned electronic improvisation outfits Landscape of Hate and Landscape of Hope. He is the director of Project SOMEONE (Social Media Education Every Day) and creator of the Grimposium festival. He holds the UNESCO co-Chair in Prevention of Radicalisation and Violent Extremism and is Associate Professor of Inclusive Practices in Visual Arts in the Faculty of Fine Arts at Concordia University.

Part I
Opening

Craftsmanship in Academia: Skilled Improvisation in Research, Teaching, and Leadership

Liora Bresler

Abstract Educators typically focus on one of three levels: *micro*, the individual; *meso*, the institutional; or *macro*, the global (Bresler, Res Stud Music Educ 11:2–18, 1998). It is unusual to find an educator who has impacted all three levels as significantly as Magne Espeland does. I begin this preface by exploring the notion of craft, the central idea behind his vision for this book, discussing its associations and possibilities, and what these mean in the context of research. I then reflect on how such aspects are manifested in his research, teaching, and leadership, including a close relationship to improvisation and responsiveness to different communities in which he practices his craft.

Educators typically focus on one of three levels: *micro*, the individual; *meso*, the institutional; or *macro*, the global (Bresler, 1998). It is unusual to find an educator who has impacted all three levels as significantly as Magne Espeland does. I begin this preface by exploring the notion of craft, the central idea behind his vision for this book, discussing its associations and possibilities, and what these mean in the context of research. I then reflect on how such aspects are manifested in his research, teaching, and leadership, including a close relationship to improvisation and responsiveness to different communities in which he practices his craft.

The Craft of Research: Giving Form to Our Souls

The notion of "craft" is a loaded term. Unlike the school subject of craft in Nordic countries, which includes creative elements (e.g., Lindstrom, 2007), North American attitudes toward craft often contrast it unfavorably with the fine arts. The flagship journal of the *Association for Supervision and Curriculum Development* (ASCD)

L. Bresler (✉)
University of Illinois at Urbana-Champaign, Champaign, IL, USA
e-mail: liora@illinois.edu

Educational Leadership, widely read by both researchers and practitioners, presented a special issue on "Teaching as Art and Craft" in January 1983, featuring 10 articles by 12 education scholars including Elliot Eisner as the guest editor, and Madeleine Grumet, Lou Rubin, and Eisner's former students, Tom Barone and Robert Donmoyer. Eisner's opening article noted the absence of attention to the art and craft of teaching: "Why is it that the arts and craft of teaching—and of school administration—should seem so quaint?" (1983, p. 6). He paired art and craft and contrasted them with science and scientific methods and models: "Teachers are more like orchestra conductors than technicians. They need rules of thumb and educational imagination, not scientific prescriptions" (Eisner, 1983, p. 5).

Madeleine Grumet, a major pioneering voice in educational feminist theory, discusses in that issue the estrangement of art and craft, pointing to their difference in prestige, as well as to their shared qualities, and grounding them in the gendered reality of teaching:

> For the object that is contained within the category of craft is destined for daily use and intended to enhance the common order, not to disrupt it. It is only with the passage of time that the works of craft achieve the function of cultural commentary, when the balance and economy that sustain daily life have changed sufficiently for the object whose form has expressed yesterday's social order to achieve the distance needed for critique. If teachers have often found themselves caught within the conventional confines of craft, artists have too. (Grumet, 1983, p. 31)

The other authors, even with "craft" in the title of this special issue, tend to ignore craft as they celebrate the creativity and inspiration of the arts. Curriculum scholar Lou Rubin, in his article "artistry in teaching"[1] claims, in line with his title: "The concept of pedagogical intelligence—as opposed to craft rules—has not been adequately advertised" (Rubin, 1983, 49). Rubin associated craft with the routine, the mundane. While Rubin acknowledges that the famous pianist Glenn Gould had both art and craft, he consistently connects vision, interpretation, and inspiration with the artistic. This view of craft was shared by many scholars, including myself in my early thinking about curriculum, not recognizing the sophisticated skill, depth of embodied knowledge, and personal investment involved in craft.

Yet art and craft can be skillfully and elegantly combined, as Tom Barone's paper portraying art curriculum in an Appalachian high school illustrates (Barone, 1983). Barone described the teaching, and later the long-term impact (Barone, 2001) of award-winning teacher Don Forrister and his pedagogies, examining the respective traditions of arts and crafts, their inherent tensions, and the skillful ways that Forrister integrates them.

In our current collection, Magne Espeland identifies the educational significance of craft to the field of music education. He invokes the English association of craft with power, physical strength, might, and skill; the meaning of the old Norse word "kraptr" as strength and virtue; and the evolution of the concept to mean something built and made. These notions are compatible with sociologist Richard Sennett's

---

[1] Rubin published a book with the same name in November 1984.

argument that there is no art without craft: the *idea* of a paper is not a paper; the idea of a musical composition is not a musical composition (Sennett, 2008, p. 65). Craft, whether in teaching or musical performance, is founded on skill, a trained practice developed to a high degree. Materials are central to the making. Becoming a teacher or a musician involves proficiency with contents and pedagogies for the former and a voice or an instrument for the latter; for a music educator, it requires proficiency in both. The craftsman's efforts to do good quality work and shape materials depend on curiosity about the material at hand, a curiosity generating (and generated by) interaction and dialogue. In this process, Sennett argues, the line between craft and art may seem to separate technique and expression, but this separation is false.

Sennett's broader understanding of craft is highly relevant to Espeland's vision. While we often imply technical accuracy and the notion of utilitarianism when we use the word craft instead of art, the Greek origin behind our use of the terms *technology*, *technique*, and *technical* suggests there is more to examine (Sennett, 2008). To the Greeks, there was no distinction between art and craft; it was all techne, a term they used to indicate that we make form visible, whether it is drama, weaving, or a music lesson. Techne, for them, meant a good fit between the form of an idea and its use (Sennett, 2008).

Sennett uses the example of pottery, where raw clay is "cooked" both by the tools that shape it into a pot and by the kiln, which does the literal work of cooking. Cooked clay provides a medium for making images that, on a pot, create a narrative as the pot is turned. This narrative can travel and be traded or sold as a cultural artifact. Clay, Sennett claims, is "good to think with," quoting Levi-Strauss that symbolic value is inseparable from awareness of the material condition of an object; creators brought the two together (Sennett, 2008, p. 129). Sennett argues that the craftsman, engaged in a continual dialogue with materials, does not suffer the divide of understanding and doing. The craftsman, writes Sennett, must be patient, avoiding quick fixes. Good work of this sort emphasizes the lessons of experience through a dialogue between tacit knowledge and explicit critique (Sennett, 2008, p. 51).

These same distinctions, skills, and dialogical processes, I suggest, are essential aspects of conducting research (Bresler, 2008). Becoming a researcher requires proficiency with the materials and the craft of research. Accordingly, craft at its best is bringing forth the form, and doing so in a manner that animates it. Indeed, observations and interviews, data analysis, and writing are critically dependent on craft. While there are plenty of guidelines to the craft of research (the type conveyed in coursework and in textbooks) to be at its best, the craftsman's deft use of tools and materials, combined with an intuition developed from practice, creates a reciprocity that animates the form. It is a matter of using cognition and skill to join intuition and emotional resonance with research, getting into questions that have vitality, as well as instigating curiosity to understand what is unknown. These qualities create powerful texts in qualitative research.[2] I suggest that craftsmen, teachers, musicians, and

---

[2] Some favorites that I have used in my teaching to exemplify these principles include Myerhoff, 1978 and Barone, 2001.

researchers can pattern themselves after the forms they create. In this process, we give form to our souls (Bresler, 2008). Espeland's vision and practice of craftsmanship is precisely of that kind, wherein lies its power.

Educational Craftsmanship as Teacher, Researcher, and Leader

It is difficult to overstate Espeland's sense of craft. He is a skillful craftsman in the diverse (and in his case, intimately connected) arenas of teaching, researching, and leadership. His deep understanding of classroom practices (e.g., Espeland, 1987); processes and products of national policies for the arts (e.g., Espeland, 1998); early and evolving uses of technology (e.g., Espeland, 2010); improvisation in music education (Aadland, Espeland, & Arnesen, 2017; Holdhus et al., 2016); and collaborative work in formal classes (e.g., Murphy & Espeland, 2005/2006) as well as between musicians and teachers in school performances (e.g., Espeland, 1987; Holdhus & Espeland, 2013) have made compelling contributions to the field of music education. This book is a clear testimony to his impact on the profession. The chapters here relate to the different facets of his work, including intricate kinds of knowledge in music teacher education: listening as an active, creative musical experience; assessment; and the aspirations and practices of music education for all. His numerous publications identify issues that are fundamental to teaching and schooling and expand our conversation as a community of music educators. These ideas have travelled widely, as the scope of countries represented in the volume testifies.[3] His writing is characterized by insightful distinctions; a deep sense of historical, cultural, and intellectual contexts; and a wise understanding of conflicting perspectives and their raison d'être. Espeland's intellectual agility in exploring new conceptual and methodological territories is noteworthy. His skillful use of diverse genres of inquiry—from formative research and experimental design to case-study and philosophical exploration—is guided by the ability of these genres to illuminate the problem at hand. The important thing is that research matters to classroom teachers and teacher educators, as well as to scholars and researchers, and that theorizing be not for theory's sake, but continually in service of teaching and learning in music education.

The point of departure for this volume was a life-long question of how the diverse and longstanding traditions of "music education crafts" respond to a rapidly changing environment in society and education. How could music education contribute to creative and sustainable solutions for societal and educational challenges created by multiculturalism, globalization, technology, and accountability? And what kind of music education skills, virtues, and rationales need to be changed, modified,

[3]Magne's influence is much broader: quite a few major scholars from Australia, Africa, South America, and Asia whose voices are not included here shared with me Magne's impact.

developed, invented, dismissed, or kept—how, and for what reasons and to what ends? The backdrop of authentic teaching and insightful scholarship generates meaningful invitations for others to grapple with these issues in their own settings.

The Power (and Playfulness) of Improvisation in Research and Research Education

The notion of locating craft within an understanding of rapidly changing environments acknowledges the importance of improvisation in teaching and, I suggest, in research. The agility involved in improvisation is not part of the stereotype (or practice) of the common researcher. In my field work in American schools, I became sensitized to the value of an improvisatory mindset that is intimately related to a heightened connection with the fluidity of what we study (e.g., Bresler, 2005). Improvisation, of course, is a big part of life. All good conversations, for example, have an element of flow and responsiveness that are at the heart of improvisation. The reason I believe that the notion of improvisation needs to be highlighted in both teaching and research is that both are often conceived as tightly codified and prescribed, so much so that they are at risk of losing the natural flow and responsiveness that creates intellectual and pedagogical vitality.

Drawing on my early fieldwork experiences, I came to appreciate the power of an improvisatory mindset in inquiry, and I aimed to cultivate it in my role as research educator (Bresler, 2018). Acknowledging that improvisation cannot be taught, I grapple with how to develop it through class assignments and modeling. The challenge is to cultivate a habit of mind that juxtaposes disciplined, systematic aspects of inquiry with alert responsiveness to what is unfolding—the ability to improvise. Among other classroom experiences toward this end, I assign structured encounters with artworks (as examples of "bounded systems"), simulating experiences of looking, generating questions, and listening in observation and interviews. Such encounters center on description, interpretation, and contextualization and, importantly, aspire to productive relationships between knowing and unknowing (Bresler, 2018). Students improvise by attending to artwork they have not seen before, considering the interplay between description, interpretation, and contextualization of both micro (artist) and macro (cultural contexts). Theory illuminates the basis for one's understanding rather than simply demonstrating one's proficiency. We reflect on the generative (and sometimes suppressive!) influence of evaluation and judgment, the expansion of understanding through listening to other viewers' interpretations as they interact with one's own, and the role and impact of one's communication with the group. This awareness is particularly important when we aspire to engage multiple audiences. Espeland's work exemplifies these processes of intensified perception, of listening and communication in the diverse academic activities he negotiates with fluidity and ease.

Subjectivity and Positioning

I first met Magne Espeland on the phone in my office at the University of Illinois, back in 1992, when he invited me to give a talk in Norway. When he asked me if I had ever been to Norway, I told him about my visit to Oslo 12 years prior, to which he retorted: "If you haven't been to Western Norway, you haven't been to Norway!" It was a beginning of a long conversation. I learned about his project on active music listening and read his paper published in the *British Journal of Music Education*, "Music in Use: Responsive music listening in the primary school" (Espeland, 1987). The aim and scope of this work, the sophistication of the curricular materials he created as well as the collaborative pedagogies in the study, and his integration of teachers' and students' voices were pioneering. He opened new ways of going about research design, practice, and communication. This was even more astonishing at a historical time when few music education scholars conducted (let alone published) this kind of classroom-centered inquiry or included children's or teachers' voices.

I have long been interested in the Dewey-inspired genre of formative qualitative research, in its mission and possibilities of improving educational practices, and in the research engaged in this quest (Bresler, 1994). One of the motivations for the emergence of qualitative research in education was to bridge disconnected theory and practice (Schwab, 1969), a disconnection that needed specific addressing in music education research. In my role as the co-organizer of the first conference on qualitative research methodology in music education (1994), I felt that Magne Espeland's insights and modeling would provide the inspiration we needed. Other keynoters were qualitative luminaries like Norman Denzin, Fred Erickson, Alan Peshkin, and Bob Stake. Eminent music education researchers Cliff Madsen, Ed Asmus, and Keith Swanwick provided their perspectives on qualitative research.

The keynote from a Norwegian perspective, quite late in the evening of a long day when the energy was at low ebb, was uplifting! The audience, some 200 people, mostly North Americans with some European figures (including Swedish music psychologist Bertil Sundin), were all drawn into Espeland's circle as he narrated stories from Norwegian classrooms, identified big issues, and grounded them in specific practices, curricular contents, and pedagogies. This keynote, "Formative research in Norwegian primary schools: A collaborative endeavor"—published in the *Bulletin of the Council in Music Education* (Espeland, 1994)—was as thought-provoking as it was compelling. There, he grappled with the very real issue of his identity as researcher and teacher and the interplay between these two roles as they operate in the conduct (and implicitly in the communication) of the project. He addressed straightforwardly, elegantly, and with wit the significance and relevance of research to teaching and to schools, raising profound issues regarding the dissemination and impact of this work. His ten points[4] ending the paper (1994, 93) are as crucial now as they were when they were written. Rereading it 25 years after my

---

[4] Magne writes: "Music education research should continue to describe its main goal as an attempt to understand and improve the teaching and learning of music, and this attempt must be visionary

initial reading in my role as an editor of that special issue, I have a renewed understanding of the courage, authenticity, and wisdom embodied by his ideas.

The qualities of engaging musicianship, intellect, and relaxed yet forceful communication with his audience were vividly manifested when we visited an elementary public school in Urbana that week, per his request. Asked on the spot by the teacher to engage the children in a musical activity, Espeland engrossed us in a musical story about Norwegian trolls. The magic was palpable. In both his scholarly keynote and classroom activity, you knew you were in the presence of a master teacher! You were captivated, and you learned important things on music as craft along the way.

Even Magne's organizational skill involved a sense of craft, with the same level of engagement, skill and communication in speaking, writing, and drafting proposals. Examples include the Improvisation in Teacher Education (IMTE); leadership of research groups and practitioners on projects at the Stord campus; and role as program chair of the 2002 International Society for Music Education (ISME) conference.

Recapitulation: The Macro, Meso, and Micro

The macro international scope of Espeland's work is clear in the many keynotes he has given around the globe and in the broad scope of his writing, published in major international journals, about topics that are of deep relevance to all music education classrooms. In his case, the international is always grounded in the local, in the way

---

and have a direction. The best way to fulfill such a goal is to strengthen the *inclusive* perspectives in the research process by:

1. including *all* aspects of the research process and treat them with equal importance;
2. paying special attention to the publication aspect and follow-ups;
3. including values and a discussion of the "good" practice;
4. giving elements close to practice (i.e., curricular materials, videos and methodological questions) high status and by making music textbooks and resource packs research-based;
5. including teachers' and students' perspectives in our descriptions and interpretations of research in the many fields of music education;
6. utilizing the *collective* competence of the teacher and the research worlds in the research process;
7. including decision-makers as a main target group for research findings and utilizing the means for political influence available in our modern democratic societies;
8. putting greater emphasis on formative and action research;
9. stimulating the development of a collective responsibility for music education, nationally and internationally;
10. persuading colleagues to be willing to abandon isolation and take part in the challenges of a *collaborative endeavor* with research groups consisting of university and college faculty *and* music teachers" (Espeland, 1994, p. 93).

that good fiction specific to cultural setting has universal resonance. Here, Norwegian identity is clear and explicit. In a special issue of Arts Education Policy Review, for example, insights on the processes of creating curriculum reform in Norway were shared (Espeland, 1998), portraying the intricate and very real aspects of deliberation within ideological and personal contexts. Likewise, in the 2009 keynote at the Research in Music Education (RIME) conference in Exeter, UK, false dichotomies that have been too long in operation were identified, situating these ideas from the perspective of a Norwegian in a globalized world (Espeland, 2010).

Making an impact at the meso, institutional level is clearly manifested in the envisioning and co-creation of a thriving Master of Arts program and a growing research community. Being part of some of those meetings, I have observed how Espeland's masterful teaching and scholarship draws on the strengths of the Stord faculty to create vibrant research projects. These projects have not been cosmetic, one-shot actions, but rather have signified a shift in culture responsive to the changes of academic vision in Nordic countries, promoting among the people involved a sense of ownership in large and small ways.

On the micro level, each of the authors in this volume addresses what Magne Espeland's work and ideas mean for them, explicitly or implicitly. His influence on my own thinking has been one of the most crucial in my professional career. While I had visited the Nordic countries in both personal and professional capacities before I ventured into Western Norway, I owe him my vital sense of connection to this part of the world. His unique combination of extraordinary mind, collaborative spirit, generous hospitality, and sense of a balanced rhythm of life has been profoundly important. Even if I am slow and sometimes reluctant to engage with new projects, his example is motivating and activates my thinking.

One of the special qualities of Espeland's work is his ability to make astute connections between the general and the particular, the distant and the near, which are crucial aspects of craft. Consider the opening of his 1998 paper on Norwegian policy in art education. What is usually impersonal becomes alive throughout the paper, where characters and processes are animated and vitally realized. Here is the beginning:

> I have a 343-page book in front of me, beautifully illustrated with 140 pictures from Norwegian and international contemporary and traditional art. I received this book from the Norwegian Ministry of Education; it contains the guidelines for the country's new national curriculum for compulsory primary (students aged 6–12) and lower-secondary (ages 13–15) education, going into effect on 1 July 1997. I now want to become a storyteller because I think there is a different and more interesting story behind this book than behind other national curriculum guidelines from Norway and other countries. At least I think the story is unique, but that could be because I have been so immersed in it. Because I was head of the music committee and a member of the group of subject leaders writing curricula and advising the Ministry of Education, this book feels very much a part of me, and that is actually quite frightening.
>
> The story is a journey into the process of shaping a national curriculum for the arts in Norway. In some ways, the trip might resemble a tour through Western Norway--moving through waterfalls and into tunnels. (Espeland, 1994, p. 11)

For those of us who believe in multiple "forms of representation," any notion of his impact and presence would greatly benefit from going beyond texts, including a film of his facilitating a group of researchers such as the Teaching and teacher education commission in the International Society for Music Education (ISME), where he regularly brought together prominent and occasionally argumentative international figures in ways that acknowledged their respective cultural and personal styles, reminding us about the bigger mission to which we are all committed. Or by an audio of his playing, in various kinds of formal and semi-formal settings, the flute, accordion, and most recently, the violin (see Eva Saether's chapter). Indeed, music-making is often a part of the gatherings organized by Magne. Music is integral to the very special conferences in his home campus at the island of Stord complete with performances in the conferences' venues, or outside on the fjord of the campus, or in a restaurant in the mountains of Western Norway. These are intensified experiences (Dewey, 1934) at their best, artistic and educational!

The field of music education is an applied one based on a close relationship between theory and practice—in effect, craft. Ultimately, we ask ourselves: does our research contribute to better teaching and learning? Magne Espeland exemplifies such interconnections in ways that expand and inspire. I feel privileged to be in that circle of influence, reminding me what a life of scholarship can be at its best.

Acknowledgement I am indebted to Eve Harwood and Betsy Hearne for their reading this paper and for their insightful comments.

References

Aadland, H., Espeland, M., & Arnesen, T. E. (2017). Towards a typology of improvisation as a professional teaching skill: Implications for pre-service teacher education programmes. *Cogent Education, 4*(1), 1295835.

Barone, T. (1983). Things of use and things of beauty: The story of the Swain County High School arts program. *Daedalus, Journal of the American Academy of Arts and Science, 112*(3), 1–28.

Barone, T. (2001). *Touching eternity*. Teachers College Press.

Bresler, L. (1994). Formative research in music education. *The Quarterly Journal of Music Teaching and Learning, 5*(3), 11–24.

Bresler, L. (1998). The genre of school music and its shaping by meso, micro and macro contexts. *Research Studies in Music Education, 11*, 2–18.

Bresler, L. (2005). What musicianship can teach educational research. *Music Education Research, 7*(2), 169–183.

Bresler, L. (2008). Research as experience and the experience of research: Mutual shaping in the arts and in qualitative inquiry. *LEARNing Landscapes, 2*(1), 267–279.

Bresler, L. (2018). Aesthetic-based research as pedagogy: The interplay of knowing and unknowing towards expanded seeing. In P. Leavy (Ed.), *The handbook of arts-based research* (pp. 649–672). New York: Guilford Press.

Dewey, J. (1934/1980). *Art as experience*. New York: Perigee Books.

Eisner, E. (1983). The arts and craft of teaching. *Educational Leadership., 40*(4), 4–13.

Espeland, M. (1987). Music in use: Responsive music listening in the primary school. *British Journal of Music Education, 4*, 283–297.

Espeland, M. (1994). Formative research in Norwegian primary schools: A collaborative endeavor. *Council for Research in Music Education, 122*, 83–93.

Espeland, M. (1998). "Once upon a time there was a minister": An unfinished story about reform in Norwegian arts education. *Arts Education Policy Review, 99*(1), 11–16.

Espeland, M. (2010). Dichotomies in music education – Real or unreal? *Music Education Research., 12*(2), 129–139.

Grumet, M. (1983). The line is drawn. *Educational Leadership., 40*(4), 29–38.

Holdhus, K., & Espeland, M. (2013). The visiting artist in schools: Arts based or school based practices? *International Journal of Education & the Arts, 14*.

Holdhus, K., Høisæter, S., Mæland, K., Vangsnes, V., Engelsen, K. S., Espeland, M., et al. (2016). Improvisation in teaching and education: Roots and applications. *Cogent Education, 3*(1). https://doi.org/10.1080/2331186X.2016.1204142.

Lindstrom, L. (2007). Swedish questions about creativity in visual arts. In L. Bresler (Ed.), *International handbook of research in arts education* (pp. 1195–1198). Dordrecht, The Netherlands: Springer.

Murphy, R. & Espeland, M. (2005/2006). *Upbeat: Music series for schools*. Dublin: Carroll Education/Gill.

Myerhoff, B. (1978). *Number our days*. New York: Simon & Schuster.

Rubin, L. (1983). Artistry in teaching. *Educational Leadership, 40*(4), 44–49.

Schwab, J. (1969). The practical: A language for curriculum. *School Review, 78*(November), 1–23.

Sennett, R. (2008). *The craftsman*. New Haven, CT: Yale University Press.

Conceptualising Music Education as "Craft": Responses to an Invitation

Kari Holdhus and **Regina Murphy**

Abstract As an introductory chapter to the volume, we take a broad view of the craft of music education and frame it within contemporary, global discourse reflected in such issues as sustainability, equality and diversity. We identify the ways in which these issues are as relevant for music educators as they are for other leaders in society. Moving beyond neoliberal and hegemonic orientations to education to focusing on teacher education in particular, we locate this work within the values of the teacher. More specifically, we hone in on the educational concept of Bildung and virtue ethics while emphasising the importance of developing sustainability-minded, virtue-oriented and reflective music educators. It is here that music education as "craft", then, may be revealed and renewed. Our chapter concludes with an introduction to each of our fellow authors in this collection, and the unique and diverse perspectives they bring to the collective idea of craft through a constellation of theories and practices of music education.

In this introductory chapter, we focus on two crucial concepts in Magne Espeland's original invitation to authors to reflect on when considering music education as craft:'sustainability' and 'virtue'. The first of these suggests the kinds of contributions that music education can bring to societal challenges in our time, while the second suggests reflection and discussion about the kind of energy and qualities that are needed for music educators to achieve such ends.

K. Holdhus (✉)
Department of Arts Education, Western Norway University of Applied Sciences, Stord, Norway
e-mail: kari.holdhus@hvl.no

R. Murphy
School of Arts Education and Movement, DCU Institute of Education, Dublin City University, Dublin, Ireland
e-mail: regina.murphy@dcu.ie

© Springer Nature Switzerland AG 2021
K. Holdhus et al. (eds.), *Music Education as Craft*, Landscapes: the Arts, Aesthetics, and Education 30, https://doi.org/10.1007/978-3-030-67704-6_2

Music Education, *Bildung* and Sustainability

Sustainability as a concept is often defined according to the ability of something or someone to persist or endure (Stephens, Hernandez, Roman, Graham, & Scholz, 2008). Educational sustainability may also include preservation and protection in general, as well as specifically protecting cultural diversity (Kemp, Parto & Gibson, 2005). A third main characteristic is "development" that meets the needs of the present without compromising the future. Sustainability in education then is a dynamic and overarching multidimensional concept that includes epistemological, methodological as well as institutional and political dimensions.

The 17 UN goals for sustainable development is a list of ground-breaking aims, e.g. the elimination of poverty and hunger (goals 1 and 2); the focus on quality education, good health and well-being for all (goals 3 and 4); the desire for sustainable cities and communities (goal 11); and responsible consumption and production (goal 12) (United Nations, 2018). The crucial question to ask is the extent to which music education is making or, rather, *can* make itself relevant to such goals—to some, or all of them? At first sight, our immediate answer may be to point to the relevance of what seems quite obvious, such as the goals relating to "good health and well-being" and "quality education". However, we shall argue that if music and music education can contribute to better health and well-being in the world—in many ways we believe—music education can also be important for achieving the sustainable goals which *depend on* good health and well-being. Likewise, even if the sub-goals for "quality education" might be understood as achievements in the so-called basics, such as providing literacy and numeracy for all, we must always remember that (a) education is a complex, multidimensional practice of teaching and learning that is widely understood as encompassing far more than basic skills; (b) being literate and numerate in various modes, especially in the representation of multi-literacies also refers to music; and (c) music education is widely used to support literacy and numeracy in the traditional sense in schools, as well as a host of other areas of human development and well-being (Biasutti, Welch, MacRitchie, McPherson, & Himonides, 2020). Thus, as we reflect in our writing process on the UN goals for sustainability and what they may mean for music education, we are convinced from the outset that they are just as relevant for music education as they are for education in general. If, therefore, both music education and the professional craft of which we are members aspire to embrace sustainability as one of its crucial concepts, there is a need for music educators to embrace a comprehensive framework and philosophy for education that can meet such claims. For us, this also means that music educators should publicly articulate their mistrust of a neoliberal, rote-oriented, competitive and test-oriented version of education. This is a framework and philosophy that may indeed be regarded as a threat, not only to individuals but also, we believe, to the fulfillment of the UN goals for sustainability. To us, these goals can only be reached by emphasising qualities such as solidarity, communal responsibility, dialogue and democracy.

We find a number of these qualities embedded in the educational concept of *Bildung* (Klafki, 2011). In its classical interpretation, Bildung as an educational philosophy is based on developing and exercising responsibility, self-determination, co-determination and capacity for solidarity in a societal sense in children and young people. Bildung can be seen as a concept that functions simultaneously in an emancipatory and educational manner as well as on the personal, social and cultural levels. Klafki (2011) claims that Bildung can neither emerge from knowledge of material objects nor from the subject alone, but must arise in a societal context.

Aesthetic and artistic utterances, experiences and participation—the very core of music education—contribute to preparing children for an ambiguous comprehension of the world and of other people (Austring & Sørensen, 2006). This is because the aesthetic, among other things, is constructed as feeling-based, sensory, bodily and complex (Shusterman, 2000). As such, it equips people with the chance to process and express constraints as well as joyful experiences in our lives. Aesthetic enterprises contribute to Bildung, because they draw on emotions, dialogue and empathy as basic aspects of dealing with being a citizen (Dewey, 1934). We suggest that music education as a craft needs to encompass the Bildung aspects of music teaching and learning continuously in order to fulfil itself and in doing so, be sustainable. Even if music education might be described as a micro-level enterprise, we believe that micro-level political actions to create impacts can exceed themselves (Schmidt, 2019).

Kemp, Parto, and Gibson (2005) view the requirements for sustainability to be multiple and interconnected. They also claim that sustainability hinges on integration. Sustainability, in their view, is about both protection and creation, and it is context-specific, local and diverse. To these writers, construction of, and work for, sustainability appear as dynamic and relational. To pursue sustainability means to accept the world and its practices as changing, while also viewing equity and democracy as vehicles for obtaining sustainability.

Music Education as a Craft: Sustainable Virtues

How should sustainability as a component of craft in music education be addressed, and why is sustainability of importance to music education as craft? A term often used as a component in etymological descriptions of craft is *virtue*. Virtue has to do with ethics and morality while at the same time being connected to strength, potency and efficacy, and thus, power. Virtue then is about enabling oneself to act and carry out good intentions, whatever they might be. Bowman (2016) contends that virtue, as part of artistic citizenship (including art educators as obvious candidates for this kind of citizenship), needs to comply with a broad ethical comprehension, focussing on "what it is *right to do*" (p. 69, emphasis in original) and activate an ethically seen, deeper approach: "what it is *good to be*" (p. 69). Virtue ethics point directly at individuals' personal integrity and resources towards acting morally. One of Bowman's points is that all situations encountered are, in some way or another, unique and should be approached as uniquely. Virtue ethics, to Bowman then, are put into play improvisationally and carried out as situational decisions and actions. Virtue ethics imply that actions and decisions need to be based on character rather than on duty. "According to virtue ethics", as Bowman (2016) writes, "people develop their capacities to discern and pursue right courses of action not by weighing the pros and cons of potential outcomes, rather by recourse to habitually developed, character-based ethical dispositions" (p. 68). Following this argument, we shall argue that students' habitually developed dispositions also are likely to be inherited from their teachers and role models. David Best (1992) claims that "No teacher can avoid the moral responsibility of deciding what to teach and how to teach it." (1992, pp. 180–181). Working with sustainability as a steering parameter, both "what to teach" and "how to teach" will be affected by teacher values.

For a music educator working in a neoliberal regime of schooling, the challenges of responsibility often are twofold: to be moral in decisions over what and how to teach while possessing the virtue to argue for the selected activities to take place (Väkevää, Westerlund, & Ilmola-Sheppard, 2017). In order to contribute to creative and inclusive solutions to societal and educational challenges, sustainability in music education necessarily must have to do with identification and discussion of contemporary issues of relevance. Such a contribution should contain reflection and critique over issues regarding music education connected to music as a phenomenon in a larger societal environment (Elliott, Silverman, & Bowman, 2016).

The Music Educator, Musical Skills and Renewal

An engaged music educator teaching on a daily basis will possibly start their practice with a reflection on: "What will I do in my next music lesson?". Even if such a reflection might appear to be functional and even superficial, teachers' decisions on what to plan and do will stem from underlying values, often only exposing themselves as music educators through their preferred actions and activities over time. These underlying values impacting pedagogical actions and decisions may be conscious and deliberate, or they may take the shape of "tacit knowledge" (Polanyi, 2009) and transact more intuitively. However, we shall argue that in the current global situation, described as the age of the Anthropocene (Ojala, 2017; Veiga, 2017), our senses have been sharpened by the COVID-19 pandemic,[1] and reinvigorated by global consciousness of systemic racism through the Black Lives Matter protest movement. We know that we have experienced a collective and significant shift in perception on many levels and that the world, as we once knew it, is changing rapidly. Our connectedness and interdependence on a human level was never more crucial, yet our capacity to sustain the constant traversing of the globe has

---

[1]A burgeoning literature continues to explore the effects of COVID-19 on every dimension of human activity and on well-being in particular (cf. Kontoangelos, Economou, & Papageorgiou, 2020).

been called into question. We have observed how the pandemic has heightened awareness of how structural inequality persists within and among nations, affecting the disadvantaged and marginalised in our communities most of all (Braveman, 2020; United Nations, 2020). The issues of social protection, representation, social justice, diversity and inclusion have never been more important in our theorising on what to teach (Murphy & Ward, 2021) and what education is for, and requires that we take an even closer look at our craft as music educators.

In teacher education, it is crucial that those who teach at all levels have opportunities to explore the assumptions that are underlying their own and others' practices through reflective practice. The thrust of reflection must be towards making beliefs and attitudes visible in order to understand the influences on practice and on teachers' own evolving identities (Hall, Murphy, Rutherford, & Ní Áingléis, 2019). Moreover, as sustainability-minded, virtue-oriented and engaged music educators, we will need to take a step further. Thus, in order to address the questions posed for this book, it will only be considered ethical and sustainable to view "virtue" as a part of "music education as craft" if values are *explicit*, subject to reflection and critique, and acted upon. Bowman (2002) exemplifies such a value-based position when he points to the necessity to educate *through* music. The opposite would be an orientation towards the learning and training of mere skills in isolation. To us, it seems that a neoliberal, educational hegemony focused on specific skills and competences might underline what Biesta (2009, p. 36) describes as "the learnification of education". Further, in arguing against neoliberal conceptions of education as mere learning, he aims at bringing "issues of value and purpose back into our discussions about education".

How are the values *we* advocate in this chapter compatible with the learning of traditional skills? To perform and teach musical skills has been a core task for music educators throughout the centuries, and this activity is, in our view, by no means outdated (Holdhus, 2019). When students are able to keep a pulse, sing, play an instrument or master a digital audio workstation, it will enhance the musical experience and contribution for everyone. By fostering such skills, however, under the umbrella of sustainability, and/or ethics and the virtuous, we make explicit, some would even say *introduce* an added value aspect in our teaching and practice. The skills taught therefore should not only be appropriated for someone's personal good, but for the common good, and support sustainable relations with others as well as with the local and global environment. Therefore, it is our view that to enable and improve playing, singing, composing and listening always will be part of a music teacher's contribution to sustainability (Holdhus & Espeland, 2018).

One aspect of sustainability is preservation, as illustrated in our discussion above, where we argue for the preservation of teaching musical skills. Sustainability, however, is also about creation and renewal. Music educators will always meet the question of what to protect and what to renew and why. Gates (2009) claims that musical life has to change within what he calls a societal ecology: "The ideas that seemed solid at one time as foundations for practice need to be challenged and changed in rapidly changing times; we need more flexible bases for rationalising creative, inspiring practices than we currently have" (p. xxii). He continues his argument this way: "We can and must build resilient, flexible rationales for practice because the times will change our students by altering the musical resources by means of how they will live their musical lives" (p. xxii).

If music educators preserve themselves from contemporary musical life, they risk "falling out of synchrony" (Gates, 2009, p. xx) and becoming museal. Music educators need to discuss how to cope with change and still be able to support accumulated knowledges and musics as relevant for student Bildung. An answer, according to Gates, is to pursue "dynamic permanence" (Gates, 1994), which, in short, means to embrace tradition as a subject to transformation. Committing to "dynamic permanence" then will be a balancing contribution to the cultural and temporal ecology of culture, education and society, instead of disturbing it or refusing to care for it. Changing teaching habits (including how we view students) will mean to deliberately enter contemporality's continuous flow of change. Such an intention, to us, is an asset to the future "craft" of music education.

As exemplified in the previous section, the elements of "music education as craft" seem to intertwine, change, morph and nourish each other. In our view, it is possible to construct a dynamic, never-ending explanation of "music education as craft" suited to address public music education as a concept in rapidly changing societies. Thus, the notion of "craft" can be viewed as a hub, pushing and pulling the wheel of music education forward, relating to culture, time and temporality as well as to values of inclusion and dialogue, pursuing sustainability.

The Chapters: Engagement with the Craft

The present book reflects the manifold and varied responses to an invitation, each of them deriving from a specific author context, providing possible answers to the question "what might music education as a craft mean to me, or us, seen from my/ our position"? Each contributor displays a profound engagement with music education and its politics and values. Our fellow writers are skilled and experienced in different fields of music education and research, and many contributors have chosen to discuss and deepen a possible concept of "music education as craft" through texts based in their own special field of interest. The variety of approaches can be seen as a polyphonic answer to the question of what "craft" might mean, as a concept to to be addressed across various fields and domains of music education and research. To us, the burning commitment, profound engagement, motivation, "fighting spirit" and deep knowledge demonstrating a multitude of diverse positions in music education emerge as important topics to discuss in the future formation of music education as a "craft" in all its forms.

This compilation of texts can be seen to address music education as representing something aesthetic and intersubjective while at the same time taking its place as profoundly societal and political. The book opens with an assembly of chapters that we view as political and societal approaches to the concept of "craft", while the ensuing chapters illustrate aspects of the "craft" of music education through teaching, transmission and transformation.

Part II: Music Education as a Sustainable Craft in Society

In his chapter "The Craft of Music Teaching in a Changing Society", Geir Johansen connects the craft of music teaching with the ideals of significant system builders of music education in the twentieth century, linking the affiliated teaching strategies with categories of knowledge. By drawing on Aristotle, he describes these craft dimensions in terms of *episteme*, *techne* and *phronesis*, whereafter connecting them with aural-motoric ways of teaching and the non-verbal realm of human cognition as reaching deeper and wider than verbal-categorising cognition. This enables a critique towards the global domination of visual-verbal priorities in everyday schooling as well educational politics and scholarship.

The overall purpose of Petter Dyndahl and Siw Graabræk Nielsen's chapter, "Crafting Music Education for All? The Composite Knowledge Base of Music Education in Times of Cultural Diversity and Social Polarisation" is to discuss the conditions for inclusive music education in times of cultural diversity and social polarisation and thus to contribute to the deconstruction of the slogan *music education for all* such that it is appropriately formulated historically and with informed, contemporary knowledge. The authors discuss why and how music educators must acquire the necessary epistemic craftsmanship to analyse, negotiate and, eventually, be able to choose the proper resources and tools in today's complex social and cultural situation.

In his chapter "Music Education in England as a Political Act: Reflections on a Craft Under Pressure", Martin Fautley claims that neoliberal political ideas currently dominate political thinking in many countries. One of the ways in which policies in education reflect this is that certain sorts of knowledge are privileged in assessment terms. In music education this can take a number of forms, but common to them is a tacit assumption that some styles and genres of music are deemed more worthy of privilege. However, doing this automatically places other musics in a less privileged position. Fautley suggests that music educators need to think through what sorts of values they wish to promote in their classrooms, and how types, styles and genres of music are not the only ways in which this is visible, but also in the pedagogic practices that are employed. It is his view that informal pedagogy contains within itself a different way of assessing progress by individual pupils, as well as within groups of learners.

The chapter "Educating Music Teachers for the Future: The Crafts of Change" by Catharina Christophersen discusses the concept of craft in relation to music teacher education from a perspective of change. A starting point for Christophersen is that the crafts of music teacher education are directly concerned with the facilitation of development and change, for example, by deliberating on what is important to keep and build on in the professional practice of music teacher education, and what is better left out. Christophersen suggests that one should take into consideration if and how educational practices of music teacher education (a) actively reflect on and productively try to contribute to the big challenges of the world; (b) explicitly address systemic bias and inequalities; and (c) provide spaces for student participation and agency.

The Lithuanian music educator, Rūta Girdzijauskienė, presents the chapter "The Craft of Music Teaching in a Changing Society: Singing as Meaning, Education and Craft: Reflections on Lithuanian Singing Practices". The chapter discusses the meaning of singing in the context of Lithuanian culture. Lithuanian singing tradition is reflected upon as integrated in the nation's lifestyle. Girdzijauskienė exemplifies this by pointing at the role of singing in critical periods of national history and singing's impact on the construction of a contemporary Lithuanian identity. Crafting people's ability to sing as a part of a nation's identity can develop a strong vehicle for expressing political views in a society, she claims.

From music therapy, Brynjulf Stige discusses "Artistic Citizenship and the Crafting of Mutual Musical Care". To Stige, the notion of artistic citizenship is of relevance both to music education and music therapy. The chapter suggests that artistic citizenship needs to be performed with both care and craft and that professional practitioners need to promote mutuality and participation in order to nurture it. This argument challenges the assumption that music educators teach *to music* while music therapists help people to grow *through music*. Stige points out that such a traditional distinction is less than clear, because, in his view, any person's interest in learning music might give new possibilities for participation in a community. Artistic citizenship requires care to be realised, and Stige views care as intricate, sometimes problematic. The possible craft of developing *mutual musical care* is therefore examined as a main point in the chapter.

Part III: Music Education Practices Reframed

The purpose of Jody L. Kerchner's chapter "Music Listening: An Evolution of Craft" is to consider contemporary theoretical, neuroscientific and pedagogical shifts in thinking about music listening, how these understandings might affect teachers' pedagogical craft and the processes by which students' develop their personal music listening craft. Discussions on pedagogical craft in this area of music education involve the development and use of observational tools with which teachers learn from students about their prior music listening experiences and with which they subsequently scaffold students' new music listening experiences. Kerchner claims that if music educators understand how, why and what students are listening to outside of school, then perhaps music teachers can come closer to crafting pedagogical strategies for enhancing music listening skill development in schools.

In "The Craft of (Re-)Presenting Musical Works", Randi Margrethe Eidsaa seeks to investigate perspectives on music listening by asking how teachers can relate to present day thinking about music and music education when presenting "musical works" in educational contexts. What aesthetic, musical, relational, ethical or social choices should be considered when selecting repertoires for different target groups? Eidsaa refers to empirical and theoretical perspectives on the craft (or crafts) of presenting musical repertoires for various participant groups, drawing on several examples from her practice as a music educator.

In her chapter "Developing Craftsmanship in Music Education in a Palestinian Refugee Camp and Lebanese Schools", Signe Kalsnes reflects upon the experience of preservice music teachers participating in a music project in collaboration with a Palestinian refugee camp. Throughout an internship period in Lebanon, Norwegian students taught music to 50–60 children and youth for 3–4 days in the refugee camp and played concerts for Lebanese pupils in schools. The empirical basis for the chapter draws on student logs from this internship period in Lebanon. Analysing the logs, Kalsnes addresses the question *What kind of experience does the Lebanon Project give students and what is the impact of this experience with regard to their subsequent professional lives as music teachers and musicians?* This specific study and the Lebanon Project form Kalsnes' basis for a more general reflection on the concept of music education as a craft.

Urbaniak, Venkatesh and Ben-Horin's chapter, "A Creative Global Science Classroom: Crafting the Global Science Opera", provides a discussion of crafts in relation to an utterly contemporary music education approach. The chapter details a narrative case study of *The Global Science Opera* (GSO), which is the first opera initiative in history to produce and perform operas as a global community. The chapter focuses on the pedagogical principles and teaching crafts that are potentially involved in an international, complex, multisite project of the kind GSO represents, as well as the formation of a relationship between what can be called arts-based pedagogical elements and science-education based elements. The study discussed in this chapter provides an opportunity to gain a deeper understanding of 15 adult participants' perceptions of the learning and transfer experiences occurring within the GSO creation and performance. Findings are discussed in relation to the arts-based and inquiry-based pedagogical approaches favoured by the creators of GSO and reified by its practitioner community.

Inquiry-based, student-dependent and facilitated teaching necessarily calls upon pedagogical improvisation, in music as well as in other educational contexts. In the chapter, "The Craft of Teaching Musical Improvisation Improvisationally: Towards a Theoretical Framework", Nick Sorensen explores the particular pedagogical challenge of how do we teach musical improvisation improvisationally? According to Sorensen, a greater understanding of the *what* and the *how* provides knowledge about the craft of teaching musical improvisation improvisationally, a unique craft that is of special significance to the discourse of music educators. A theoretical framework that views teaching musical improvisation improvisationally as a hybrid craft enriches this discourse. Sorensen's framework is intended to unite the theory and craft of musical improvisation with the findings of empirical research into the improvisational craft of teacher expertise.

Tiri Bergesen Schei presents the chapter: *"Phronesis* in Music Education". She believes it is the task of a music educator to find ways to support learning and liberate creative potential in performers. However, educational theory, research knowledge and teaching traditions cannot take a teacher, a coach or a performer all the way, or provide a prefabricated solution to the individual learner's particular problem. Schei draws on Aristotle's concept of *phronesis*, usually translated as practical wisdom, which denotes a kind of knowledge that allows a teacher, coach or performer to sense what may be suitable goals and devise the means to fulfil them, in praxis situations, characterised by social interaction. Aristotle termed *phronesis* an "intellectual virtue", the development of which depends on experience and individual character development. A virtue can be defined as an acquired disposition to do what is good. A *phronimos* is a virtuous person, characterised by perceptivity, flexibility and creativity manifested in concrete action. Aristotle's insights are reflected in Kierkegaard's observations on what it takes to be a helper: In order to help someone effectively, one must understand what he understands, in the way he understands it. If not, one's own understanding, however correct, scientific and wonderful, will be of no help. Schei claims *phronesis* and craft to be complex concepts that can force music educators to rethink what knowledge is and to reflect on how little we know about how we make the decisions that underpin our actions in teaching. A question then is whether the development of *phronesis* is in itself a kind of craft.

In the chapter "Approaching Vulnerability Through Contemporary Music: The Gelland Approach" Erkki Huovinen argues that music education should address human incompleteness and ambiguity—as especially evident in contexts involving vulnerability. Music has often been seen as an indicator, but also as a means of overcoming unwanted psychological or social vulnerabilities. From another point of view, vulnerability may also be understood as a desired quality of openness needed for creativity and education—a quality that nevertheless requires appropriate safety mechanisms. Huovinen illustrates these facets of vulnerability through the work of the Swedish-German *Duo Gelland*, one of the world's foremost classical violin duos. Using brief contemporary compositions, the Gellands elicit children's associative imagery, incorporating it in subsequent interpretations of the music in which the children may take part as conductors or musicians. Through interviews and observations from school workshops in Germany, Huovinen displays how the Gellands create musical contexts in which children's vulnerabilities can be safely exposed and transformed. He claims that in providing a neutralising arena for children's sometimes frightening and violent realities, the Gellands demonstrate a model and craft for "health musicianship", challenging sharp distinctions between artistic, pedagogical and therapeutic realms.

The aim of the narrative approach adopted by Eva Sæther in "The *Kraptr* of Aging Folk Musicians: Mental Practice for the Future" is to illustrate the ethical dimensions of sharing knowledge, including the experience that comes with age. Sæther reflects here on a question for a sustainable future concerning if and how education can enhance a sense of coherence. This is done when analysing practice habits and methodologies among older folk musicians, their reasons for engaging in a physically and mentally demanding practice, the motivation that drives them to continue such regimens over time and most importantly, the implications for our understanding of future oriented *kraptr* that can be found from a study on and with aging fiddlers. The chapter centres on participant observation and interviews from *Malungs Folkhögskola*, the distance education *"Folkmusik fiol"*, led by the doyen of Swedish folk music pedagogy, Jonny Soling. With his life-long experience of fiddle education for grown-ups, Soling possesses unique knowledge on holistic fiddle didactics. What is it that inspires aging folk musicians to invest time and energy in undertaking challenging further training? And what aspects of coherence and tradition can be explored within a frame of sustainable music education, Sæther asks.

Finally, we conclude our collection with a very comprehensive chapter by Magne Espeland titled "Music Education as Craft: Reframing a Rationale" that reaches right to heart of this publication. In tackling some of the age-old conundrums of music education, Magne brings breadth and depth of experience to the theory and practice of teaching and research as he explores some of the "old chestnuts" that essentially demarcate the nature of the crafts of music education. Theorists are interweaved in the discussion from across borders, cultures and time. Drawing on philosophy, psychology, sociology and new materialism, as well as personal and professional experiences from national and international settings, he illuminates some of the more challenging debates in curriculum, pedagogy and assessment and sets them within historical and contemporary discourses. Clearly, the craft of music education continues to evolve and engagement with debate on its relevance was never more important.

References

Austring, B. D. & Sørensen, M. (2006). *Æstetik og læring: Grundbog om æstetiske læreprocesser* [Aesthetics and learning: Primer on aesthetic learning processes]. Copenhagen, Denmark: Hans Reitzel.

Best, D. (1992). *The rationality of feeling: Understanding the arts in education.* London: Falmer Press.

Biasutti, M., Welch, G. F., MacRitchie, J., McPherson, G. E., & Himonides, E. (Eds.). (2020). *The impact of music on human development and well-being.* Lausanne: Frontiers Media SA. https://doi.org/10.3389/978-2-88963-683-9

Biesta, G. (2009). Good education in an age of measurement: On the need to reconnect with the question of purpose in education. *Educational Assessment, Evaluation and Accountability, 21*(1), 33–46.

Bowman, W. (2002). Educating musically. In R. Colwell & C. Richardson (Eds.), *The new handbook of research on music teaching and learning: A project of the Music Educators National Conference [MENC]* (pp. 63–84). Oxford, NY: Oxford University Press.

Bowman, W. (2016). Artistry, ethics, and citizenship. In D. Elliott, M. Silverman, & W. Bowman (Eds.), *Artistic citizenship: Artistry, social responsibility, and ethical praxis* (pp. 59–80). New York: Oxford University Press.

Braveman, P. (2020). COVID-19: Inequality is our pre-existing condition. *UNESCO Inclusive policy lab.* https://en.unesco.org/inclusivepolicylab/news/covid-19-inequality-our-pre-existing-condition

Dewey, J. (1934). *Art as experience.* New York: Penguin.

Elliott, D., Silverman, M., & Bowman, W. (Eds.). (2016). *Artistic citizenship: Artistry, social responsibility, and ethical praxis.* New York: Oxford University Press.

Gates, J. T. (1994) *Dynamic permanence as a professional construct in doing music education history*. Paper read at the National convention of the music educators national conference, April. Cincinnati, OH.

Gates, J. T. (2009). Introduction: Grounding music education in changing times. In T.A. Regelski & J.T. Gates (Eds.), *Music education for changing times* (pp. xix-xxx). Dordrecht, The Netherlands: Springer.

Hall, K., Murphy, R., Rutherford, V., & Ní Áingéis, B. (2019). Mentoring and assessing student teachers on school placement: Integrating theory and practice. *Education Research and Perspectives, 46*, 75–107.

Holdhus, K. (2019). When students teach creativities: Exploring student reports on creative teaching. *Qualitative Inquiry, 25*(7), 690–699.

Holdhus, K., & Espeland, M. (2018). Music in future Nordic schooling. *European Journal of Philosophy in Arts Education (EJPAE), 2*(2), 85–118.

Kemp, R., Parto, S., & Gibson, R. B. (2005). Governance for sustainable development: Moving from theory to practice. *International Journal of Sustainable Development, 8*(1–2), 12–30.

Klafki, W. (2011). *Dannelsesteori og didaktik: Nye studier* [Bildung theories and didactics: New studies]. Klim.

Kontoangelos, K., Economou, M., & Papageorgiou, C. (2020). Mental health effects of COVID-19 Pandemia: A review of clinical and psychological traits. *Psychiatry Investigation, 17*(6), 491–505. https://doi.org/10.30773/pi.2020.0161.

Murphy, R., & Ward, F. (2021). Connecting social justice to the teaching of music. In A. M. Kavanagh, F. Waldron, & B. Mallon (Eds.), *Teaching for social justice and sustainable development across the primary curriculum*. Routledge.

Ojala, M. (2017). Hope and anticipation in education for a sustainable future. *Futures, 94*, 76–84.

Polanyi, M. (2009). *The tacit dimension*. Chicago: University of Chicago Press.

Schmidt, P. (2019). *Policy as practice: A guide for music educators*. New York: Oxford University Press.

Shusterman, R. (2000). *Pragmatist aesthetics: Living beauty, rethinking art*. Lanham, MD: Rowman & Littlefield Publishers.

Stephens, J. C., Hernandez, M. E., Román, M., Graham, A. C., & Scholz, R. W. (2008). Higher education as a change agent for sustainability in different cultures and contexts. *International Journal of Sustainability in Higher Education, 9*(3), 317–338.

United Nations. (2018). The millennium development goals report 2018. United Nations.

United Nations. (2020). *COVID-19 and human rights: We are all in this together*. https://www.un.org/victimsofterrorism/sites/www.un.org.victimsofterrorism/files/un_-_human_rights_and_covid_april_2020.pdf

Väkevä, L., Westerlund, H., & Ilmola-Sheppard, L. (2017). Social innovations in music education: Creating institutional resilience for increasing social justice. *Action, Criticism, and Theory for Music Education, 16*(3), 129–147.

Veiga, J. E. D. (2017). The first Antropocene Utopia. *Ambiente & Sociedade, 20*(2), 227–246.

Part II
"Music Education" as a Sustainable Craft in Society

The Craft of Music Teaching in a Changing Society

Geir Johansen

Abstract In this chapter, I connect the craft of music teaching with the ideals of some of the significant system builders of music education in the twentieth century, linking affiliated teaching strategies with categories of knowledge. These categories include music teachers' knowing how and tacit knowledge, sometimes made explicit by language tools such as those afforded by, for example, Donald Schön or Lee Shulman. By drawing on Aristotle, I first describe these craft dimensions in terms of *episteme*, *techne* and *phronesis* and then connect them with aural-motor ways of teaching and non-verbal realms of human cognition, reaching deeper and wider than verbal-categorising cognition alone. This enables a critique of the global domination of visual-verbal priorities in everyday schooling as well as in educational politics and scholarship. Finally, I discuss whether seeing the craft of music teaching this way entails a potential to operate within a changing society in ways that contribute to social change. I suggest that in order to move in that direction, music teaching must transform into a reflective practice wherein the craft of music teaching and the changing society are continuously reflected in each other.

Introduction

The scholarship on music education rarely addresses the notion of craft. Still, discussions about what it entails to be and become a good music teacher frequently reveal craft dimensions. For example, the skill of performing the reversed pattern of an Orff instrument ostinato in front of a class, because you choose to face the students instead of turning your back to them, entails such a craft dimension. Introducing a rhythmically complicated passage by ear and hand clapping, before showing your instrumental student how it looks in the relevant sheet music, demonstrates another.

G. Johansen (✉)
Norwegian Academy of Music, Oslo, Norway
e-mail: Geir.johansen@nmh.no

© Springer Nature Switzerland AG 2021
K. Holdhus et al. (eds.), *Music Education as Craft*, Landscapes: the Arts,
Aesthetics, and Education 30, https://doi.org/10.1007/978-3-030-67704-6_3

In this chapter, I intend to depict some central craft dimensions of music teaching in terms of categories of knowledge. When reflected in the philosophy of knowledge (Gustavsson, 2000), they also provide connections with theories of social science as well as the sociology of education. After presenting some possible interpretations of "craft", I will describe how craft dimensions are visible in the shape of aural-motor teaching strategies within the traditions that follow some of the most significant system builders of music education in the twentieth century. Thereafter, I connect those craft dimensions to the philosophy of knowledge with a particular focus on Aristotle's concepts *episteme*, *techne* and *phronesis*. Acknowledging that theories of teaching by necessity must be comprehended with the related learning in mind (Hanken & Johansen, 2013), I then draw some connections between aural-motor craft dimensions of teaching and the comprehensive field of non-verbal human cognition. This is followed by a discussion of how such craft perspectives relate to theories of cognitive psychology and phenomenology, indirectly opposing the tendency of reducing human development to a single-dimensioned relationship between cognition and verbal language. Then, I point to how connections emerge between the described craft dimensions of music teaching, and sociological theories addressing the complexity of the contemporary society. Finally, by drawing on works within the sociology of education, I discuss the extent to which those craft dimensions, when reflected in the theoretical perspectives, can play a role within processes of social change.

Dimensions and Discourses of "Craft"

My introductory examples of craft dimensions in music teaching do not represent the only way to interpret "craft". Dictionarywise,[1] at least a second and third way of seeing it are thinkable. The second way entails craft as strength, demonstrating a direct line to its Germanic origins in the word "kraft" along with Old Saxon and Northumbrian "*cræft*" and Old Norse "*kraptr*", existing today as *Kraft* in German as well as Scandinavian languages. Understood this way, craft points to the possible impact music education can make on students as well as their surroundings. For example, we often tell ourselves that music education can have vast influences on students' identity formation, and we discuss the potential strength of music education in contributing to recognising the necessity of the arts in society. The third way of conceiving "craft" points to it as a verb entailing the skill in making something by hand, as in handcraft, or metaphorically in examples such as "how to craft a good textbook" or "a carefully crafted teaching plan". Within such wide possibilities of a definition, in this chapter I concentrate on the skill and process dimensions of craft as my point of departure, or the *noun* designating what you know (e.g. a teaching strategy) along with the *verb* pointing to what you do (when carrying out that strategy in the teaching situation). Both dimensions include aspects of music teachers'

---

[1] See: https://en.oxforddictionaries.com/definition/craft as well as https://www.etymonline.com/word/craft

knowing how (Ryle, 1949) with elements of tacit knowledge (Polanyi, 1966). Moreover, these tacit skill and process dimensions can be made explicit by language tools such as those afforded by Donald Schön (1987), entailing teachers' ability to select and adapt to the dynamics of practical contexts as reflection-in-action. Lee Shulman (1987), on his side, affords naming them as elements of pedagogical content knowledge, whilst Gunnar Handal and Per Lauvås (2000) suggest that they can be seen as parts of teachers' practical vocational theories.

Crafts and their performance, as expressed and demonstrated by music teachers, come from somewhere: there are good reasons for suggesting that music teachers do not invent their actions on the spot. On the contrary, a music teacher's actions as well as action rationales, explicit or tacit, can be seen as anchored in her or his knowledge base. In turn, this knowledge base is connected with historically and collectively developed subject traditions and standards, including dimensions of craft. Hence, even the manifestations of music teachers' reflections-in-action (Schön, 1987) which, at a first glance may appear as intuitive, can be conceived as being founded within the frames of what they conceive as possible actions and craft ideals. From a discourse perspective (Nerland, 2004), music teachers can be described as knowledge agents, acting on behalf of particular ideas about knowledge and development, or systems of thought and action operating through them. In other words, we can comprehend the crafts of music teachers, as well as their own comprehension of "craft", as intertwined with such discourses.

Several discourses of music teaching have been confirmed as valid within our historically developed subject traditions. By structuring the frames of what teachers conceive of as possible ways of operating, they have set standards for the crafts of teaching. Here, I will direct the attention towards some of those that have brought aural-motor craft dimensions to the fore. This is the case with the works of some of the most influential system builders of our field in the twentieth century.

Systems of Non-verbal Music Teaching

Some particular skill and process dimensions of craft lie at the heart of the discourses of music teaching connected with systematic approaches such as those constructed by Émile Jaques-Dalcroze, Carl Orff and Zoltán Kodály (Campbell & Scott-Kassner, 1995; Choksy, Abrahamson, Gillespie, Woods, & York, 2001). Here, the craft of music teaching is connected with a focus on aural-motor learning processes. Jaques-Dalcroze manifests this emphasis in the teaching strategies of *Eurythmics* combined with *solfège*. In this system, the craft of teaching is about making students perceive, perform, create and experience music by responding to it and reflecting it in and through the body, in a combination of gross motor skills and fine motor skills, along with singing the repertoire using absolute solfège syllables. Aural-visual processes (i.e. knowing how something sounds before learning how to read or write it) or visual-motor processes (i.e. seeing a note and pushing the right key, valve or flap) take place only when a solid foundation of aural-motor,

non-verbal experiences have been established[2] in the shape of embodied knowledge. Carl Orff's *Schulwerk* and its practices take care of this principle by the
teacher knowing the repertoire by heart in order to teach the ostinato patterns by
imitation. Thus, successful teaching enables the students to experience the sounds
of instruments such as xylophones, glockenspiels, metallophones and hand drums
by ear and as connected with the body movement of arms and hands in striking the
instruments. Similarly, Zoltán Kodály prioritised teaching strategies, enhancing the
connections between song, relative solfège syllables and a system of hand movements, which together with Jaques-Dalcroze were inspired by the works of Sarah
Ann Glover and John Curwen in the 1840s (Sadie, 1980). Whilst music educational-
ists may associate these aural-motor craft dimensions with classroom music teaching, we should bear in mind that Jaques-Dalcroze primarily constructed his system
in order for conservatoire students to improve their skills in aural training, and Orff
as well as Kodály developed strategies for instrumental teaching as well as the
classroom. In addition, other successful instrumental teaching systems such as the
Suzuki concept (Hanken & Johansen, 2013) are based on the same principles to a
large degree. In this way, teaching strategies that involve mirroring aural-motor
learning processes carry the craft ideal of what I suggest to call non-verbal teaching,
entailing doing instead of saying, and explaining in music instead of explaining in
verbal language.

Seen as knowledge agents operating within the discourses originating in the subject traditions of Jaques-Dalcroze, Orff, Kodály or Suzuki, teachers are known to
practice non-verbal teaching by introducing and rehearsing musical patterns with
their students as alternatives to giving verbal instructions, often taking the shape of
response-based music games. For example, by playing or singing a descending
minor third in order to have the students sit down instead of telling them to do so,
and the opposite in order for them to stand up, the students are trained in bodily
responding to falling and rising parts of melody lines, developing a basic, aural-
bodily knowledge ground. In addition, they are aural-bodily introduced to the
descending minor third as a basic element in pentatonic scale construction and recognition, which is pointed to by several scholars as a core element of child music
culture generally (Bjørkvold, 1992; Sundin, 1998; Walker, 2007). Some teachers
develop aural-motor teaching strategies into sophisticated systems or scripts ensur-
ing that most communication during a music lesson or session happens in music
instead of verbal language.

---

[2] For an elementary textbook promoting this principle, see Micheal Houlahan & Philip Tacka's
(2012) *From Sound to Symbol: Fundamentals of Music.*

Craft as Knowledge

The craft of aural-motor teaching strategies can be described in terms of knowledge by drawing on Aristotle's (1999, see also Gustavsson, 2000) concepts *episteme*, *techne* and *phronesis*. *Episteme* entails Ryle's (1949) "knowing that" as opposed to "knowing how", or in other words *episteme* entails the explicit, systematic and often scientific knowledge of a subject field. *Episteme* points to the verbal knowledge about aural-motor strategies in the way I describe them in this chapter. It is a challenge that music teachers, to some extent, need epistemic knowledge about these strategies in order to reflect on them in deliberate ways, even if the traditional way of acquiring them is by being trained in their execution without much further explanations or reflections. Partly, this is a consequence of the tacit nature (Polanyi, 1966) of this kind of practical "knowing how" (Ryle, 1949). Making them explicit in terms of epistemic knowledge enables their clarification as a category that has rarely been identified and described within music education scholarship.

Carrying out aural-motor teaching strategies in the everyday practical teaching context corresponds with Aristotle's *techne,* pointing to technique as well as arts sides of teacher competence (see Varkøy, 2013), also entailing components of tacit knowledge (Polanyi, 1966). Moreover, Heidegger's (Varkøy, 2013, p. 9) point of view that *techne*— beyond interpretations pointing to aspects of technique and art, entails a way in which to have knowledge—is worth noting. In other words, teachers, as well as students, acting out and learning through aural-motor strategies demonstrate ways in which to have musical knowledge, primarily manifest in bodily action and not necessarily made explicit in a secondary important medium such as verbal language.

However, knowing, naming and being able to carry out aural-motor teaching strategies is not enough if the teacher is supposed to be more than a sheer clerk, "expected to implement a system's accounting procedures [...]" (Westbury, 2000, p. 17), or a technician trained to mechanically carrying out a set of techniques in a more or less unreflective way. On the contrary, as part of their teaching craft, in order to enhance student learning, teachers need to carry out those strategies with practical wisdom, or in Aristotle's words, *phronesis*. It is worth noting that Aristotles designated practical wisdom as a particular category of knowledge, thus contributing significantly to what we in the twentieth and twenty-first century have pointed out as questioning the hegemony of scientific knowledge, even in discussions about postmodernity (Lyotard, 1984). Complying with the ideal of *phronesis*, the craft of music teaching includes paying attention to the students' personal and sociocultural preconditions as well as to the context specific, situational factors of a lesson or course of lessons when making decisions on the spot, as reflection-in-action (Schön, 1987).

Whilst descriptions of aural-motor processes in verbal-categorising terms, or in other words, as *episteme*, represent a way of knowing *about* them, actually demonstrating the relevant competences in action represents a way of *knowing* them with the body, entailing a particular, however different way "in which to have knowledge" (Heidegger, as cited in Varkøy, 2013, p. 9). Following this train of thought, aural-motor teaching strategies and processes point directly to the core of music, its inherent or intersonic meaning (Green, 2008; Johansen, 2010) and thereby possibly to the "layers of meaning in the musical object" (Nielsen, 1998, p. 136).[3] In contrast, epistemic descriptions would point only to what we might know *about* music, or its delineated meaning (Green, 2008).

Non-verbal Cognition

Connecting the aural-motor craft dimensions of music teaching with *techne* and *phronesis* (Aristotles, 2011; Gustavsson, 2000) reveals their relationship with the, often unnoticed, extremely comprehensive domain of non-verbal human cognition and experience which reaches far beyond our intellectual, verbal-categorising possibilities (Nielsen, 1998).

Frede V. Nielsen (1998) suggests that one way of conceiving and understanding this non-verbal realm of human cognition and experience is to express or attend to it non-verbally, in non-verbal forms and structures (p. 112) such as those represented by the arts. Consequently, Nielsen (1998) suggests that art, equally with science, affords tools for human cognition and recognition. The differences between art and science, or in Nielsen's (1998, p. 111) words, the *ars* and *scientia* dimensions of the basis for music teaching, are at least threefold. First, they differ in the ways they express these cognitions and recognitions. Second, they differ in the degree to which they are capable of doing this unambiguously; and third, they differ with respect to the parts of our reality about which they are able to express something. Tangentially, John Dewey (1930, see Johnson, 2011, p. 147) highlights *scientific inquiry* and *artistic inquiry* as two forms of inquiry basic to human living. Whilst the first typically searches for "generalizations over a circumscribed set of phenomena", the second focuses on "grasping the qualitative unity of a situation".

Thus, being connected with the non-verbal realm of human cognition and reasoning, the aural-motor craft dimensions of music teaching enhance a particular, situated way of human thinking. Whilst proponents of language based theories of human development tend to reduce human thinking to mainly include verbal-intellectual categorisations, in music verbal language formations represent only secondarily significant dimensions of the brain's processing of information. This is what Keith Swanwick (1994) points to when differentiating between intuitive and logic-analytic musical knowledge, designating intuitive knowledge as the basic, primary form within which logic-analytic knowledge has to be anchored. Davidson and Scripp (1992), on their side, suggest that Vygotsky's model of social interaction in cognitive development carries little meaning for musicians as it lies outside musical practice (p. 392). The craft of music teaching in the aural-motor tradition thus

---

[3] My translation.

represents a way of enabling and stimulating a significant way of human cognition, which is complementary to verbal-categorising cognition. If we look away from the potential of aural-motor and non-verbal teaching approaches to fostering human thinking, we run the risk of—to paraphrase Anna Sfard (1998)—knowing two metaphors of human cognition and exposing ourselves to the dangers of choosing just one.

Music Teachers' Toolkits

Taking a sociocultural perspective of learning (Bruner, 1996; Vygotsky, 1978; Wertsch, 2004) as mentioned above, we might argue that aural-motor strategies of teaching constitute parts of a music teacher's "toolkit and procedures" (Bruner, 1996, p. 8) for helping students "understanding and managing [the] world" (p. 8). Moreover, these toolkits and procedures are clearly context specific and should be regarded as such, since the context wherein they are situated (Lave & Wenger, 1991) are significantly different from other educational contexts. The importance of regarding them this way seems supported by other educational-psychological perspectives as well. When *surveying the coordinates of cognitive skills in music*, Davidson and Scripp (1992) point to an increased recognition among the scholars of cognitive psychology in the 1980s, that "[T]he connection between thinking and the specific context in which thinking occurs becomes a critical factor in research" (p. 392). Particularly significant in this respect are "the disciplines in which [those cognitive skills] are used" (p. 393).

Body Dimensions

Drawing on Heidegger's point of view (Varkøy, 2013) in relation to the Aristotelian *techne*, music teachers' aural-motor competences can be identified as manifestations of bodily ways in which to have knowledge. So, too, can the aural-motor competences in their teaching, when successful, enable in their students. We find support for this idea within phenomenology of the body as well as cognitive psychology. Teaching for bodily experience with music resonates with Maurice Merleau-Ponty's (1979) thoughts about the body as an instrument for experiencing the world. Accordingly, bodily response to music is comprehended as a way of being in the music. Human perception is a bodily process itself, Merleau-Ponty suggests. We express our knowledge with our body, by our bodily actions (see also Gustavsson, 2000). Correspondingly, Mark Johnson (2011), discussing how artists make contributions to the growth of human understanding and knowledge, describes how cognitive psychology highlights the importance of bodily experiences as a ground for knowledge development processes. He reports that among recent cognitive psychology approaches studying "the bodily basis of meaning, conceptualizing and reasoning", there is a "new 'embodied cognition' view on knowledge" (p. 145) which is emphasising the importance of recognising "especially our sensory-motor processes [...] in our capacity for understanding and knowing" (p. 145).

Johnson (2011, p. 148) underlines his point by citing neuroscientist Don Tucker, who summarises the view of cognitive psychology in the relevant domain by stating that:

> Complex psychological functions must be understood to arise from bodily control networks. There is no other source for them. This is an exquisite parsimony of facts [...]. We can then specify the structure of abstract conceptualization as a structure of mind based on bodily forms.

Highlighting the aural-motor strategies of music teaching, then, illustrates the craft of music teaching as empowering a unique form of human cognition and thus underlines the unique contribution of music in educational contexts as a core issue in the debate on the justification of music education. This debate has been enlightened by scholars separating between musical and non-musical outcomes (Mark, 2002), intersonic and delineated musical meaning (Green, 2008) and between learning *music* and learning *about* music as I have done here. Moreover, music has been positioned within the realm of arts education, as a subject with an aesthetic core that constitutes its main distinction from other subjects. Teaching then aims at enabling aesthetic experiences and fostering aesthetic development in students, with teaching strategies training the listening and analysis of "great works". By attending to the aural-motor "gateway" to non-verbal, human cognition, we might argue that the craft of aural-motor teaching strategies adds another, not frequently addressed dimension to the search for uniqueness. Releasing this potential requires us to expand our notion of the craft of music teaching to entail a reflective practice wherein its *techne* and *phronesis* dimensions are deliberately reflected in *episteme* whilst not reducing them to epistemic categories but making them explicit by describing their uniqueness.

Criticism, Social Change and Complexity

Suggesting that the aural-motor and non-verbal craft dimensions of music teaching connect tightly with what music essentially is about implies taking a stand, that students' aural-motor, non-verbal cognition constitutes the most basic dimension of music learning. Consequently, the practice of aural-motor teaching strategies include an often covert musically based criticism of notions connecting human development with verbal language, overemphasising human thinking as being mainly connected with verbal-categorising cognition (Nielsen, 1998). This point of view is strongly supported by John Finney (2011, p.18). By drawing on Susanne Langer's notion of the non-discursive, he reminds us that music can be conceptualised as "thought in itself" and that "to think music" is different from "thinking about music".[4]

Do such aural-motor and non-verbal craft principles of teaching music in public school have the potential to operate within, relate to and handle the complexity of its societal environment in ways that contribute to constructive social change? The road from conducting aural-motor teaching strategies to arriving at social change seems long, and the scholarship of music education is gradually recognising the dangers of over-romanticising its potential of serving non-musical priorities (Johansen, 2017, 2019; McPherson, 2018). Hence, it is fairly reasonable to suggest that if aural-motor teaching strategies and their connected, theoretical foundations may contribute to social change; it would be as a smaller part of larger forces aiming at restoring the status of intuitive, sensory-motor, non-verbal and bodily forms of knowledge in society generally. In turn, these forces might constitute parts of an even larger mosaic of counterhegemonic thought and action.

An urgent question is then, of course, what kind of hegemony would those counterhegemonic actions be directed against? In order to identify the relevant hegemony, a turn to theories of modernity might be fruitful. Within the condition of late modernity (Giddens, 1990) described by characteristics such as social complexity (Johansen, 2010, 2016; Luhmann, 1995), liquidity and uncertainty (Baumann, 2012), reflexivity and risk (Beck, 1994) and contradictory identities (Hall, 1992), values such as those connected with the aural-motor craft dimensions of music teaching are under pressure. This is due to that even if, to some extent, different values apparently exist on equal terms in the late modern society, such as those connected with religious practices, gender priorities, cultural preferences, aesthetic practices and sexual orientations, discursive struggles about hegemony constantly goes on. In education, such struggles take place among discourses competing about filling floating signifiers (Laclau & Mouffe, 2014) such as "good teaching", "deep learning", "effective schooling" and "relevance" with meaning. Scholarly works within the sociology of education (Apple, 2007, 2013, 2015), curriculum studies (Smith, 2003) as well as the sociology of music education (Wright, 2011) describe the clearly hegemonic position of certain ideologies over others, along with their educational consequences on society's macro as well as micro level. These hegemonic ideologies include neoliberalism and the neopositivist ideals of the new managerial class, all congregated under Michael W. Apple's (2007, 2013, 2015) category of conservative modernisation.

However unintended, theories overemphasising and thereby reducing human thinking to entail verbal-categorising cognition have come to support the hegemony of verbalisation that constitutes the dominant basis for neopositivist and neoliberal notions of education, and thereby teaching, in the contemporary society. They therefore directly support the priorities of target-means and measurement-based educational ideologies, making values and principles that cannot be formulated in verbal categories slide out of focus. Encompassed in this are narrow conceptions and strict

---

[4] See also Kanellopoulos (2021).

"rules" of how to formulate educational aims and objectives as well as assessment criteria such as those, for example, practiced by OFSTED in Great Britain (Fautley, 2016). Included is a one-dimensional concept of epistemic knowledge that has manifested its hegemony in school and society, oppressing *techne* and *phronesis* knowledge dimensions and favouring teaching as a visual and verbal activity at the cost of aural and motor strategies. In part, this reductionist notion of knowledge and teaching has found support within the conceptualisation of school quality underlying the PISA[5] test results which has been widely debated in several Western societies since the beginning of the twenty-first century (Karlsen & Johansen, 2019).

I suggest that what is needed in order to contribute in a counterhegemonic mosaic aiming at constructive social change is that the craft of music teaching becomes a reflective practice (Westbury, Hopmann & Riquarts, 2000) wherein that craft, in all its dimensions and nuances, as well as its constantly changing social environment, are reflected in each other. In this way, the second interpretation of craft that points to the possible impact music education can make on students as well as its environment can come closer to a realisation, in two ways: a more powerful justification of music in public school and a more powerful impact of music education on social change.

References

Apple, M. (2007). Whose markets, whose knowledge? In A. R. Sadovnik (Ed.), *Sociology of education. A critical reader*. New York: Routledge.

Apple, M. (2013). *Can education change society?* New York: Routledge.

Apple, M. (2015). Educational realities and the tasks of the critical scholar/activist. *Finnish Journal of Music Education, 02*(18), 8–19.

Aristotle. (2011). *The Nicomachean ethics*. Chicago, IL: University of Chicago Press.

Baumann, Z. (2012). *Liquid modernity* (2012th edition). Cambridge, MA: Polity press.

Beck, U. (1994). Reflexive modernization. In U. Beck, A. Giddens, & S. Lash (Eds.), *Reflexive modernization*. Cambridge, MA: Polity Press.

Bjørkvold, J. R. (1992). *The muse within: Creativity and communication, song and play from childhood through maturity*. New York: Harper Collins.

Bruner, J. S. (1996). *The culture of education*. Cambridge, MA: Harvard University Press.

Campbell, P. S., & Scott-Kassner, C. (1995). *Music in childhood: From preschool through the elementary grades*. New York: Schirmer.

Choksy, L., Abrahamson, R., Gillespie, A. E., Woods, D., & York, F. (2001). *Teaching music in the twenty-first century* (2nd ed.). Upper Saddle River, NJ: Prentice Hall.

Davidsson, L., & Scripp, L. (1992). Surveying the coordinates of cognitive skills in music. In R. Colwell (Ed.), *Handbook of research on music teaching and learning* (pp. 392–413). New York: Schirmer.

Fautley, M. (2016). Policy and assessment in lower secondary school music education: The English experience. In C. Hung-Pai & P. Schmidt (Eds.), *Proceedings of the 18th international seminar of the ISME commission on music policy: Culture, education, and mass media*. Birmingham, UK: Birmingham City University.

---

[5] Programme for International Student Assessment.

Finney, J. (2011). John Paynter, music education and the creativity of coincidence. *British Journal of Music Education, 28*(1), 11–26.

Giddens, A. (1990). *The consequences of modernity*. Stanford, CA: Stanford University Press.

Green, L. (2008). *Music on deaf ears. Musical meaning, ideology and education* (2nd ed.). Bury St. Edmunds, UK: Arima Publishing.

Gustavsson, B. (2000). *Kunskapsfilisofi* [The philosophy of knowledge]. Stockholm, Sweden: Wahlström & Widstrand.

Hall, S. (1992). The question of cultural identity. In S. Hall, D. Held, & A. McGrew (Eds.), *Modernity and its futures* (pp. 274–316). Cambridge, MA: Polity in association with the Open University.

Handal, G., & Lauvås, P. (2000). *Veiledning og Praktisk Yrkesteori* [Supervision and practical vocation theory]. Oslo, Norway: Cappelen Akademisk.

Hanken, I. M. & Johansen, G. (2013). *Musikkundervisningens didaktikk* [The *didaktik* of music teaching]. Oslo, Norway: Cappelen Damm Akademisk.

Houlahan, M., & Tacka, P. (2012). *From sound to symbol: Fundamentals of music* (2nd ed.). New York: Oxford University Press.

Johansen, G. (2010). Musikdidaktik and Sociology. In R. Wright (Ed.), *Sociology and music education* (pp. 207–221). Aldershot, UK: Ashgate.

Johansen, G. (2016). Educating for the music teacher profession in a complex world. In R. Wright, B. A. Younker, & C. Benyon (Eds.), *21st century music education: Informal learning and non-formal teaching approaches in school and community contexts* (Canadian Music Educators' Association, Biennial Book Series, Research to Practice) (Vol. VII). Waterloo, ON: Canadian Music Educators' Association.

Johansen, G. (2017). Hva er selvkritisk musikkpedagogikk, og hvordan skal vi forholde oss til den? [What is Self-Critical Music Education, and how should we relate to it?]. In K. Stenseth, G. Trondalen & Ø. Varkøy (Eds.), *Musikk, handlinger, muligeter* [Music, Actions, Possibilities]. Festschrift to Even Ruud. Oslo, Norway:Norwegian Academy of Music.

Johansen, G. (2019). Music, universality and globalization. Some challenges for music education in the decades to come. In D. Hebert & T. B. Hauge (Eds.), *Advancing music education in Northern Europe* (pp. 81–91). London, UK: Routledge.

Johnson, M. (2011). Embodied knowing through art. In M. Biggs & H. Karlsson (Eds.), *The Routledge companion to research in the arts*. Oxon, UK: Routledge.

Kanellopoulos, P. (2021). Cage(d): Children, creativity and 'the contemporary' in music education—A sociological view. In Wright, R., Johansen, G. & Schmidt, P. (Eds.). *The Routledge handbook to sociology of music education*. New York: Routledge.

Karlsen, S. & Johansen, G. (2019). Assessment and the dilemmas of a multi-ideological curriculum: The case of Norway. In D. J. Elliott, M. Silverman & G. McPherson (Eds.). *The Oxford handbook of philosophical and qualitative perspectives on assessment in music education* (pp. 447–463). New York: Oxford University Press.

Laclau, E., & Mouffe, C. (2014). *Hegemony and socialist strategy. Towards a radical democratic politics* (2nd ed.). London, GB: Verso.

Lave, J., & Wenger, E. (1991). *Situated learning. Legitimate peripheral participation*. Cambridge, UK: Cambridge University Press.

Luhmann, N. (1995). *Social systems*. Stanford, CA: Stanford University Press.

Lyotard, J. F. (1984). *The postmodern condition. A report on knowledge*. Minneapolis, MN: University of Minnesota Press.

Mark, M. L. (2002). Nonmusical outcomes of music education: Historical considerations. In R. Colwell & C. P. Richardson (Eds.), *The new handbook of research on music teaching and learning* (pp. 1045–1052). New York: Oxford University Press.

McPherson, G. (2018). A life's journey through music. Keynote address at *ISME 33. World Conference*. Baku, Aserbajdsjan, 15–20 July.

Merleau-Ponty, M. (1979). *Phenomenology of perception*. London, GB: Routledge.

Nerland, M. (2004). Kunnskap i musikkpedagogisk praksis [Knowledge in music education practice]. In G. Johansen, S. Kalsnes & Ø. Varkøy (Eds.). *Musikkpedagogiske Utfordringer* [Challenges of music education] (pp. 46–56). Oslo, Norway: Cappelen Akademisk.

Nielsen, F. V. (1998). *Almen Musikdidaktik* [General *Musikdidaktik*]. Copenhagen, Denmark: Academic Publications.

Polanyi, M. (1966). *The tacit dimension.* London, GB: Routledge & Kegan Paul.

Ryle, G. (1949). *The concept of mind.* London, GB: Hutchinson.

Sadie, S. (Ed.). (1980). *The new grove dictionary of music and musicians.* London, GB: Macmillan.

Schön, D. A. (1987). *Educating the reflective practitioner: Toward a new design for teaching and learning in the professions.* San Francisco, CA: Jossey-Bass.

Sfard, A. (1998). On two metaphors for learning and the dangers of choosing just one. *Educational Researcher, 27*(2), 4–13.

Shulman, L. S. (1987). Knowledge and teaching: Foundations of the new reform. *Harvard Educational Review, 57*(1), 1–22.

Smith, D. G. (2003). Curriculum and teaching face globalization. In W. Pinar (Ed.), *International handbook of curriculum research* (pp. 35–52). Hillsdale, NJ: Erlbaum.

Sundin, B. (1998). Musical creativity in the first six years. A research project in retrospect. In B. Sundin, G. McPherson, & G. Folkestad (Eds.), *Children composing.* Lund, Sweden: Malmö Academy of Music.

Swanwick, K. (1994). *Musical knowledge. Intuition, analysis and music education.* London, GB: Routledge.

Varkøy, Ø. (2013). Technical rationality, techne and music education. In E. Georgii-Hemming, P. Burnard, & S.-E. Holgersen (Eds.), *Professional knowledge in music teacher education* (pp. 39–50). Aldershot, UK: Ashgate.

Vygotsky, L. S. (1978). *Mind in society: The development of higher psychological processes.* Boston, MA: Harvard University Press.

Walker, R. (2007). *Music education: Cultural values, social change and innovation.* Springfield, IL: Charles C. Thomas.

Wertsch, J. V. (2004). *Voices of collective remembering.* Cambridge, GB: Cambridge University Press.

Westbury, I. (2000). Teaching as a reflective practice: What might *didaktik* teach curriculum? In I. Westbury, S. Hopmann, & K. Riquarts (Eds.), *Teaching as a Reflective Practice. The German Didaktik Tradition.* Hillsdale, NJ: Erlbaum.

Crafting Music Education for All?
The Composite Knowledge Base of Music Education in Times of Cultural Diversity and Social Polarisation

Petter Dyndahl and Siw Graabræk Nielsen

Abstract In this chapter, the authors argue for employing a composite and multidimensional notion of the music education crafts. This concept is broadly framed and justified by a number of traditions and positions from knowledge and learning theory, as well as from philosophy, sociology and pedagogy, which are thoroughly examined throughout the chapter. The overall purpose is to discuss the conditions for inclusive music education in times of cultural diversity and social polarisation and thus to contribute to the slogan *music education for all* being formulated historically appropriately and with informed, updated knowledge. This is accomplished by indicating why and how music educators must acquire the necessary epistemic craftsmanship to analyse, negotiate and, eventually, be able to choose proper resources and tools in today's complex social and cultural situation.

Preamble: Knowledge, Crafts and Complexities

Our ethical point of departure in this chapter is that unequal or imbalanced offers and opportunities for music education on the basis of gender, sexuality, age, ability, ethnicity and/or social class are a democratic problem and should be recognised and treated as structural challenges and not primarily classified as issues that must be sorted out on an individual basis. This implies both analyses of social structures and knowledge dimensions affecting music education in general as well as more specific aspects, including what could be considered as the crafts of music education,

P. Dyndahl (✉)
Inland Norway University of Applied Sciences, Hamar, Norway
e-mail: petter.dyndahl@inn.no

S. G. Nielsen
Norwegian Academy of Music, Oslo, Norway
e-mail: Siw.G.Nielsen@nmh.no

© Springer Nature Switzerland AG 2021
K. Holdhus et al. (eds.), *Music Education as Craft*, Landscapes: the Arts, Aesthetics, and Education 30, https://doi.org/10.1007/978-3-030-67704-6_4

indicating that such crafts should be part of a composite knowledge concept that must reflect and apply to musical learning and upbringing.

It follows that we believe that the concept of knowledge is complex and dynamic, leading to questions such as what kinds of knowledge are relevant to today's music students and what knowledge-related issues should music teachers, teacher educators and researchers keep track of and be able to deal with in contemporary culture and society. The last question refers to the application-oriented crafts dimension that will be emphasised in the following discussion. In the next section, we give the first account of a multidimensional concept of knowledge from an epistemological perspective. This will be further developed from different angles in subsequent sections.

As for the chapter title indication that we live in times of cultural diversity and social polarisation, we build on the premise that cultural diversity is a permanent condition. However, diversity encompasses far more than ethnic and national variety and difference. Equally important—but often overlooked in the context of music education—is the inclusion of social class, gender, sexual orientation, age/generation and so on. Moreover, in our time—partly as a result of economic and political crises, populism and radicalisation—social polarisation has increased. This, of course, takes place within the realm of the material economy, but also in what might be characterised as a symbolic or cultural economic dimension, which in some situations even finds expression as so-called culture wars. Despite this, music education has a strong tradition of emphasising music's harmonising and consolidating properties for building interaction and community. This is all well and good, but the question must be raised whether it thus can contribute to a discursive formation that obscures conflicting interests and frictions between social groups and cultural forms of expression in education and society, as this is also reflected in the field of music. These issues will be elaborated later in detail.

Against this background, we argue that in order for the slogan *music education for all* to be formulated historically appropriately and with informed, updated knowledge, music educators must acquire the necessary epistemic craftsmanship to analyse, negotiate and, finally, be able to choose proper resources and tools in today's complex social and cultural situation.

Part I Dimensions and Nuances: Types and Forms of Knowledge

In the *Nicomachean Ethics*, Aristotle (Aristotle/Ross, 2009) divided knowledge into five intellectual virtues: *episteme* (scientific knowledge), *techne* (craftsmanship), *phronesis* (practical wisdom), *sophia* (theoretical wisdom) and *nous* (understanding). The Aristotelian concept of knowledge is thus diverse and complex and contains theoretical, practical and ethical dimensions. However, this division does not consist of discrete units. For example, *sophia* refers to a combination of *episteme* and *nous*. Hence, theoretical wisdom should be regarded as scientific knowledge plus understanding. *Nous*, in turn, is seen as belonging to another more intuitive principle than the others. Thus, it can be argued that over the course of time, the Aristotelian concept has been reduced to a threefold division of knowledge (i.e. into scientific knowledge, craftsmanship and practical wisdom), for instance, in the process of being "rediscovered" and reformulated by Wittgenstein (1953). Here, according to Wittgenstein's terminology, the three types of knowledge are often referred to as *propositional, practical* and *implicit*. As Wittgenstein applies these to music, propositional knowledge would involve explaining what a musical instrument is in descriptive, factual terms. Practical knowledge would be about mastering the art of playing the instrument in question, while the implicit knowledge, which is a more intransitive form of knowledge that is built up over time, would be about knowing something without necessarily being able to say what it is. While both the propositional and practical knowledge can be expressed in words, it is not so easy to explain the implicit knowledge verbally. It is therefore often referred to as *tacit knowledge*, a term attributed to Polanyi (1967), which is based upon forms of pre-linguistic or non-linguistic comprehension. Wittgenstein's example is to recognise the sound of a particular musical instrument (Wittgenstein 1953, §78), but even more subtle distinctions can be added, for example, the ability to assess whether a performer is playing well or badly on it. The latter aspect points to a musical pedagogy operationalisation of Wittgenstein's implicit knowledge concept, but it would not be difficult to exemplify also propositional and practical knowledge in relation to music education. What is more, McGuinness (1989) argues that Wittgenstein emphasised the importance of understanding philosophical thinking as:

> a craft, a discipline [...] and its value consisted in its being well done. So one should do it well and not preach about it: [...] showing not saying was important. Like all crafts, its exercise at its highest produces beauty, a beauty which requires an intellectual effort to grasp [...]. (McGuinness, 1989, p. 77)

In this context, it is interesting to observe how the applied craftsmanship is highlighted as an important perspective on epistemology and philosophy.

A similar tripartite scheme of knowledge as that of Wittgenstein underlies Nielsen's (2007) views on forms of music knowledge as a combination of aspects from the arts, practice-based knowledge and research. Nielsen (1994) argues that one dimension of knowledge in music stems from the immediate "perceptual experience of music" and is "practice-based knowledge without any direct dependency on verbal–linguistic experiences" (p. 106, our translation). He defines this as the *ars* dimension of music knowledge. A second dimension stems from "the verbal-linguistic experiences" of music, defined as the *scientia* dimension of knowledge (p. 106). Although these dimensions appear as discrete and distinct forms of knowledge, Nielsen also puts forward the notion that these dimensions may form opposite ends of a continuum and, as such, to a certain degree overlap each other in some musical activities. For example, in the context of music education, Nielsen (1994) defines five central activities in which these dimensions are emphasised differently but may still be present in varying degrees. The activities are reproduction,

production, perception, interpretation and reflection. An understanding of music education as rooted in music as art emphasises the ars dimension of music knowledge that is teaching "music in music's own medium and on its own terms" (p. 115, our translation) by letting students perform and create music or by students' listening to music. However, when music is made an object for teaching and learning, the need to talk about and to verbally articulate the content—the music—emerges, and, as such, the importance of the scientia dimension in activities such as analysing and interpreting music in non-musical forms and channels or in reflecting upon music's cultural or historical dimensions is emphasised.

Together, the above perspectives add to a true composite and multidimensional concept of knowledge, not least in music and music education. Moreover, the explicit inclusion of crafts justifies that so far we can operate with a comprehensive notion of the music education crafts, including epistemic craftsmanship. A question to be raised, however, is what this concept might be missing in relation to cultural diversity, social polarisation and music education for all. We will come back to this.

Part II Ontologies and Metaphors: Music, Education and Music Education

Claiming that today's music reality is diverse is no exaggeration. The media landscape allows all kinds of music to be immediately present, and music can be linked to virtually any situation and occasion. This diversity means that questions about what music is or may be need to be answered in many different ways. This is something Bohlman (2001) characterises as *multiple ontologies of music*, meaning that people are implementing a number of assumptions and beliefs about what kind of phenomenon music is, what it is good for and what qualities it possesses. Bohlman's main point is that any ontology must be situated in specific contexts, cultures and values. Similar forms of diversity and variety are expressed by a number of thinkers, but with different emphases and intentions. For example, Small (1998) opposed a basic understanding of music as an object when he launched an alternative conception of music that claims that it is first and foremost activities or practices. In that sense, it becomes logical to replace the concept of music with the notion of *musicking*. This is not just a matter of creating or exercising music, but in principle any activity that can be linked to music, including negotiations of musical values. Frith (1996) assumed that different music is valued differently, for example, by various musical authorities, when he criticised what he described as the prevailing perception that classical music primarily conveys aesthetic values, while popular music is more inclined to be understood and interpreted by virtue of its social functions, such as providing social identity and group affiliation. Opposite to this, he argued that all kinds of music are both aesthetic and functional and that these aspects are inseparable and necessary for the music to have an impact on people's lives. In the description of the distinction between classical music and popular music, Frith basically built on Bourdieu's (1984) social analysis of high and low culture, offering different amounts of cultural capital respectively. We return to this later in the chapter, but can already infer that what offers cultural capital is also related to situational factors such as time, place, cultural status inequalities and social class.

A similar multiple ontologisation that has been described in music should perhaps also apply to the understanding of what education might be in today's society. Biesta (2010) has attempted to meet this issue by launching a multidimensional concept of education. He believes that education in general should fill three different but interrelated and overlapping functions, namely, *qualification*, *socialisation* and *subjectification*. Biesta sees qualification as one of organised education's major functions. According to the role education plays in providing students with knowledge, crafts and skills that prepare them for working life, the qualification function is an important justification for public education in society. Moreover, when he describes socialisation as a function of education, Biesta draws attention to the processes of internalising society's norms and values. In addition, Biesta claims that, regardless of intentions, any education will always have a socialising function and thus play an important role in the perpetuation of culture and tradition. Furthermore, Biesta believes that education has a crucial function in the student's process of becoming a subject, and this is what he denotes as subjectification. He ascribes greater significance to the ways students may become more autonomous and independent in their thinking and acting through subjectification than through the other two functions, which he believes tend to overshadow subjectification in today's education policies. Our position is that together these dimensions can act as important aspects of the music education crafts also in times of cultural diversity and social polarisation. However, in that case they must be released from Biesta's own tendency to consistently emphasise the subjectification feature of the concept at the expense of the others. Although he claims to have good reasons for this in today's political context, it will be crucial to hold on to the reciprocal link between social, cultural and individual functions related to our purpose (see Dyndahl, 2021).

Similar to the diversity of the music education crafts, the multiplicity in concepts and thinking regarding music and education is also present in widespread learning metaphors. Looking into how different aspects of learning may complement each other is essential in our work as educators, Sfard (1998) argues, and therefore "too great a devotion to one particular metaphor can lead to theoretical distortions and to undesirable practices" (Sfard, 1998, p. 4). Her main argument relies on introducing two overarching metaphors that operate across different theories of learning and which "educational research is caught between" (1998, p. 5), namely, the *acquisition* and the *participation* metaphors. As Sfard states, "since the dawn of civilisation, human learning is conceived of as an acquisition of something" (1998, p. 5) and thus as something being acquired as the individual's private knowledge. As Sfard finds it, this privatisation of learning and seeing knowledge as something permanent "has persisted in a wide spectrum of frameworks, from moderate to radical constructivism and then to interactionism and sociocultural theories" (1998, p. 6). However, in more recent theories of learning, "the permanence of *having* gives way to the constant flux of *doing*", as Sfard (1998, p. 6) conceives it. By emphasising the learner's participation in different learning communities, "learning a subject is now conceived of as a process of becoming a member of a certain community", whereby both the participants and the community may "affect and inform" each other (Sfard, 1998, p. 6).

Lahn and Jensen (2008) take up Sfard's discussion on the metaphors for learning in relation to communities of learning and argue that the literature concerning learning communities downplays the importance of abstract and material aspects of learning in addition to how practitioners accomplish their professional knowledge, crafts and skills. They therefore launch a comprehensive *tool metaphor*, by which they, on the one hand, articulate a professional-oriented perspective on *epistemic tools*, based on Engeström's (1987) activity and expansive learning theories. On the other hand, the tool concept is developed as a *material tool* perspective, based on Latour's (2005) actor-network theory, where the argument is that human cognition has lost its privileged status in learning and the production of knowledge. This is by far in line with our claim that now learning and knowledge must be considered as complex crafts.

These significant aspects of musical and educational ontologies and metaphors thus represent important input to the music education crafts. However, they also raise questions about where this leaves us in relation to questions about the uses and functions of music education in times of cultural diversity and social polarisation. In the next section we follow this path towards a more in-depth examination of the relationship between knowledge and action.

Part III Conflict and Transcendence: Fundamental Epistemologies

So far, we have looked at how different theories imagine what knowledge and crafts can be. Ontologically (and metaphorically) speaking, we have recognised that this is a complex and composite epistemological field, and we have put forward various ideas or metaphors for knowledge, learning and education. All of this we have attempted to relate to music and music education, and we have also begun discussing it in relation to cultural diversity and social polarisation. Now it is time to take a closer look at the relationship between knowledge/crafts and action, and the possibility that epistemic craftsmanship can act as a liberating force, in particular as this is interpreted completely differently within the contradiction between subjectivist and objectivist social theories.

Central to Bourdieu's social theory is that scientific knowledge must exceed everyday knowledge if liberation is to be possible (Bourdieu, 1977, 1990). He thus denies purely inductive knowledge approaches, such as grounded theory, and believes theory is necessary to develop concepts that transcend intuitive knowledge. At the same time, he estimates that the sociology before him has been characterised by what he, on the one hand, calls *social phenomenology* and, on the other, *social physics*. With the former, he points to a subjectivist understanding of knowledge, according to which creative and independent actors in an unobstructed and rational way seem to be able to construct the social world and the knowledge of it from the bottom up. Examples of such theories are micro-interactionism and rational choice theory. On the other hand, on social physics he refers to objectivist theories which, as their starting point, aim at objective, social structures that exist independently of the individual actors and determine their range of action and possibilities. In this context, Bourdieu has, in particular, functionalism and post-structuralism in mind.

The above approaches have been left in a confrontational relationship to each other. Bourdieu's solution to the conflict is that he transcends both and instead conceives a social theory that incorporates both subjectivist and objectivist perspectives (Bourdieu, 1977, 1990). This action represents at the same time his way of solving the classic sociological dichotomy between structure and agency, especially as expressed in his attempt to unite them in the notion of *habitus*. The dual character of the concept is evident in that Bourdieu, on the one hand, sees habitus as something external that is forced upon us through upbringing and location within given social structures. Thus, one could say that society takes residence in our bodies and minds. On the other hand, however, habitus also gives the individual an intelligible position in society and the world: a place from which the subject can act on the basis of intuition and a practical sense (Bourdieu, 1977, 1990)—agentic capacities that Bourdieu understands as collectively and socially shaped. This means that habitus is strongly regulated by structural conditions and class-based classification systems. Hence, this must also apply to the music education crafts, since they are closely related to the person's qualification, socialisation and subjectification. However, notwithstanding this fact, habitus also holds an enabling potential, which opens the way for the practical sense to be exercised, and this might be regarded as Bourdieu's expression of agency. Accordingly, the practical sense must be an operative feature of the music education crafts as well. This potential is important in relation to this field in particular, as Bourdieu and Passeron (1977) attribute a certain relative autonomy from structural coercion precisely within social fields such as art and education.

In the next section, we attempt to locate some of the above tensions in relevant Norwegian higher music education examples. It is therefore necessary to go into detail of how music education is always situated in certain contexts, cultures and values, as Bohlman (2001) claims these apply to multiple ontologies of music also. And—not least—it will be necessary to introduce a concept of power in the examination of the music education crafts.

Part IV Music Education in Culture and Society: Situated Knowledge, Situated Learning and Gender

In her 1988 essay "Situated Knowledges: The Science Question in Feminism and the Privilege of Partial Perspective", Haraway emphasises how one is always bodily and materially situated in the ways one represents the world. No representations objectively reflect a stable world. Representations are always linked to our situation and derived from practice, where it is not clear who creates and whom is created. All scientific practice is characterised by specific situations, and knowledge production contributes in its ways to characterise the situation. It follows that the production of knowledge is always *gendered*. Situated knowledge is thus a critique of masculine science, which implicitly claims that this particular tradition is assumed to be free from social and biological ties that can interfere with the ability to remain unbiased in the study of reality. In Haraway's feminist philosophy of science, it is rather the case that the researcher's gaze is always bodied. This means that since the body has a gender, an age, a variation of functionality and an ethnicity, these factors contribute to shaping the researcher's experience and understanding of the world. As situated knowledge manifestations, the music education crafts are bound to be developed at the intersection of the same factors.

For Lave and Wenger (1991), an essential point is that the different elements of knowledge/crafts and professional culture should not be viewed in isolation from each other. They build their concept of situated learning—obviously inspired by Haraway (1988)—on a comprehensive study of how apprentices learn to master the craftsmanship of their profession while taking part in more and more professional activities under the master's supervision. Thus, the apprentice is incorporated into what Lave and Wenger call *legitimate peripheral participation*, through which learning takes place through the practice and the situation it relates to.

Theories of situated knowledge and situated learning emphasise the need, as many of the other theorists we have employed have also expressed, to always interpret and understand knowledge and crafts in the specific forms and contexts in which they appear. As Haraway in particular indicates, these will also be charged with power. The theorist who has primarily been concerned with the relationship between knowledge and power is Foucault. For him, power and knowledge are considered to be mutually constitutive. However, he argues that power is not only repressive but also productive and that it penetrates all relations and levels of society:

> This form of power that applies itself to immediate everyday life categorizes the individual, marks him by his own individuality, attaches him to his own identity, imposes a law of truth on him that he must recognize and others have to recognize in him. It is a form of power that makes individuals subjects. There are two meanings of the word "subject": subject to someone else by control and dependence, and tied to his own identity by a conscience or self-knowledge. Both meanings suggest a form of power that subjugates and makes subject to. (Foucault, 2001, p. 331)

In the same way as with Bourdieu's habitus concept, Foucault maintains a duality that makes it possible to unify the dichotomy structure–agency, as regards both the concept of power and the subject. And, as stated above, we also place the notion of the music education crafts within a duality that refers both to the dichotomies of structure–agency and of power–knowledge.

Since 2013, both of us have been part of a research group that, among other things, has investigated Norwegian higher music education and music research through the lenses of a concept we have entitled *musical gentrification*. In this, we have attempted to operate the above dichotomies in a nuanced manner as well as keeping a glance at the power dimension that, for example, concerns what is included and excluded in music education and research. Adapted and recontextualised from urban geography and planning, the musical gentrification metaphor indicates that—from a certain point in the history of higher music education in Norway—it became increasingly attractive for students, teachers and researchers to include music, musical practices and musical cultures that had previously had too low a cultural status to be considered relevant as teaching and research objects in this context (Dyndahl, Karlsen, Skårberg & Nielsen, 2014). This is first and foremost about popular music's introduction to and, in turn, significant presence in Norwegian music academia. We have therefore researched when, how, why and what kind of popular music (as well as any music tradition, genre and style) has been included in Norwegian higher education and research by examining all master's theses and doctoral dissertations approved in any academic music discipline throughout the century from 1912 to 2012, a total of 1695 theses (Dyndahl, Karlsen, Nielsen & Skårberg, 2017). The results show that the first entrance of a thesis focusing on popular music was in 1974, with a work on modern/contemporary jazz written within one of the country's musicology programmes. Since then, an ever-increasing proportion of theses has been related to popular music. Already in 1981, popular music theses occupied about 20% of the total amount of academic output at this level, and from 2006 the percentage rose above 30%, a level that remained stable as long as our data reaches—that is, until 2013—but there is reason to believe that it is still ascending.

With this, one could believe that higher music education is "democratised" and that all kinds of music are now included. In comparison to the overall dominant position Western classical music had previously, an inclusive expansion has obviously also taken place. However, in the same way as urban gentrification is exercised by people with higher status than the original inhabitants of the neighbourhoods that become objects of their attraction and therefore also tends to expel the original residents, musical gentrification also has exclusionary or marginalising effects. This is expressed in several ways. First of all, not all popular music styles are being gentrified. Thus, new genre hierarchies arise. It is not surprising, therefore, that jazz was both the first genre that was included and that it is very well represented in the overall picture. At the opposite end of the scale, we find Scandinavian dance band music, which is a widespread music genre and cultural practice in Norway and Sweden, but which is not represented in the investigated material at all. Postgraduate students, as future music teachers and/or potential music researchers, apparently do not wish to be associated with music that has such a clear working-class affiliation. However, musical gentrification is not just about what is included and excluded, respectively. Equally important is how it is done. By using sufficiently sophisticated theory and conceptual apparatus, it seems that virtually any music (with a few notable exceptions) can be lifted up to legitimate culture and provide opportunities to reap—in this case—academic capital. Thus, one can also say that the gentrification changes the music (including its reception) that is exposed to it, just as the former workers' homes are transformed by middle- and upper-class habitus in urban gentrification. In other words, this is an example of academics' practice of their agency or adequate practical sense for the purpose of accumulating cultural capital according to the structural norms and values set or constantly being re-set within dynamic classification systems. As such, it is reminiscent of both Aristotelian techne and phronesis, but for research to analyse it and put it towards useful concepts, not least for liberating action, episteme is also needed. In this context, it is therefore reasonable to also describe such practices as variants of the composite concept of the music education crafts.

Another challenge refers to the unequal and imbalanced offers and opportunities for music education based on gender. At first glance, it seems that there is full gender equality in Norwegian music academia. There has been an equal gender distribution between female and male students in higher music education for a long time, and there are more female staff members now than ever before at higher educational institutions (Borgen et al. 2010). Nonetheless, by examining our data from the above survey study more closely, we find some features that point in other directions. We have conducted three studies on gender aspects in the academisation of higher music education in Norway. In the first, Dyndahl et al. (2017) found that the uptake that applies especially to popular music appears to be strongly gendered and that there is an overall strong male dominance in the gender of the popular music theses' authors in the investigated period. In the second study, Nielsen (2021) discusses the gendered divisions in the music educational field as a process of *gender-fication* that takes place in parallel with the processes of musical gentrification. With the backdrop of Bourdieu's theories on masculine domination and studies of genderfication processes in urban gentrification (van den Berg, 2012), Nielsen (2021) coins musical genderfication as "the production of gender norms and gendered divisions within this specific social space, which also unfolds hierarchies of 'high' and 'low' culture" (2021, p. 111). Looking into how these gendered divisions may evolve over time, Nielsen (2021) finds, for example, that the male dominance in authorship of popular music had been visible from quite early on, while female dominance in authorship within Western classical music had evolved over time by a "shift in gender dominance" from male to female from 1984 and onwards (2021, p. 116). Other genres and topics have also experienced such gendered shifts. Recently, Nielsen and Dyndahl (2021) have questioned metaphorically "which 'rooms' are available for women in the music academia household, which positions have been kept hidden in the dark interior of the house and which have been brought out into the light at the front" (2021, p. 344), referring to Bourdieu's (1977) analysis of the structural dominance exercised by men over women in the *Kabyle house*. They argue that "the use of symbolic violence maintains and reproduces masculine domination and a gender order within music academia" (Nielsen & Dyndahl, 2021, p. 348). One result of genderfication tendencies within musical gentrification might be that the number of female full professors in higher music academia does not reflect the abovementioned development that indicates an equal gender distribution between female and male students as well as a record number of female staff members in general. The relatively low number of women who have reached the top of the academic hierarchy also applies when compared to other disciplines within the country's higher education system (Committee for Gender Balance and Diversity in Research, 2018–2021).

Part V Summary and Conclusion

In this chapter, we have attempted to draw attention to the epistemological, ontological and metaphorical diversity of the compound knowledge concept of music education crafts. We have also supported theories that claim that knowledge must be linked to power and that fundamental perceptions of knowledge/crafts can stand against each other in conflictual relationships. Here, however, it has been important to argue that there are also sustainable social theories that seek to transcend those contradictions in ways that show the possibility of action. A basic premise is still that the music education crafts are always situated in specific contexts and thus are the bearer of particular interests and power. Moreover, through examples from our own research on Norwegian higher music education, we have demonstrated how complex and paradoxical these issues can be, which emphasises the need for further epistemic reflection. In times of cultural diversity and social polarisation, this is a demanding task, and whatever action is taken will have social and cultural consequences always—already being impregnated by power. Music education and research, as well as teaching and teacher education, however, have no choice but to respond actively and ethically to this challenge by constantly (re-)negotiating the music education crafts. This is about nothing less than music education's credibility in achieving the aim of music education for all.

References

Aristotle. (2009). *The Nicomachean ethics*. (D. Ross, Trans., L. Brown, Ed). Oxford University Press. (Original work published c. 340 BC).

Biesta, G. (2010). *Good education in an age of measurement: Ethics, politics, democracy*. Boulder, CO: Paradigm Publishers.

Bohlman, P. V. (2001). Ontologies of music. In N. Cook & M. Everist (Eds.), *Rethinking music* (pp. 17–34). Oxford, UK/New York: Oxford University Press.

Borgen, J. S., Arnesen, C. Å., Caspersen, J., Gunnes, H., Hovdhagen, E., & Næss, T. 2010. *Kjønn og musikk: Kartlegging av kjønnsfordelingen i utdanning og arbeidsliv innenfor musikk* [Gender and music. A survey on gender balance in education and labor market in music]. NIFU: Rapport 49/2010.

Bourdieu, P. (1977). *Outline of a theory of practice*. Cambridge, UK: Cambridge University Press.

Bourdieu, P. (1984). *Distinction: A social critique of the judgement of taste*. London/New York: Harvard University Press.

Bourdieu, P. (1990). *The logic of practice*. Stanford, CA: Stanford University Press.

Bourdieu, P., & Passeron, J.-C. (1977). *Reproduction in education, society and culture*. London: Sage.

Committee for Gender Balance and Diversity in Research. (2018–2021). Kifinfo. Retrieved from http://kifinfo.no/en/content/statistics

Dyndahl, P. (2021). Music education as qualification, socialisation and subjectification? In R. Wright, G. Johansen, P. Kanellopoulos, & P. Schmidt (Eds.), *The Routledge handbook to sociology of music education* (pp. 169–183). Abingdon, UK: Routledge.

Dyndahl, P., Karlsen, S., Nielsen, S. G., & Skårberg, O. (2017). The academisation of popular music in higher music education: The case of Norway. *Music Education Research, 19*(4), 438–454.

Dyndahl, P., Karlsen, S., Skårberg, O., & Nielsen, S. G. (2014). Cultural omnivorousness and musical gentrification: An outline of a sociological framework and its applications for music education research. *Action, Criticism, and Theory for Music Education, 13*(1), 40–69.

Engeström, Y. (1987). *Learning by expanding: An activity-theoretical approach to developmental research*. Orienta-Konsultit Oy: Helsinki, Finland.

Foucault, M. M. (2001). The subject and power. In J. D. Faubion (Ed.), *Essential works of Foucault 1954–1984: Vol. 3: Power* (pp. 326–348). Penguin Books.

Frith, S. (1996). *Performing rites: On the value of popular music*. Cambridge MA: Harvard University Press.

Haraway, D. (1988). Situated knowledges: The science question in feminism and the privilege of partial perspective. *Feminist Studies, 14*(3), 575–599.

Lahn, L. C., & Jensen, K. (2008). Profesjon og læring [Profession and learning]. In A. Molander, & L. I. Terum, (Eds.), *Profesjonsstudier* [Professional studies] (pp. 295–305). Universitetsforlaget.

Latour, B. (2005). *Re-assembling the social: An introduction to actor-network theory*. Oxford, UK: Oxford University Press.

Lave, J., & Wenger, E. (1991). *Situated learning: Legitimate peripheral participation*. Cambridge, UK: Cambridge University Press.

McGuinness, B. (1989). *Wittgenstein, a life: Young Ludwig*. London: Duckworth.

Nielsen, F. V. (1994). *Almen musikdidaktik* [General music *Didaktik*]. København: Christian Ejler's Forlag.

Nielsen, F. V. (2007). Music (and arts) education from the point of view of Didaktik and Bildung. In L. Bresler (Ed.), *International handbook of research in arts education* (pp. 265–286). Dordrecht, the Netherlands: Springer.

Nielsen, S. G. (2021). Musical gentrification and 'genderfication' in higher music education. In P. Dyndahl, S. Karlsen, & R. Wright (Eds.), *Musical gentrification and socio-cultural diversities: An analytical approach towards popular music expansion in egalitarian societies* (pp. 109–124). Abingdon, UK: Routledge.

Nielsen, S. G. & Dyndahl, P. (2021). Music education, *genderfication* and symbolic violence. In R. Wright, G. Johansen, P. Kanellopoulos, & P. Schmidt (Eds.). *The Routledge handbook to sociology of music education* (p. 343–353). Abingdon, UK: Routledge.

Polanyi, M. (1967). *The tacit dimension*. London: Routledge.

Sfard, A. (1998). On two metaphors for learning and the dangers of choosing just one. *Educational Researcher, 27*(27), 4–13.

Small, C. (1998). *Musicking. The meanings of performing and listening*. Hanover, NH/London: The University Press of New England.

van den Berg, M. (2012). Femininity as a city marketing strategy: Gender bending Rotterdam. *Urban Studies, 49*, 153–168.

Wittgenstein, L. (1953). Philosophical investigations. (G. E. M. Anscombe, Trans.). Oxford, UK: Basil Blackwell.

Music Education in England as a Political Act: Reflections on a Craft Under Pressure

Martin Fautley

Abstract Assessment in music education is an issue which dominates discourse in many jurisdictions. This chapter argues that assessment needs to be seen against a political backdrop. Assessment is never neutral and value-free; it cannot be by definition. The focus for this chapter is the teaching and learning which takes place in music classrooms. Neoliberal political ideas currently dominate political thinking in many countries. One of the ways in which policies in education reflect this is that certain sorts of knowledge are privileged in assessment terms. In music education, this can take a number of forms, but common to them is a tacit assumption that some styles and genres of music are deemed more worthy of privilege. However, doing this automatically places other music in a less privileged position. Governmental intervention that controls curriculum can also control thinking. With increasing controls of curriculum-as-content, there are also increasing checks on teacher freedom. This chapter suggests that music educators need to think through what sorts of values they wish to promote in their classrooms and how types, styles, and genres of music are not the only ways in which this is visible, but also in the pedagogic practices that are employed. The rise of informal pedagogies contains within itself a different way of assessing progress by individual pupils, as well as in groups of learners. This chapter provides food for thought for music educators on this issue.

Introduction

This chapter proposes that music education, curriculum, and assessment, focussing on the specific context of the lower secondary school, are sites of contestation and hegemonic intervention. The ways in which this situation has come into being are explained and related historical aspects discussed. This chapter takes as its starting point the observation made by Magne Espeland that:

M. Fautley (✉)
Birmingham City University, Birmingham, UK
e-mail: martin.fautley@bcu.ac.uk

© Springer Nature Switzerland AG 2021
K. Holdhus et al. (eds.), *Music Education as Craft*, Landscapes: the Arts, Aesthetics, and Education 30, https://doi.org/10.1007/978-3-030-67704-6_5

> Knowledge is the basis for power and power produces knowledge. Curricular reforms are…
> examples of a process where there is a close connection between the production of knowl-
> edge and power. (Espeland, 1999, p. 177)

Curriculum and assessment in music education are both issues that dominate discourse in a number of jurisdictions across the globe. Whilst music education may
seem an unlikely site for political activity, and of the politics of knowledge, nonetheless it is the case that this is so. Sometimes discourse in this arena takes the form
of tacit and unarticulated valorisation, and the very music educators directly
involved in it can be unaware that this is occurring. This chapter focuses on teaching, learning, and assessment in the generalist music classroom and considers how
political views on these matters affect the day-to-day working of the music teacher.
It takes the perspective from England as the main focus, as it is there that these matters have played out significantly in terms of how teachers work and how they are
required to act. The overarching theme of this book is *music education as craft*, and
the idea of "craft" is an important one to bear in mind when thinking about this
music education context in England. The notion of *craft* in the English situation has
become complex, and possibly obfuscated, by a steady stream of political intervention and of interference in ways of working.

Music Education and Curriculum in England

The statutory nature of music education has become increasingly fractured over the
years. England got its first National Curriculum in 1992 (Department for Education
and Science, 1992), but this was the result of much political and sociological fighting in terms of both approach and content. In the run-up to its publication, a high-
profile argument took place, often played out in the columns of national newspapers.
This quote, for example, from *The Times* in 1991, as the draft National Curriculum
was being considered:

> Music education in the state sector has been in a mess for 20 years. These new recommen-
> dations only codify the confusion. Old certainties of the post-1944 era classroom singing, a
> traditional grounding in classical music history and the rules of harmony and counterpoint
> were swept away in the late 1960s. Some reform was necessary; only a tiny minority of
> children was benefiting fully from this rigorous academic framework. But what has replaced
> the old buttresses?
>
> The new recommendations enshrine a tired form of anything-goes egalitarianism, of letting
> children "express their feelings" and "discover things for themselves". Musical literacy is
> no longer seen as the key to true creativity or musical appreciation; rather, it is presented as
> a marginal option. Yet when it comes to active participation in musical activity, no amount
> of access to expensive synthesisers, or "project work" on the life and times of Michael
> Jackson, can prepare a child half as well as the certain knowledge that All Cows Eat Grass.
> It is as basic to musical growth as teaching the meaning of tens and units is to numeracy.
> (Morrison, 1991)

The reference to "All Cows Eat Grass" was a coded description of the ways in which many pupils in England were (and still are) taught the names of notes in the bass clef, A-C-E-G being the mnemonic for the notes in the spaces of the stave which arise from this. The fact that Morrison does not feel that he needs to explain what this means is a link forward to a work that has come to dominate the thinking of English Politicians in early years of the twenty-first century, namely, E. D. Hirsch's, "Cultural literacy: What every literate American needs to know" (Hirsch, 1987). In this book, Hirsch argues that in order to fully understand what is being written or discussed, children and young people need a thorough grounding in cultural matters:

> "Cultural literacy," the grasp of background information that most writers and speakers assume their readers and listeners already have, is the key to effective education, Hirsch says. That background information, even when much of it is rather vague, is what enables us to grasp the point of a magazine article or make sense of a television news broadcast because it allows us to make connections between new information and what we already know, without stopping to check an encyclopedia or dictionary or almanac every few words. (Lauermann, 1987)

What is particularly relevant in the context of this current book is that Magne Espeland had encountered the work of Hirsch in the Norwegian context in 1994. He was later to describe his feelings after hearing Hirsch speak at a conference:

> At that time very few Norwegians had heard about Hirsch's work. At the conference, he presented his ideas about cultural literacy and the necessity of strengthening the body of shared general knowledge in education. For the few of us who knew a little about Hirsch's ideas, the link to the minister's ideas about a core curriculum became obvious. The teachers and the academics present seemed puzzled when Hirsch severely criticised the progressive movement in education, calling it "romantic educational formalism".
>
> My notes from that day are not very optimistic. I was worried about what the combination of core curriculum and severe criticism of the progressive movement in education could lead to in terms of guidelines for the coming curriculum process, including the creation of subject syllabuses. Was it going to be a turning point? Would it lead to a weakening of arts education and a turn "back to the basics"? (Espeland, 1997, p. 12)

Maybe Magne Espeland was right to feel uneasy; certainly with regard to music education in England, there do seem to be echoes of his concerns. The influence of Hirsch will be picked up later in this chapter, but for the moment, to return to the Morrison piece quoted above, the author did not feel he needed to explain "All Cows Eat Grass" to his literate, culturally endowed *The Times* of London readership. But it is a number of the other background constructs to this Morrison comment piece that warrant unpicking somewhat, as they have remained more or less constant since that time. These can be categorised in two main areas:

1. Music literacy means being able to read western classical staff notation. (This carries the implication that any music which does not utilise this is probably inferior.)
2. Allowing children and young people to "express their feelings" and "discover things for themselves" is a bad thing.

The view of item 1, that of music which does not employ western classical staff notation, was amplified a little later by another article, this time in *The Sunday Times*, when it was observed that:

> Classical music is in danger of disappearing from school timetables, with pupils learning instead about the greatest hits from the world of rock, rap and reggae. Government-appointed education experts have turned their backs on tradition and excluded the names of Beethoven, Bach and other great composers from the national curriculum.

> Teachers will be free to choose Madonna and MC Hammer over Mahler and Haydn, in spite of government promises that new guidelines on what should be taught would strengthen the already perilous position of the classics. (Hymas, 1991)

Whilst Madonna and MC Hammer may no longer be the contemporary icons which appeal to young people today, nonetheless the sentiment of valorisation has continued. The rationale behind the ire aimed at the authors of the National Curriculum is to do with a number of factors. These include the ways in which various types of music are considered and what the perceived statuses of these different types of music are. The attitudes displayed in *The Times* articles from the last decade of the previous century are often not too far in the background today, as politicians and commentators become involved in the teaching and learning of music in schools.

The Privileging of Knowledge

The attitudes displayed in the articles considered so far in this chapter reveal a hankering after what were felt to be, as Morrison put it, "old certainties of the post-1944 era" which were now felt to be in danger of being dissolved. But in cultural terms, this view is likely to have always been the case, with what many have thought of as a previous "golden age" being just out of sight around the last corner of looking back into the past. After all, back in 1885, the librettist W S Gilbert placed similar sentiments into the mouth of Ko-Ko, in the Gilbert and Sullivan Operetta "The Mikado":

> Then the idiot who praises, with enthusiastic tone,

> Every century but this, and every country but his own...

But this "golden age" notion is very appealing to politicians, who can show how their recent predecessors from different political parties presided over a lowering of standards and that, as the song has it, "things aren't what they used to be". This is an appealing tactic for politicians, as it taps into a zeitgeist of dissatisfaction.

In England and Norway, the work of the American, E. D. Hirsch, has already been noted as being influential. Indeed, a long-serving education minister in the 2017 Conservative government, and the preceding Conservative and coalition governments, Nick Gibb, has observed that: "No single writer has influenced my thinking on education more than E. D. Hirsch" (Gibb, 2015).

What Hirsch work involved, coming as he did, from an American context, was to produce a list of things that, as the title of his book states, "What every literate American needs to know" (Hirsch, 1987). This publication established Hirsch's position, and he then went on to help found the "Core Knowledge Foundation" which produced school curricula that were based on his ideas. Similar activities took place in England.

In music education, we are in a highly problematic situation with regard to notions of cultural literacy, and, to borrow Hirsch's phrase, "what every educated child needs to know" at the end of their school music course. There are many reasons for this, and sometimes these are in conflict with each other. An obvious example of this is that the knowledge required for classroom music is very likely to be of a different type and order to the knowledge required for instrumental music learning. Indeed, so complex can these areas be that it is possible to think of them as entailing different content domains. A highly simplistic division of music teaching and learning encounters would entail a range of these aspects (Table 1).

There are undoubtedly more possibilities than this list entails, but even with these ten variations, it should be clear that the knowledge types involved in each of these can offer distinctly different ways of musical thinking, learning, and doing. The knowledge required for formal instrumental teaching from the learner may well involve a range of different aspects from that required by a group of young people getting together in one of their dads' garages to work out how to play some favourite songs on instruments they have only just acquired.

Table 1 Music teaching and learning encounters

1.	Classroom music	Where whole classes in schools have a generalist music education, including singing, playing, composing, listening, history, theory
2.	Formal instrumental teaching	Where an individual child learns how to play a musical instrument. Can take place in or out of school
3.	Group instrumental teaching	As above, but in a group
4.	Whole class ensemble teaching	WCET in England, combines elements of 3 and 1 above, whole classes learn to play an instrument together. (See Hallam (2016) for a discussion of the WCET programme in England.)
5.	Theory of music	Separate classes focussing solely on this aspect
6.	In school informal learning	Where teaching and learning focus on building up competencies in areas the children and young people choose
7.	Out of school informal learning	As 6, but undertaken entirely out of school, e.g. learning songs together in garage bands
8.	Formal ensemble playing	Where children and young people in receipt of lessons in 2 and/or 3 above come together to perform, directed by an expert
9.	Informal ensemble playing	As above, but potentially more ad hoc, e.g. in churches, folk groups, jam sessions
10.	Specialist music learning	Takes place out of normal school, although in some jurisdictions replaced by focusing on a selected elite

The reason that these matters become contested issues is that some in society want to place different cultural values on these activities. This means that what is being done is that a hierarchic taxonomy or lexicon of knowledge types is either overtly produced, as in the case of Hirsh's book, or tacitly assumed, as in the case of the newspaper articles cited above. For those who do not have to work with or alongside children and young people, this need not be a problem; they can issue their diktats from afar; but for teachers whom needs must work with the same young people on a daily basis, this creates a problematic relationship from the outset. We know that children and young people are constantly making value judgements about what they like, as Sefton-Green observed back in 2000:

> I don't think in the end it's a question of whether you teach it or not [aesthetic judgement], it's the easiest thing in the world to get kids to make aesthetic judgements. They do it all the time. The hardest thing in the world is to stop them. Oasis are better than Blur. Eastenders is better than Brookside. The question is how well they articulate it ... and distinguish between the things which are personal and the things which are not necessarily universal or transcendental but are shared. (Sefton-Green, 2000, p. 21)

Where this becomes problematic is when it becomes central to curriculum content discussions with these same children and young people. Another English politician, Michael Gove, at the time the Conservative minister for education made the observation that:

> ...I am unapologetic in arguing that all children have a right to the best. And there is such as thing as the best. Richard Wagner is an artist of sublime genius and his work is incomparably more rewarding – intellectually, sensually and emotionally – than, say, the Arctic Monkeys. (Gove, 2011)

This is a straightforward statement for a politician to make and will appeal to the constituency of the newspaper article authors and associated readership cited above. But for a teacher working with children and young people who enjoy the music of the Arctic Monkeys, or whoever is trending at the time, there is a danger that this can become a slanging match of the "mine is better than yours" variety. This then places the learners in the situation of being perceived as having inferior tastes and that the teacher is there to help them rise above the poor choices they have made in terms of the music they like. At the very heart of this is the notion of what counts as "good" music and, related to this, who says so. It seems highly unlikely that class of young people are going to be terribly impressed by what a politician tells them to like, and so it is doubtful that having read Michael Gove's thoughts on the matter they would immediately see the error of their ways and start listening to *Tristan and Isolde*!

The mistake that commentators can make is summed up in the well-known English phrase "I know what I like, and I like what I know". This applies to the ways in which popular music could be approached in the school curriculum. Writing back in 1994, Shepherd and Vulliamy noted this:

> The value of music could not be judged across cultures according to a scheme of absolutes taken to be objective, but only in relation to criteria developed as an integral aspect of the socially constructed reality of the group or society creating the music to be evaluated.

> Popular music as introduced into the secondary school curriculum could not therefore be
> judged according to an 'objective' set of criteria – which without exception turned out to be
> abstracted from the technical and aesthetic criteria of music of the established Western
> canon – but only according to criteria which were much more closely associated with those
> who created and appreciated the music. (Shepherd & Vulliamy, 1994, p. 29)

This is an important observation, as the technical and aesthetic criteria which
Shepherd and Vulliamy are describing here are clearly related to the sorts of music
which the commentators cited above are familiar with. Again, presenting children
and young people with judgements of why their music falls down, Shepherd and
Vulliamy's aforementioned phrase, "according to a scheme of absolutes taken to be
objective" (but which is in fact nothing of the sort!), makes this a particularly difficult way for education to proceed.

Shepherd and Vulliamy went to point out that music creates meanings which are
relevant for the audiences they were intended for. This is bound up with what we
think of today as musical identity, but nonetheless what they wrote all those years
ago still resonates today:

> … while music is powerfully affective in a direct and concrete yet symbolic manner, the
> route from music's sounds to 'music's meanings' is more slippery and elusive than hitherto
> supposed. The construction of affect and 'meaning' through music-the processes through
> which students in classrooms engage with the sounds of music – seem to be much more
> complex than debates of either a political or intellectual nature have hitherto supposed.
> (Shepherd & Vulliamy, 1994, p. 38)

And it is this that matters to the listeners of such music that the meanings it creates
for them, in their lives, in their contexts, and in their situations are what matters to
them. It is this aspect which Lucy Green was describing when she wrote about
delineated meaning that music has for the listener:

> Images, associations, memories, queries, problems and beliefs inspired in us by music are
> musical meanings that, rather than inhering in musical materials and pointing only to them-
> selves, point outwards from music and towards its role as a social product, thus giving it
> meaning as such for us. Music communicates. It does so not only through its inherent inter-
> relations as they pass in time, but it also communicates its social relations as they are
> through history. Music delineates a profile of its position in the musical world amongst
> these social relations, and thereby also delineates ideas of social relations and social mean-
> ings to us: I will call these *delineated musical meanings*. (Green, 1988, p. 28)

Green distinguished such delineated meanings as being separated from what she
saw as the *intrinsic meaning* contained within the music, both in and of itself. These
delineated meanings matter for the individuals, and they matter especially for children and young people who are still maturing and for whom identity construction,
especially with how they are regarded by others, particularly in their peer groups, is
a key and evolving part of their growing up.

All of these issues, as we have seen, will affect how teachers are able to engage
with their learners. This will also be influenced by the fact that many teachers will
themselves be sympathetic to the musical tastes of the children and young people in
their charge. This may be especially observed to be the case in England, which has
one of the youngest teaching workforces in Europe. This is different from the

situation in many other countries, as the Organisation for Economic Co-operation and Development (OECD) noted:

> The relatively young teaching force in the UK stands in stark contrast to the situation in many European countries where inflexible employment conditions coupled with declining youth populations have led to ageing teacher populations. (OECD, 2013, p.6–7)

However, alongside their comparative youthfulness, the music teachers in the UK are likely to have come through an education and training route which has continued to emphasise the western classical element of music, a point noted by Wright and Davies:

> The vast majority of teachers at present working in school music are still products of a musical training firmly embedded within the western art-music tradition. In Bourdieu's terms, as western art music tends to advantage children possessing middle-class habitus, schooling's reproductive processes assure that many of these teachers are themselves from a middle-class background ... While this is not to say that all school knowledge is middle-class knowledge and that, for this reason, it is inevitably rejected by working-class pupils, it is being argued that there are habitus/class code issues about recognition and acceptance of curriculum content, particularly in the creative domain, extending from the acceptability of the canon in literature to the standing of musical genres. (Wright & Davies, 2010, p. 46)

This matter of personal background will be more of an issue in some schools than others. The sorts of music listened to, and participated in, by pupils in schools in England should not be considered to be uniform. It will not only vary from place to place but will also vary within schools, between school year groups, and within school classes. All of which makes presenting a viable unitary music curriculum a singular issue, which is probably best addressed by each teacher thinking about what is and what could and should be taking place in their school, in their classes, with their learners. This point was recognised back in the nineteenth century, when the author of a celebrated piano teaching method, Mrs. Curwen, produced a set of maxims for the teacher. One of these was: "Proceed from the known to the related unknown" (Curwen, 1886). This is a way in which many teachers have worked with their charges in order to move the learners' knowledge of music into new and hitherto undiscovered directions for them. Of course, this is not the only way to do this, but in many cases contextualisation matters. As a profession, we found out in the middle of the last century that music appreciation lessons as a way of getting children and young people to appreciate the canon might not always be a good thing. Music as a social improver has a long history, but, with increased attention to youth voice, becomes harder to sustain over time.

The Place of Assessment

At its simplest, assessment can be considered in two modalities, assessment which arises from curriculum and assessment which leads curriculum. These two modalities can be easily spotted in music education. Graded instrumental music examination, such as those in the United Kingdom offered by the Associated Board of the

Royal Schools of Music (ABRSM) (see gb.abrsm.org) and Trinity College London (see trinitycollege.com), will often lead to a teaching programme constructed so as to enter the young musician for the examination, in other words assessment which leads to curriculum. In the UK classroom, generalist music in the lower secondary school, normally for children aged from 11 to 14 years old, will often be constructed by the music teacher in a school according to National Curriculum strictures, but with individual elements and progression frameworks designed by that teacher. This will be an example of assessment which arises from curriculum, as in these instances it is the teacher who constructs and administers any such assessment. This aspect is returned to later in this chapter.

In the cases of curriculum which arises from the assessment, there is the possibility of what is referred to as *backwash* in the assessment literature, arising from the assessment back onto the teaching and learning programme. This is not a pejorative view of either assessment or curriculum construction, indeed, as Biggs, one of the first to describe this phenomenon, noted back in 1996:

> Backwash is no bad thing, particularly if it can be harnessed from the centre outwards, so that performance indicators send out the kind of messages to teachers that teachers say they want to send out to their own students. (Biggs, 1996, p. 14)

This is not only going to be the case in instrumental musical learning, but also for those aspects of musical teaching and learning where there will be some form of significant or high-stakes examination at the end of the programme of study, in the case of England, these will be GCSE exams at age 16 and A-level at age 18. What it does mean, however, is that in cases where curriculum arises from assessment, then the choice of materials that will be examined will have a significant impact upon the nature of what will be taught. Examination bodies will be writing a syllabus which sets out the content of the examination. The various sorts of examinations that we have in music education all have their own range of materials. Thus a graded music performance examination will specify the repertoire, the pieces of music that need to be played at each grade point for that examination board. General Certificate of Secondary Education (GCSE)[1] and A-level[2] music examination boards will decide on topics for content in historical studies and which pieces of music will be required as set works for study and analysis. What this means is that the choices of these materials will have a significant impact on what is taught and learned in music lessons in those schools. Thus if an examination board chooses music from the Baroque era to be studied, with a corresponding set work, for example, Purcell's *Dido and Aeneas*, then this is what will be studied. Timetabled opportunities being limited for teaching and learning in all school subjects, it would take a brave music teacher to venture too far from this topicality and teach a unit on Reggae, for example,

---

[1] The General Certificate of Secondary Education (GCSE) is a set of exams taken in England, Wales, Northern Ireland, and other British territories. They are usually taken by students aged 15–16, after 2 years of study.

[2] A-level is a qualification in a specific subject typically taken by school students aged 16–18, at a level above GCSE.

knowing full well it would not feature in the examination. Indeed, it could be argued that such behaviour would be reckless and inappropriate! The effects of this are that the contents of various examination syllabi operate a form of hegemony as well as backwash on the curriculum content of what is being taught and learned.

This in itself might not seem to be a substantive issue, but the backwash effects can be much greater than simply in the choice of materials for examination groups. In England about 7% of pupils take the GCSE music examination each year (Cambridge Assessment, 2016) at age 16, after a programme of study that they have been studying since the age of 14. What this means is that some 93% of pupils are not taking up music as an optional subject at this stage and cease their formal studies in music as a school subject at this juncture. The effects of backwash on the lower secondary school curriculum, however, mean that many schools topics appear which are clearly there in preparation for the examination. In a 2016 study in London, and a 2018 study in Birmingham (Fautley, 2016; Fautley, Kinsella & Whittaker, 2018), it was found that a number of teachers are teaching topics in the lower secondary school which figure in examination syllabi. This may be no bad thing, after all we would want teaching and learning in the lower secondary school to lead seamlessly to exam preparation in the upper school. Where it becomes a problem is if such a programme is designed solely for the benefit of the 7% who will take the optional examination course and ignores the wants and needs of the 93% who will not do so.

Although, as we have seen above, there is a National Curriculum in operation in England, it is actually very slight for music, with the outline of what children and young people aged between 11 and 14 should be taught coming in at a little over 200 words. What this means is that teachers in England can produce their own schemes of work, and so long as they involve composing, listening, and performing, they are likely to conform to the strictures of the National Curriculum. With this degree of freedom, it might be considered surprising, therefore, that as the London and Birmingham research cited above shows, there is not that much difference between many schools. What we see in the instances outlined above is a complex circularity wherein assessment and curriculum have a troubled relationship one with another. The notion of teachers deciding what it would be appropriate for the learners in their schools to be working on is replaced by one wherein teachers feel that they have to prepare the majority for a public examination which they will never take. This seems to be a sad situation, when there is so much in music that can be taught and learned, played and sung. This is also problematic when it comes to producing new musical and pedagogic ideas, which may fall foul of dominating hegemonic discourses, which openly favour historically conservative musical notions, particularly those that fall under the heading of western art music.

Suggestions for the Craft of Music Education

In England, many music teachers are concerned with a range of worries, from *what* to teach to *how* to teach it. Music education does not contain a neat set of pre-ordained content segments; it is a living and dynamic art form. With the ways in which neoliberalism spreads across countries and systems, it would be helpful for music teachers to be able to wrestle control of the curriculum back from politicians. The problem with this is that by the time policy reaches schools, it seems distant. It is to be hoped that just as children and young people will always want to make music, there will always be teachers in positions to guide and educate them and that this can be done in a *musical*, not simply one that panders to the whims of whoever is in political power at the time. After all, music teachers will still be there long after those politicians have moved on to other positions – so there is hope!

Conclusion

Taken together, what these various elements show is that music curriculum, and its associated assessment in English secondary schools, is a highly contested arena and has been so for a number of years. The *craft* of music teachers involves a well-intentioned attempt to touch the lives of young people. Unfortunately, what can all too often happen is that the desires of music teachers, and the wants and needs of children and young people, are thwarted by the outworkings of policy constructed by those whose own backgrounds often lie far from the very classrooms they are legislating for. The need for music education to move towards a truly inclusive curriculum and examination system which involves more than preparation for a bygone age seems to be an important role for the twenty-first century. Suggesting this is not an abdication of responsibility, but a recognition that things are moving on, and we want our children and young people to be prepared for the future. Of course this involves learning about the past, but it also involves learning *from* the past and applying these lessons to music that has not yet been created.

References

Biggs, J. (1996). Assessing learning quality: Reconciling institutional, staff, and educational demands. *Assessment and Evaluation in Higher Education, 21*(1), 5–16.

Cambridge Assessment (2016). Uptake of GCSE subjects 2016: Statistics report series No. *114* Retrieved from: http://www.cambridgeassessment.org.uk/Images/420406-uptake-of-gcse-subjects-2016.pdf

Curwen, A. J. (1886). *The teacher's guide to Mrs. Curwen's pianoforte method (the child pianist): Being a practical course in the elements of music.* London: Curwen's Edition.

Department for Education and Science [England]. (1992). Draft order for music, Her Majesty's Stationery Office.

Espeland, M. (1997). Once upon a time there was a minister: An unfinished story about reform in Norwegian arts education. *Arts Education Policy Review, 99*, 11–16.

Espeland, M. (1999). Curriculum reforms in Norway: An insider's perspective. *Arts and Learning Research Journal, 15*(1), 172–187.

Fautley, M. (2016). *Teach through music: Evaluation report*. Birmingham, UK: Birmingham City University and Trinity Laban Conservatoire of Music and Dance.

Fautley, M., Kinsella, V., & Whittaker, A. (2018). *Birmingham music hub: Secondary school music teachers survey 2018*. Birmingham, UK: Birmingham City University.

Gibb, N. (2015). How E. D. Hirsch came to shape UK government policy. In J. Simons & N. Porter (Eds.), *Knowledge and the curriculum: A collection of essays to accompany E. D. Hirsch's lecture at Policy Exchange*. London: Policy Exchange.

Gove, M. (2011, Nov. 25th). *Speech: Michael Gove to Cambridge University*. Department for Education (Ed), London, DfE. Retrieved from: https://www.gov.uk/government/speeches/michael-gove-to-cambridge-university

Green, L. (1988). *Music on deaf ears*. Manchester, UK: Manchester University Press.

Hallam, S. (2016). Whole class ensemble teaching (WCET) Final Report 2016. Music Mark and UCL.

Hirsch, E. D. (1987). *Cultural literacy: What every literate American needs to know*. Boston, MA: Houghton Mifflin.

Hymas, C. (1991, July). *The great composers expelled from school*. London: The Sunday Times.

Lauernman, C. (1987, Sep 6th). Are we a nation of cultural illiterates? You bet your Jeremiad, says a professor and critic of our educational system. *Chicago Tribune* (Pre-1997 Fulltext); Chicago, Illinois.

Morrison, R. (1991, Feb 13th). *A generation drummed out*. London: The Times.

Organisation for Economic Co-operation and Development [OECD] (2013). *Education at a glance 2013: United Kingdom*. OECD Indicators. OECD Publishing.

Sefton-Green, J. (2000). *Evaluating creativity*. London: Routledge.

Shepherd, J., & Vulliamy, G. (1994). The struggle for culture: A sociological case study of the development of a national music curriculum. *British Journal of Sociology of Education, 15*(1), 27–40.

Wright, R., & Davies, B. (2010). Class, power, culture and the music curriculum. In R. Wright (Ed.), *Sociology and music education (pp. 35–50)*. London: Ashgate.

Educating Music Teachers for the Future: The Crafts of Change

Catharina Christophersen

Abstract In light of current global educational reforms and neoliberal discourses, it is timely to ask about the future direction of music education. This chapter discusses the concept of "crafts" in relation to music teacher education, more particularly from a perspective of change. A starting point for this chapter is that the crafts of music teacher education directly concerns the facilitation of development and change, for example, by deliberating on what is important to keep and build on in the professional practice of music teacher education and what is better left out. When deliberating on questions of traditions and change, I suggest that one should take into consideration if and how the educational practices of music teacher education (a) actively reflect on and productively try to contribute to the big challenges of the world; (b) explicitly address systemic bias and inequalities; and (c) provide spaces for student participation and agency.

Introduction

Music is part of every culture ever known. People around the world "use music to create and express their emotional inner lives, to span the chasm between themselves and the divine, to woo lovers, to celebrate weddings, to sustain friendships and communities, to inspire political mass movements, and to help their babies fall asleep" (Turino, 2008, p. 1). Music thus serves important personal and social functions, such as expression and regulation of emotions, communication and mediation between self and others, symbolic representation, and coordination of actions (Clayton, 2016). Music can be a leisure activity, a job, an industry product, a part of everyday soundscapes, or substantial to transpersonal experiences. Consequently, music is unquestionably a part of people's lives and has therefore also been considered a natural part of general education as well as of teacher education in many parts of the world.

C. Christophersen (✉)
Western Norway University of Applied Sciences, Bergen, Norway
e-mail: crc@hvl.no

© Springer Nature Switzerland AG 2021
K. Holdhus et al. (eds.), *Music Education as Craft*, Landscapes: the Arts, Aesthetics, and Education 30, https://doi.org/10.1007/978-3-030-67704-6_6

Notwithstanding the lip service the educational value of music has been given, it is probably fair to say that music has never been a major part of school curricula, even back in the eighteenth century when its main purpose was to support hymn singing in church. Still, in the last decades, global educational reforms have, not surprisingly, marginalised arts and humanities in many educational systems (Prest, 2013; Rusinek & Aróstegui, 2015; Sahlberg, 2016). This is also the case in Norway where the neoliberal discourse in connection with pre-determined learning goals, corporate management models, test-based accountability practices, as well as decreased funding of the arts in schools and teacher education have contributed further to this predicament.

In light of these developments, it is timely to ask about the future directions of music education, in this book framed through the concept of "crafts". In this chapter I will discuss "crafts" from a music teacher education angle and more particularly from a perspective of change. A starting point for this chapter is that a critical and conscious dealing with traditions is necessary. I will discuss why this change is inevitable, and I will also suggest a framework for discussion and decision-making relating to change in music teacher education.

Music Teacher Education: A Mostly Norwegian Snapshot

Having been a music teacher educator for two decades, I have visited quite a few teacher education institutions in Norway as well as in other countries. Enter the music department of a teacher education institution anywhere, and the chances are that this is what you will find:

> The music department has one or two large rooms with generous floor space and a collection of Orff and various percussion instruments such as marimbas and xylophones, djembes and congas, claves, cowbells, shakers, rainmakers, boom whackers, and triangles, to name but a few. There are probably one or two smaller rooms, one of which may have tables. These large and smaller rooms will probably have a computer and/or smart board for audio- and video-presentations, a piano, a collection of drums on the floor, some bandstands, a few acoustic and electric guitars (maybe even ukuleles) hanging on the wall, and a garage band rig in a corner. The rooms will have stacks of chairs on one side. On the other side of the room, there will be shelves and cupboards containing songbooks, CDs, additional small instruments, cables, musical toys/games, possibly costumes, or other accessories. The music department may have a dedicated computer lab, or possibly a small studio, and, finally, some rehearsal rooms for individual practice or small ensemble rehearsals.

The rooms of this imaginary yet experienced music teacher education department bear witness of collective classroom music making, individual or small-group performances, as well as activities connected to music theory and analysis. The equipment indicates that several musical genres are represented, although there might be a slight emphasis on popular music making.

This is exactly what Jon Helge Sætre describes in a comprehensive mixed-methods study of Norwegian music teacher education (Sætre, 2014). Sætre's study describes Norwegian music teacher education as characterised by a fragmented course structure, as being highly influenced by Western conservatoire traditions, where popular music has been included as repertoire, but where the teaching discourses are traditional, teacher centred, and performance oriented (Sætre, 2014, 2017). Notwithstanding occurring attempts at innovation and renewal within music teacher education programmes, such attempts take place within fairly restrained structures, thus limiting the impact and level of change (Sætre, 2017): As Sætre (2014) states, "Despite development in a range of areas, a course structure representing tradition is kept, suggesting an accumulative logic of recontextualizing rather than one of transformation" (p. 14). In other words, traditions seem to prevail, and structures are reproduced in Norwegian music teacher education.

Zooming Out

Looking to music education research and scholarship internationally, it is widely acclaimed that music teacher education is influenced by Western classical music traditions (Bowman, 2007; Burnard, 2013; Hess, 2018; Pellegrino, 2009; Rusinek & Aróstegui, 2015). A study of music teacher education programmes across 27 European and 17 Latin-American countries (Aróstegui, 2011; Aróstegui & Cisneros-Cohernour, 2010; Rusinek & Aróstegui, 2015) finds that despite variations between countries,[1] there are by and large strong traditions internationally for emphasising musical content within music teacher education. In the Nordic context, though, popular music has been a natural part of educational programmes since the mid-1970s, and studies suggest that popular music, particularly garage band music, now represents an inverted hegemony in Nordic music education (Georgii-Hemming & Westvall, 2010; Lindgren & Ericsson, 2010; Westerlund, 2006). While Sætre's Norwegian study suggests that music teacher educators are more progressive than the structures they work within, a Swedish study suggests that student music teachers have developed far more progressive educational and musical attitudes than their educators due to extensive contact with general education programmes (Georgii-Hemming & Westvall, 2010).

The conservative educational discourses and practices described in previous studies could be seen as examples of the "musico-pedagogical practice model" (Laes & Westerlund, 2018) where performative practices of music take precedence over educational practices. Musical diversity, then, may be considered important. However, adding content, as in including new styles of music, does not necessarily mean that pedagogies change to reflect these styles (Christophersen & Gullberg, 2017). Musical diversity does not necessarily equal pedagogical diversity within a musico-pedagogical practice model because of the emphasis on prescriptive

---

[1] Aróstegui and Cisneros-Cohernour (2010) claim to find examples of a reasonably balanced relationship between musical content and educational perspectives within European music education (especially in Sweden and Finland), more than in Latin American countries, where there is a particularly strong emphasis on musical content.

teaching and learning, often through the master-apprentice-model that is so pervasive within the field of music. Further, the musico-pedagogical model leads to a performance-oriented and "ableist" focus, where students' talents and skills come to the forefront. Consequently, student selection methods become important, specifying "who is entitled to learn and to perform music" (Laes & Westerlund, 2018, p. 35). The same goes for the eligibility requirements for becoming a music teacher, since access to many teacher education programmes are indeed sometimes also regulated through auditions and entrance exams.

I have discussed auditions and other screening procedures with fellow music teacher educators on several occasions. After many years of concern about student music teachers' alleged steadily decreasing musical skills, one institution finally managed to implement screening procedures for applicants, among other things documentation of music reading skills and a self-recorded video of a musical performance. I asked if the screening procedures could involve an exploration of students' motivation to become teachers, for example, by asking the applicants to include in their video a brief reflection on their teaching motivation and possible prior teaching experience. My suggestion was declined, as students' personal motivation was considered subjective and too difficult to assess. Assessing the qualities of musical performance, on the other hand, was considered neither subjective nor problematic. Following the logic of the musico-pedagogical practice model, a sufficient mastering of an instrument was in this situation considered the most important pre-condition for entering teacher education.

The focus on certain content and prescriptive pedagogies supporting the transmission of such content "pushes the profession towards the sustenance of the past and preservation of traditions" (Westerlund & Karlsen, 2017, p. 81). Such issues described above are not necessarily exclusive to the field of music, though. Scholars have described teacher education practices as content oriented. Lin Goodwin, Smith, Souto-Manning, Cheruvu, Reed, and Taveras, (2014) purport that content specialisation, in many cases, is considered the most important factor when teacher educators are hired, suggesting that "the assumption is that knowledge necessary for teacher educating is not so much about teacher education pedagogies but about content or discipline knowledge" (Lin Goodwin et al., 2014, p. 296). The picture is of course more nuanced, since many teacher educators have backgrounds as schoolteachers (Ulvik & Smith, 2016). Still, teacher education is a complex educational practice that may require a particular teacher education pedagogy, as Loughran (2014) notes:

> the work of teacher education it is not about 'upskilling' staff to perform in new ways in response to mandated changes in curriculum, policy, or practice, it is about an ongoing process of learning, development, and change driven by the players central to that work— teacher educators. (p. 273)

There is a danger that the lack of a systematic knowledge base for teacher education (see, e.g. Darling-Hammond, 2006; Futrell, 2010; Loughran, 2014; Zeichner, 2005) could reduce teacher education to transmission of content without critical reflection and self-reflection, thus possibly producing stable pedagogies that are resistant to change.

Why Change?

As the editors have discussed elsewhere in this book, the concept of "crafts" in music education is closely connected to future directions of music education, which suggests the idea of development and change. The idea of change does not necessarily include revolution or radical altering of positions. Change could be viewed as an inevitable flux, a permanent trait of existence, and therefore also an integral part of education (Biesta, 2007; Jorgensen, 2003; Moss, 2014). Things evolve, things develop, things change, as Kratus (2015, p. 340) notes: "The contexts in which we live and teach, continue to change, and so must we in order to survive". Change and stability then pre-suppose each other: Not only is change necessary for the sustenance of education, but traditions are also necessary for change to happen:

> As one generation gives way to the next, it is necessary to decide which beliefs and practices to preserve and which to change (…). Without schooling, socialization and enculturation, a group would be without the means to transform itself". (Jorgensen, 2003, p. 19)

From the perspective of transformation, change implies flux, gradual development, where some things are kept and some things are replaced. A conscious transformation of education implies decision-making in the desired direction, deciding what to keep and what to get rid of. Such decisions are difficult as they connect to purposes, beliefs, and values, which belong to the philosophical domain of education.

On a large scale, the purpose of education could be said to "prepare people to live well in a world worth living in" (Kemmis, Wilkinson, Edwards-Groves, Grootenboer, & Bristol, 2014, p. 27). A slightly wordier version of the same purpose:

> …education ought to be humane. It ought to be directed toward such ideals as civility, justice, freedom, and inclusion of diverse peoples and perspectives. It ought to take a broad view of the world's cultures and human knowledge and prepare the young to be informed and compassionate citizens of the world. (Jorgensen, 2003, p. 20)

Educational philosopher Gert Biesta articulates a three-pronged concept of educational purpose, that of qualification (acquisition of necessary knowledge and skills), socialisation (learning the ways of existing orders and developing identity), and subjectification (the ability to live outside the existing orders, which imply freedom and autonomy) (Biesta, 2017).

Educational purposes are enshrined in laws and regulations. The mandatory basis for teacher education, for example, is to qualify teachers to work in schools. According to Norwegian teacher education regulations, teacher education programmes should be grounded in the Education Act[2] and in current primary and lower secondary curricula (Regulations Relating to the Framework Plan for Primary and Lower Secondary Education,[3] §1). The same regulations state that teacher

---

[2] The Primary and Lower Secondary Education Act (2010).

[3] https://lovdata.no/dokument/SF/forskrift/2010-03-01-295?q=L%C3%A6rerutdanning

training should qualify teachers to do professional work in a society characterised by diversity and change (§2).

The mandate of teacher education is elaborated through the objectives of the Education Act, which state that education among other things is to promote intellectual freedom, respect for individual convictions, local and international cultural traditions, equality, solidarity, democracy, critical thinking, ethical action, environmental awareness, joint responsibility, and the right to participate. Education should further combat all forms of discrimination (Education Act, section 1-1[4]). These objectives are what generalist music teachers should be able to contribute to and therefore ideally something that pre-service music teachers should be prepared for through their teacher training, also in music. These objectives further point to pressing issues for education, which in my view could be seen as essential to encircling the crafts of music teacher education. I will elaborate on this below.

A Framework for Discussing Change

Making changes in education may be considered necessary when purposes are distorted or unfulfilled, for example, by injustice, by rigid routines, by stifling traditions, by lack of knowledge, and so on. Purposes, however, are abstract entities and could be interpreted in a number of different ways. Warranting changes in music teacher education could be considered controversial. Considering cutbacks in resources and recent technological changes, some educators may feel there has been enough change already. Some educators may not want to change since the way they already teach music in teacher education seems to work well. Others may not welcome change because change represents something uncertain and inevitably challenges the familiar. Once something is changed, it may not be possible to go back, however well-intended, since change "carries with it the possibility of inadvertent disaster, and change does not come with a money-back guarantee" (Kratus, 2015, p. 340).

Change, then, is connected to beliefs, values, and possible discursive positionings. Change is not only a matter of implementation, rather, as Bruner (2018) states, "what is fundamental is the normative and political question about the quality of the change" (p. 123). There may not be a shared perception of what such quality is or how change should play out in certain situations. Claims for change rest on certain beliefs and values of what is good and desirable. By extension, matters of transformation and change may be perceived differently by different institutions and different people.

Still, I assume that the idea of education as contributing to the making of a better world is not up for discussion. I will therefore start from the idea of making a better world, as included in the purposeful objectives of the aforementioned Education Act

---

[4] https://lovdata.no/dokument/NL/lov/1998-07-17-61?q=opplæringslov

(2010) and suggest a framework for discussion and decision-making relating to change in music teacher education.

Change Informed by Global Issues

The objectives of the Education Act point to the very big issues of this world. The twenty-first century challenges of globalisation, migration, climate change, and technological innovation affect us all. The world is rapidly changing, and education must reflect and take on the challenges brought on by such changes. The United Nations' sustainable development goal for education is to ensure inclusive and equitable education and lifelong learning opportunities for all.[5] While Norway is privileged education-wise compared to other countries in other parts of the world, improvement of education is a never-ending task for all societies. For example, educational target 4.5 specifically mentions equal access to education for vulnerable groups including the disabled, while target 4.7 notes the aim of the United Nations by the year 2030 as being:

> [To] ensure that all learners acquire the knowledge and skills needed to promote sustainable development, including, among others, through education for sustainable development and sustainable lifestyles, human rights, gender equality, promotion of a culture of peace and non-violence, global citizenship and appreciation of cultural diversity and of culture's contribution to sustainable development. (UN Sustainable development target 4.7)

It is obvious that teacher training has a role to play here, and we have to ask ourselves how music teacher training programmes can contribute to these bigger, pressing issues, and what kinds of issues we want to address in our music teacher programmes. Those questions could, and maybe even should, inform a debate on what should be done in music teacher education programmes to ensure they support the United Nations sustainable development goals.

Change Informed by Systemic Issues

The objectives of the Education Act call for education to address and act upon systemic issues in our societies and institutions. This certainly applies to education in general, but there are also issues pertaining particularly to music education. However, the broader field of music education has been criticised by critical and social justice scholars for reclusiveness and for actively ignoring issues surrounding the educational programmes and institutions. According to these scholars, music education has typically been justified by referral to the aesthetic qualities of music (Bowman, 2007), as emotional growth (Jorgensen, 2007) or self-improvement

---

[5] https://sustainabledevelopment.un.org/?menu=1300

(Vaugeois, 2013), which creates a passive, naive disinterestedness, that is, the "intent to stay unaware or disinterested in world events and the systems that shape our society" (Hess, 2018, p. 19).

There are issues of race, gender, ableism, cultural appropriation, and colonialism that should be addressed within music teacher education programmes (Wright, 2019). Bowman (2007) asks the pertinent question as to who is to be considered the "we" in music education. In so doing, he also points to the ways that a sense of "we" form basis for certain perceptions of professionalism that could result in a systematic exclusion of certain music and therefore also of people. Music education, no matter the institution, will always be a political and ethical endeavour. Bowman further describes a procedure of circularity that serves to reproduce existing values and traditions within institutions:

> (1) Start with an understanding of music derived from and well-suited to one particular mode of musical engagement and practice. (2) Craft a definition of musicianship derived from its basic tenets and demonstrable primarily on instruments that have evolved in its service. (3) Privilege curricula and pedagogies that serve to nurture that kind of musicianship. (4) Select students for advanced study on the basis of criteria well-suited to these modes of practice. (5) Hire faculty to serve the needs and interests of such students. And (6) assess success in terms of the extent to which the norms and values of that tradition and its conventions are preserved. (p. 116)

This goes to show that music teacher education institutions may very well function as "silos" for the reproduction and sustainment of values, beliefs, and practices (Väkevä, Westerlund & Ilmola-Sheppard, 2017), a claim that is corroborated by Sætre's study (2014) of Norwegian music teacher education. Such circularity serves to shut out and stifle alternative voices and practices within music teacher education (Westerlund & Karlsen, 2017, p. 18). This begs the questions of how to promote and facilitate just, open, and diverse music teacher education programmes. In order to do so, one needs to ask what are the systemic issues in our programmes and in our institutions and what can possibly be done about it.

Change Informed by Agentic Issues

The objectives of the Education Act also recognise students' voice, participation, and agency as fundamental to education. An important task for a music teacher educator is to help future music teachers develop professional agency, that is, the ability to influence and take control over their professional circumstances. Agency is a "temporally embedded process of social engagement, informed by the past (in its habitual aspect) oriented towards the future (as a capacity to imagine alternative possibilities) and 'acted' out in the present" (Emirbayer and Mische, 1998, p. 970 in Priestley, Biesta & Robinson, 2015, p. 24). This flux between past, present, and future implies that music teacher education could indeed play an important role in the development of such agency and that pre-service teachers should be able to experience a sense of professional agency also as pre-service music teachers.

I have mentioned the conscious selection of which traditions to pass on as an important dimension of the crafts of music education. Randall Allsup (2016, p. 65) polemically poses the question: "Do we (…) teach a tradition, or do we teach a child?", or in this case a grown-up pre-service music teacher. Traditions and people are of course not mutually exclusive categories. Traditions are essential when it comes to forming professional identities that enable and motivate professional action, but they can also stifle development. Educators need to be particular when choosing which traditions to hold on to. In the words of educational philosopher Gert Biesta:

> …the crucial educational question is about what (or better: who) is coming towards us from the future, so to speak. The educational question is about the 'newness' that is trying to come into the world. Who is it that is trying to come into the world? It is here that we can locate educational responsibility and the responsibility of educators, as a responsibility for the coming into the world of 'newcomers,' of 'new beginnings' and 'new beginners'. (Biesta, 2007, pp. 31–32)

Learning to know our students better is thus essential. The cultural and musical resources that students bring to their education may however not be recognised as competence. As teacher educators, we may observe that some of today's students do not read music as well as students did a few decades ago, but do we know what they know instead? What do they bring to the table, how can we recognise and build on it, and how can we work alongside the students to develop the educational practices of music teacher education? If losing sight of the people one tries to educate, if ignoring their lives and experiences, if not acknowledging the human, musical, and cultural resources they represent, the people we presume to educate then become incidental to our music education practices. Considering we are trying to qualify future music teachers that are going to work with future generations of citizens, the ramifications may be far-reaching.

A pertinent question, then, is how music teacher education can contribute to opening spaces for "radical listening" (Kincheloe, 2008; Tobin, 2009), where pre-service teacher's voices could be heard and where action is possible, thus possibly providing opportunities for students to experience that they can indeed affect their circumstances. Are we as music teacher educators willing to listen to students and, if necessary, change our practices as a result thereof?

Crafting Change: Concluding Remarks

The crafts of music teacher education, as I see it, directly concerns the facilitation of development and change, for example, by deliberating on what is important to keep and build on in the professional practice of music teacher education and what is better left out. When deliberating on questions of traditions and change, I have suggested that one should take into consideration if and how the educational practices of music teacher education (a) actively reflect on and productively try to contribute to the big challenges of the world, (b) explicitly address systemic bias and inequalities, and (c) provide spaces for student participation and agency.

It is important to say, though, that educational change does not happen by reflection alone. Trying to alter thoughts and beliefs could be a good start but is hardly enough. Educational change must happen in different dimensions and on different levels (Fullan, 2016). Educational practices are, for example, comprised of language and discourses that regulate our understandings, by physical resources that regulate our actions and by social-political arrangements that regulate the way things in our immediate surroundings are organised and relate to each other, thereby creating rules and practical agreements (Kemmis et al., 2014). Change could be difficult to achieve, at least immediate change. The perceived achievability of new alternatives should not constrain discussion of viability. What is immediately not achievable may be so in a near future, and providing "compelling accounts of viable alternatives to existing social structures" (Wright, 2007, pp. 32–33) could be a way of stretching the limits of achievability. If the crafts of music (teacher) education is indeed connected to future directions, then the concept of crafts should also include the ability to envision alternatives thereby "enlarging the space of the possible" (Osberg, 2009).

Acknowledgement This work was supported by the Norwegian Research Council and developed within the research project "Music Teacher Education for the Future" (FUTURED 2019–2022).

References

Allsup, R. E. (2016). *Remixing the classroom*. Bloomington, IN: Indiana University Press.

Aróstegui, J. L. (2011). *Educating music teachers for the 21st century*. Rotterdam, the Netherlands: Sense.

Aróstegui, J. L., & Cisneros-Cohernour, E. (2010). Reflexiones en torno a la formación del profesorado de música a partir del análisis documental de los planes de estudio en Europa y América Latina. *Profesorado: Revista de curriculum y formacion del profesorado, 14*(2), 179–189.

Biesta, G. (2007). The education-socialization conundrum or "who is afraid of education?". *Utbildning och demokrati, 16*(3), 25–36.

Biesta, G. (2017). The future of teacher education: Evidence, competence or wisdom? In M. A. Peters, B. Cowie, & I. Menter (Eds.), *A companion to research in teacher education* (pp. 435–453). Singapore: Springer.

Bowman, W. (2007). Who is the "we"? Rethinking professionalism in music education. *Action, Criticism and Theory for Music Education, 6*(4), 109–131.

Burnard, P. (2013). Problematizing what counts as knowledge and the production of knowledges in music. In E. Georgii-Hemming, P. Burnard, & S.-E. Holgersen (Eds.), *Professional knowledge in music teacher education (pp. 97–108)*. Surrey, UK: Ashgate.

Burner, T. (2018). Why is educational change so difficult and how can we make it more effective. *Forskning & Forandring, 1*(1), 122–134.

Christophersen, C., & Gullberg, A.-K. (2017). Popular music education, participation and democracy: Some Nordic perspectives. In G. D. Smith, Z. Moir, M. Brennan, P. Kirkman, & S. Rambarran (Eds.), *The Routledge research companion to popular music education* (pp. 425–437). Abingdon, UK: Routledge.

Clayton, M. (2016). The social and personal functions of music in cross-cultural perspective. In S. Hallam, I. Cross, & M. Thauth (Eds.), *The Oxford handbook of music psychology* (pp. 46–59). Oxford, UK/New York: Oxford University Press.

Darling-Hammond, L. (2006). Constructing 21st century teacher education. *Journal of Teacher Education, 57*(3), 300–314.

Emirbayer, M., & Mische, A. (1998). What is Agency? *American Journal of Sociology, 103*(4), 962–1023.

Fullan, M. (2016). *The new meaning of educational change.* New York: Routledge.

Futrell, M. H. (2010). Transforming teacher education to reform America's P-20 education system. *Journal of Teacher Education, 61*(5), 432–440.

Georgii-Hemming, E., & Westvall, M. (2010). Teaching music in our time: Student music teachers' reflections on music education, teacher education and becoming a teacher. *Music Education Research, 12*(4), 353–367.

Hess, J. (2018). Equity and music education: Euphemisms, terminal naivety, and Whiteness. *Action, Criticism, and Theory for Music Education, 16*(3), 15–47.

Jorgensen, E. (2003). *Transforming music education.* Bloomington: Indiana University Press.

Jorgensen, E. (2007). Concerning justice and music education. *Music Education Research, 9*(2), 169–189.

Kemmis, S., Wilkinson, J., Edwards-Groves, C., Grootenboer, P., & Bristol, L. (2014). *Changing practices, changing education.* Singapore: Springer.

Kincheloe, J. (2008). *Critical pedagogy primer.* New York: Peter Lang.

Kratus, J. (2015). The role of subversion in changing music education. In C. Randles (Ed.), *Music education: Navigating the future* (pp. 340–346). New York/London: Routledge.

Laes, T., & Westerlund, H. (2018). Performing disability in music teacher education: Moving beyond inclusion through expanded professionalism. *International Journal of Music Education, 36*(1), 34–36.

Lin Goodwin, A., Smith, L., Souto-Manning, M., Cheruvu, M. Y., Reed, R., & Taveras, L. (2014). What should teacher educators know and be able to do? Perspectives from practicing teacher educators. *Journal of Teacher Education, 65*(4), 284–302.

Lindgren, M., & Ericsson, C. (2010). The rock band context as discursive governance in music education in Swedish schools. *Action Criticism and Theory for Music Education, 9*(3), 35–54.

Loughran, J. (2014). Professionally developing as a teacher educator. *Journal of Teacher Education, 65*(4), 271–283.

Moss, P. (2014). *Transformative change and real utopias in early childhood education: A story of democracy, experimentation and potentiality.* Oxon, UK: Routledge.

Osberg, D. (2009). "Enlarging the space of the possible" around what it means to educate and be educated. *Complicity: An International Journal of Complexity and Education, 6*(1), iii–x.

Pellegrino, K. (2009). Connections between performer and teacher identities in music teachers: Setting and agenda for research. *Journal of Music Teacher Education, 19*(1), 39–55.

Prest, A. (2013). The corporatization of schooling and its effects on the state of music education: A critical Deweyan perspective. *Action, Criticism, and Theory for Music Education, 12*(3), 31–44.

Priestley, M., Biesta, G., & Robinson, S. (2015). *Teacher agency: An ecological approach.* London: Bloomsbory.

Rusinek, G., & Aróstegui, J. L. (2015). Educational policy reforms and the politics of music teacher education. In C. Benedict, P. Schmidt, G. Spruce, & P. Woodford (Eds.), *The Oxford handbook of social justice in music education* (pp. 78–90). New York: Oxford University Press.

Sætre, J. H. (2014). Preparing generalist student teachers to teach music. PhD Dissertation, Norwegian Academy of Music, Oslo.

Sætre, J. H. (2017). Music teacher education: A matter of preservation or innovation? In R. Girdzijauskiene & M. Stakelum (Eds.), *Creativity and innovation: European perspectives on music education 7* (pp. 215–228). Innsbruck, Austria: Helbling.

Sahlberg, P. (2016). The global educational reform movement and its impact on schooling. In
    K. Mundy, A. Green, B. Lingard, & A. Verger (Eds.), *The handbook of global education policy*
    (pp. 128–144). New York: John Wiley & Sons.
Tobin, K. (2009). Tuning into others' voices: Radical listening, learning from difference, and
    escaping oppression. *Cultural Studies of Science Education, 4*(3), 505–511.
Turino, T. (2008). *Music as social life: The politics of participation.* Chicago: University of
    Chicago Press.
Ulvik, M., & Smith, K. (2016). Å undervise om å undervise – Lærerutdanneres kompetanse sett
    fra deres egen og fra lærerstudenters perspektiv. *Uniped, 36*(1), 61–77.
Väkevä, L., Westerlund, H., & Ilmola-Sheppard, L. (2017). Social innovations in music education:
    Creating institutional resilience for increasing social justice. *Action, Criticism, and Theory for
    Music Education, 16*(3), 129–147.
Vaugeois, L. C. (2013). *Colonization and the institutionalization of hierarchies of the human
    through music education: Studies in the education of feeling.* PhD Dissertation, University of
    Toronto.
Westerlund, H. (2006). Garage rock bands: A future model for developing expertise. *International
    Journal of Music Education, 24*(2), 119–125.
Westerlund, H., & Karlsen, S. (2017). Knowledge production beyond local and national blindspots:
    Remedying professional ocularcentrism of diversity in music teacher education. *Action,
    Criticism and Theory for Music Education, 16*(3), 78–107.
Wright, E. O. (2007). Guidelines of envisioning real utopias. In S. Davidson & J. Rutherford
    (Eds.), *Soundings 36: Politics and market.* London: Lawrence & Wishart.
Wright, R. (2019). Envisioning real Utopias in music education: Prospects, possibilities and
    impediments. *Music Education Research, 21*(3), 217–227.
Zeichner, K. (2005). Becoming a teacher educator: A personal perspective. *Teaching and Teacher
    Education, 21*(2), 117–124.

Part III
Music Education Practices Reframed

The Craft of Music Teaching in a Changing Society: Singing as Meaning, Education, and Craft – Reflections on Lithuanian Singing Practices

Rūta Girdzijauskienė

Abstract In this chapter, the craft of singing is discussed in terms of the meaning of singing in the context of Lithuanian culture and the specifics of Lithuanian musical education. The Lithuanian singing tradition is introduced as the way in which singing reflects the lifestyle of the nation and its role in the critical periods of national history as well as the construction of the contemporary Lithuanian identity. Singing is acknowledged to be the basis of Lithuanian musical education. Moreover, the realisation of the functions of singing in formal and non-formal musical education and the teacher's role and competences in teaching children to sing are presented as the basis for craftsmanship in singing.

Introduction

Visitors to Lithuania are often surprised at, and fascinated by, Lithuanian singing traditions. They are impressed by the performance of choirs and vocal ensembles as well as by regional and national events representing the culture of singing. A more attentive onlooker will notice the ability of singers of different generations to experience communion in singing when people from different regions, of different professions, and from different social strata together perform several dozens of songs. What is the secret of the phenomenon? How did this singing tradition of the Lithuanian people maintain the craft in Lithuanian singing traditions in schools and society?

In the present chapter, I seek to justify the idea that singing is not merely "the production of musical tones by means of the human voice" (Encyclopedia Britannica, online). That is a complex and multifaceted phenomenon, covering various cultural, educational, musical, and personal variables and relationships between them. The relationships are best explained by Csíkszentmihályi's *Systems Model of Creativity*

R. Girdzijauskienė (✉)
Klaipeda University, Klaipeda, Lithuania
e-mail: girdzijauskiene.ruta@gmail.com

© Springer Nature Switzerland AG 2021
K. Holdhus et al. (eds.), *Music Education as Craft*, Landscapes: the Arts, Aesthetics, and Education 30, https://doi.org/10.1007/978-3-030-67704-6_7

(2016), in which he defines creativity as a sociocultural structure with the components of the domain, the field, and the individuals. The author explains the domain as symbolic or cultural aspects of the environment (events, means, procedures, knowledge, rules) and the field as a social aspect (individuals who practice a given domain). According to Csíkszentmihályi, all components are closely related with each other:

> ...a set of rules and practices must be transmitted from the domain to the individual. The individual must then produce a novel variation in the content of the domain. The variation then must be selected by the field for inclusion in the domain. (Csíkszentmihályi, 1999, p. 315)

The Lithuanian singing tradition can also be defined as a system whose uniqueness is predetermined by the sociocultural context, a singing-based system of musical education, and the professionalism of individuals fostering the singing tradition. The first section of the chapter focuses on the historical, cultural, and social causes that predetermined the formation of the singing tradition. The second section reveals how the said factors influenced the formation of a singing-based system of musical education. The third section attempts to demonstrate the essential moments of the craft of singing and the craft of teaching to sing. Each section starts with the narratives of 16–17-year-old pupils, focusing on their singing experience in various contexts, and comments on them. The short narratives reveal a variety of attitudes towards singing and also link individual pupils' experiences through historical, cultural, social, and educational variables.

The Meaning of Singing in the Context of Lithuanian Culture

Singing is not an independent cultural activity. It is related to socially recognised values and expectations as well as to other cultural domains. According to Csíkszentmihályi (2016), in any historical period, some domains tend to become more eagerly recognised and predominant. Ethnomusicologists, music historians, and choir leaders agree that the Lithuanian singing tradition has been predominant for several centuries and formed under the influence of historical circumstances, the sociocultural context, the system of musical education, and great personalities in the music field (Šmitienė, 2010). Founder of the Lithuanian musical education system, Balčytis (2012), argued that people's singing was not biologically programmed, rather that was a deeply sociocultural phenomenon. People sing in certain places or situations, purposefully or led by subconscious motives, and by song they express their attitude to what is happening to themselves and around them. In the following section of the chapter, the interplay of singing and of song will be discussed in relation to the cultural and historical context of Lithuania.

Singing as a Way of Life

> *My Granny and I were returning to my native town by bus. We were coming together with about fifteen people of different ages, different professions, and hardly knowing each other. I was the youngest one. As soon as we set off, somebody started singing. The others joined in and continued: the first song was followed by another one, and another one... I knew almost all of the songs from family celebrations and could sing some of them. The songs were different – folk, written by popular composers, or romances. We kept singing for two hours.* (Roma, 16 years)

The story contains at least several moments that can be defined as typical for Lithuania. First, on gathering into a large group, it is rather common for Lithuanians to sing. Irrespective of the variety of people and situations, singing is an activity expressing commonality and practiced together. Second, regardless of the region or the place of gathering, there always will be songs that people of different ages or professions know and are able to sing, and not just one or two, but a number of them.

The ability and the desire to sing have deep historical traditions. As argued by ethnomusicologist Trinkūnas (2009), singing for Lithuanians was like a rite, equivalent to a religious ritual and contributing to the preservation of the tradition of pagan religion, which was basically polytheistic with elements of animism and pantheism. Consequently, all Lithuanian songs abounded in symbolic situations. They often juxtaposed the human and the natural worlds: a maiden was compared to an apple or a linden tree and a young man to an oak or a maple tree. Natural phenomena in the songs warned of future events or conveyed human relations: when the men went off to war, the leaves of the trees were trembling, and the wind witnessed an impending disaster. When the practices of paganism went into decline, songs preserved the Baltic ethnic religion.

As testified by the sources of folklore, in the consciousness of presenters, singing was fixed as an activity providing security and psychological comfort and suppressing anxiety (Maceina, 1993; Šmitienė, 2010). The comforting, refreshing, and communality-supporting effect of singing is emphasised. That is also related to the manner of singing: there are no individual singers or leaders, with the rest of the singers acting as the background or support. A Lithuanian folk song is basically a community song, which is reflected both in its content and its collective performing.

The thematic and genre variety of folk songs reveals that Lithuanians used to sing everywhere and on any occasion. In terms of content, Lithuanian songs do not differ from those of other nations: birth and death, love and marriage, and war and work. The lyrics of folk songs do not have a uniform rhythmical pattern, and the text does not present a poem with a clear storyline. The actual object of Lithuanian folk songs is the inner world of an individual rather than the objective world or an eventful story (Razauskas, 2013). A folk song must have become an integral part of the life of Lithuanians due to the narrative style of the text and the presentation of people's inner, instead of the outer, world. Much in the tradition of singing has been preserved up to the twenty-first century. In the consciousness of Lithuanians, the meaning of songs and singing has not changed much.

Singing as a Way of Preserving National Identity

> *Our choir went to the USA. Our programme included the Mass in a Washington church
> which had a small Lithuanian chapel. After the Mass, we sang several Lithuanian songs in
> it. I could not hold back my tears. In each line and each melody, I felt Lithuania. I had never
> felt being a Lithuanian so strongly as when singing thousands miles away from home.* (Ana,
> 16 years)

The story demonstrates how singing can be an instrument of strong feelings about
the nation. Like any small country, Lithuania, geographically surrounded by big
states, experienced the influence of its neighbours and had repeatedly been dramati-
cally constrained in terms of its national culture. In each of the periods, folk culture,
and particularly singing, served as a way of preserving national identity.

A memorable stage of history was the period (1864–1904) when the Lithuanian
word was banned, Lithuanian schools did not exist, and no books were published in
Lithuanian. During the period, Lithuanian culture is believed to have been preserved
in the cultural layer created by peasants: in particularly rich folklore and folk singing traditions (Nakienė, 2015). A similar situation occurred after the Second World
War, when Lithuania had been occupied by Soviet Russia (1940–1990). As a form
of resistance to the imposed ideology, the meanings opposing the Soviet ideology
and awakening the national and historical memory that the audience was expected
to recognise were encoded in songs (Čepaitienė, 2009). The so-called Aesopian
language was created: the prohibited topics were discussed through encoded symbols, motives, hints, and hush ups, "between the lines".

A disguised way to preserve the national identity in the Soviet years was choral
singing. Choirs became a tool of resistance to the occupational regime and the policy of the Soviet Russification, and they helped to protect Lithuanian customs, the
national culture, and the national spirit supported by Lithuanian songs. Understanding
the emotional effect and importance of choirs for Lithuanians, the Soviet system
supported the choral culture, while the choirs resourcefully applied the principles of
the Aesopian language and promoted the national culture and spirit. After paying a
certain tribute to the Bolshevik propaganda repertoire, the choirs performed folk
songs of their regions and popularised the compositions of Lithuanian classics
(Balčytis, 2012).

The significance of the Song Festival as informal cultural resistance in the years
of Soviet occupation was special from the civic and political viewpoints. In the
Song Festivals of the Soviet period, about 15,000 people sang. Song Festivals were
the main form of expression through which the ideas of independence and national-
ity were conveyed. Despite the strict ideological control of the festivals in the Soviet
times, most of the compositions were Lithuanian, and, after the events, the participants organised mass singing on the streets. In that way, Song Festivals became a
way for Lithuanians to defend the aspirations of independence (Gudelis, 2014).

In the period of 1988 to 1991, when the Baltic states sought independence from
the USSR, singing become as a weapon of national resistance. During numerous
demonstrations and meetings, Lithuanian songs were sung. Singing was one of the

most significant components of the "soft power" of Lithuania when representing its uniqueness as a country with its own values, specificities, customs, and choices. From the perspective of the present, the Singing Revolution is to be regarded as a major event: not only did it contribute to the restoration of independence, but actually became its symbol (Martinelli, 2015).

Singing as the Basis of Musical Education

Due to the deep traditions of singing, closely related to the way of life and the preservation of the national identity, it is not surprising that singing, and especially choir singing, became an important part of national culture and musical education. How did we conclude that singing became one of the major modes of musical practices? In the systems model of creativity (Csíkszentmihályi, 2016), the right to design the field belongs to the gatekeepers, professionals and authorities, practicing in a certain field and recognised to be competent connoisseurs of it. The first Lithuanian professional composers were either choirmasters or singers with an excellent feeling of folk singing. They became the authors of the first syllabi of musical education and had the greatest impact on the singing-based concept of Lithuanian musical education.

Realisation of the Functions of Singing in Formal and Non-formal Musical Education

> *Singing? In music lessons. We sing different songs and take part in projects. I am not good at singing, so I make presentations. I find it interesting to collect materials, arrange them into a presentation, and tell my classmates about them. It is enough for me to know about folk songs. (Justas, 16 years)*

Justas' narrative is short and revealing his specific relationship with singing. Just like many boys of his age, Justas is in a post-voice-mutation period and finds it difficult to manage the changed voice. Even if he does not sing, Justas finds a way to participate in music lessons. A theoretical approach, i.e. collection and analysis of information, is interesting for him. Cognitive involvement helps Justas to feel a full and equal member of singing without raising the question: to sing or not to sing.

Singing has always played a key role in the Lithuanian syllabi of music teaching. When in 1918 Lithuania declared independence, its system of education was developed on the basis of national culture (Petrauskaitė, 2009). Singing became the basis of learning music, and the first textbook of music published by Žilevičius and Andriulis in 1927 was called *A Young Singer*. The priority of singing over other activities was accounted for by the fact that textbooks were developed by choirmasters. The teaching materials were based on abundant Lithuanian folk songs. The rich heritage of folk songs and their diversity were used to introduce pupils to the notation.

After Lithuania had regained independence in 1991, folk songs played the key role in the development of children's musical culture, their abilities, and artistic taste (Velička, 2017). Folk songs were sung by ear, solmisated in one or several voices, and used to introduce to the typical features of Lithuanian culture. An analysis of music textbooks suggested that, in each form, pupils were to learn on average 20–25 songs. The vast majority of them were Lithuanian and, more than a half, Lithuanian folk songs.

Research found that singing was the most important part of a music lesson (Girdzijauskienė, 2012). Upon observing 150 music lessons for different age groups, singing was found to occupy on average one fourth of the time (11 min). On average, 2–3 songs were sung in a lesson, and almost all lessons began with vocal exercises.

Singing is also a predominant activity in non-formal musical education. Over one third of the extracurricular activities in comprehensive schools are related to music. Vocal training activities (lessons of solo, ensemble, and choir singing) are available in every school. A wide range of non-formal education institutions also offer a rich choice of musical groups. Singing is one of the most popular areas chosen by pupils (Girdzijauskienė, 2013). Various national and international events (celebrations, competitions, and festivals) contribute to the popularisation of singing. The aforementioned Song Festivals with the participation of tens of thousands of choir singers are held periodically. No less popular are events of solo and ensemble singing.

To sum up, the singing tradition in the context of Lithuanian music education can be defined as a multi-faceted phenomenon that occurs in a very broad context of formal and informal education. The content of music textbooks, the structure of the music lesson, the variety of after-school musical activities, and the abundance of musical events are naturally pervaded by the singing tradition. What outcomes of singing do pupils discern and what does singing mean to contemporary young people?

Singing Outcomes: Pupils' Point of View

> Still, I am most impressed by Song Festivals. When I come to the Vingis Park and see all those people having arrived from different parts of Lithuania, when I sing in the choir with thousands of other singers, the feeling is great. At the end of the Festival, we sang an anthem and knew that thousands of Lithuanians were singing it in different countries of the world, all at the same time. I felt like in outer space, feeling all of us united by singing. (Asta, 17 years)

The narrative featured several topics. One of them was the feeling of national identity when singing; another was the experience of participation in the Song Festival and performing with several thousands of other singers. On surveying 816 pupils-participants of the Song Festival of 2009, it turned out that, in accordance with the intensity of the experienced emotions, the event far exceeded other musical experiences. During the Song Festivals, the feelings of national identity and the communion with other singers were the strongest (Girdzijauskienė, 2013).

Similar findings were obtained from other studies. Diržinauskytė (2015) noted that senior pupils attached great importance to communication and collaboration with other singers. Girdzijauskas (2012) found out that the meaning of participation in musical activities was related by pupils to self-expression, purposeful leisure and recreation, unexpected insights, the experience of success, and the development of musical abilities. The most abundant emotional experiences came from music making and giving concerts, especially of classical music. Moreover, the pupils of the choir singing-promoting schools had deeper internal motivation and values-based orientation and were more creative.

Learning to sing happens not only at school but also in spaces where pupils actually live their lives. In other words, the singing tradition lives in a much wider context than just school. As proved by one of the latest research projects on pupils' singing (Girdzijauskienė, 2020), the majority of the respondent pupils indicated singing outside the school environment (concerts, festivals, family or friend gatherings) as the most striking experience. Students associated singing and themselves with their own participation in musical activities. A fairly small segment of pupils named singing or listening to music as their own individual activity, when alone at home, outside the house, or on a trip. A trend to relate singing to a group as a community activity was evident.

Upon discussing the historical, cultural, and educational context of singing, it is also important to focus on individuals, i.e. as Csíkszentmihályi would put it, the individuals who maintain/create the singing tradition and accept the responsibility for its authenticity and quality. In other words, the relationship of singing as a cultural phenomenon and the pursuit for excellence should be revealed.

Singing as a Craft

Sociologist Sennett (2008) defined craftsmanship as a human impulse to do the job well in a certain community or a field of activity. Having a beautiful voice is not sufficient for the excellence in singing. It is necessary to know the rules, means, and conventions of the field. To achieve excellence, one needs proficiency in the singing technique, the knowledge of the historical performance practice and aesthetic norms, as well as a precise and detailed analysis and expert interpretation of the work of music (Kramer, 2013). Craftsmanship has obviously many faces. That's why the popularity of singing in Lithuania is influenced not only by the traditions of singing but also by the efforts of qualified music teachers able to give engaging and fun vocal classes.

Teachers' Competence in Teaching Children How to Sing

Once just a few pupils came to a music lesson. We started discussing singing with the music teacher and she, in order to show how the song should be performed, sang it in an opera voice and left us open-mouthed. It was beautiful and unexpected – a great voice not somewhere on the stage, but right here in the classroom, and it belonged not to a professional singer, but to our teacher. (Rima, 16 years)

The fact that teachers have great vocal skills is not surprising. From among all the necessary competences, teachers prioritise the ability to work with musical groups of pupils (Girdzijauskienė, 2008). On the one hand, that is because of the systematic attention to the issue of vocal education. Thus, e.g. over the last decade, the Lithuanian Association of Music Teachers (www.lmma.eu) held 24 seminars for music teachers, including one fourth (6) devoted to vocal education, while in half of them (11), singing was in one or another way integral part of the event. Seminars devoted to singing are the most popular with music teachers, and, when asked about desirable topics for seminars, they insist on the events of professional development in the field of singing. Even if they are sufficiently competent in leading pupil groups, they are willing to grow further.

On the other hand, a clear dominant of vocal education in the training of prospective music teachers is worth noting. When applying to the studies of music pedagogy, applicants have to demonstrate their singing skills which account for 40% of the grade in the entrance exam. The emphasis on singing and on the competence to lead pupils' vocal groups remains during the studies (Balčytis, 2004; Lasauskienė, 2013; Girdzijauskienė, 2017). Even though different schools implement different study programmes, classes devoted to singing or learning to lead vocal groups (choir, vocal ensemble, solo singing, and conducting) occupy one third of the time assigned to music subjects. When formulating career opportunities for prospective music teachers, it is indicated that graduates of the programme of music pedagogy can work as music teachers or leaders of music groups in various types of educational institutions (kindergartens, primary and basic schools, music schools, and gymnasiums). Thus, when preparing for the career of a music teacher, students start their studies with the intention to work as leaders of musical groups in the future and are trained for that kind of work all during the studies.

In terms of higher education from the viewpoint of vocal education, it is worth mentioning the professional preparedness of university teachers and the topics of ongoing research. Presently, two thirds of (12 out of 18) holders of doctorate degrees teaching in the programmes of music pedagogy in Lithuanian higher schools have the qualifications of a choirmaster or a singer. One third of the aforementioned staff combine academic, scientific, and choirmaster's activities. Therefore, it is natural that the research topics either focus on or are related to vocal education in various aspects. Nearly two thirds of the doctoral dissertations in music pedagogy defended between 1968 and 2014 were related to the issues of vocal education (Šečkuvienė, 2014). It is possible that the research interests of the academic staff and their artistic activities affect the character of teaching and the orientation of the content of studies towards vocal activities, in the same way that the meaning of singing orients young researchers towards in-depth studies of the area.

Singing Between Craft and Artistic Aspirations

When I teach pupils to sing, I focus on voice formation, good intonation, clear pronunciation, and a sense of style. If these are properly formed, then half the work is done. Unfortunately, there is not enough time to achieve performance excellence and to reveal the meanings of music. (From a music teacher's conversation. Girdzijauskienė, 2018)

The interview quote, recorded in fieldnotes during the research, makes it fairly clear that, when it comes to teaching singing, the singing technique is a priority. The teacher often faces the dilemma of devoting lesson time to the development of a vocal technique or of artistry. The former requires constant practice and systematic work and therefore more time and attention. Artistry is associated with a personal attitude, emotionality, spontaneity, and individual variables. Kramer (2013) identifies three approaches towards defining their relation: craftsmanship as the basis for artistry, craftsmanship as a practical means of realising artistic ideas, and craftsmanship and artistry as independent categories. Concerning singing in the case of Lithuania, the first approach, which makes it possible to achieve high quality of singing, is undoubtedly predominant. However, the historically established social and cultural meanings of singing, which distinguish the Lithuanian singing tradition from that of other countries, remain in the background.

Excellence in singing requires time, dedication, instruction, and regular practice. A singing tradition is associated with the orientation towards product, high technical standards, ranking, and competition in the field. As McCarthy argues:

if music educators focus on the social and cultural dimensions of musical meaning and value, then time and energy devoted to these aspects may detract from the development of high performance standards; or, accommodating the belief that the integration of social and cultural contexts into the study of music is indeed within the purview of music educators, and not exclusively the work of social studies, history, or literature teachers. (McCarthy, 2009, p. 30)

On the other hand, the cultural and social contexts of singing are integral part of music art. Therefore, it depends only on the professionalism of the teacher what priorities he has and how he is able to follow them. Professionalism does not mean knowing more teaching techniques. This is a certain form of thinking needed to create artistically crafted work.

Conclusions

Singing is undoubtedly one of the most important areas of musical activity. Throughout the centuries, we will not find a single culture that has never practiced singing. The significance of singing is still evident today. The question is only which moments of the craft of singing are highlighted as significant for the individual, society, and culture. By focusing on the vocal technique, the specifics of music performance, and the singing style or genre, high standards of music performance are likely to be achieved. However, in such a case, the risk is to "close the singing in oneself" and leave it for a narrow circle of fans and connoisseurs to enjoy.

The present chapter aims to show that singing is a deeply social practice, as the concept of singing in society is shaped by historical, social, and political circumstances. In this way, singing becomes much more than a daily activity: it reflects the character and the way of life of the nation and becomes a means of the national identity preservation and a form of struggle for independence. Understanding the meaning of singing by general public as well as preservation of the singing tradition and a diversity of new ways of creation present the context in which the craftsmanship of singing can reach the highest standard both in terms of the quality of performance and a meaningful mode of human expression.

What insights can we offer in order to improve the craftsmanship of singing and to preserve the singing tradition? The experience of singing with others is one of the most valuable outcomes of musical education. The nature of the Lithuanian way of singing is of a communal character: when singing in a group, not only pleasure is experienced but also commonality, nationalism, patriotism, and a pride in one's nation and in oneself (Maceina, 1993; Šmitienė, 2010; Balčytis, 2012; Girdzijauskas, 2012). Of course, in the twenty-first century, the character of musical education has been significantly changed by contemporary technologies. The possibilities of music making in a group decrease, and singing loses the majority of its meanings relevant several decades ago (Girdzijauskiene, 2017). For that reason, the significance of musical education at school as a process of uniting people and providing the feeling of community tends to increase. Singing together with others in a lesson or in a choir becomes a significant tool for the implementation of the social function of music. It is necessary to relate what is learnt at school to the pupils' life outside school and to associate the music learning outcomes with the widest possible context, thus making musical education open geographically and situationally and accessible for everyone.

References

Balčytis, E. (2004). Muzikos mokytojų rengimo Lietuvos aukštosiose mokyklose studijų programų lyginamoji analizė [Comparative analysis of Pre-Service Music Teachers' study programs in Lithuanian universities]. *Tiltai, 20*, 34–41.
Balčytis, E. (2012). *Muzikinio ugdymo labirintais* [The labyrinths of music education]. Šiauliai: Šiaulių universiteto leidykla.
Čepaitienė, R. (2009). Sovietinės kultūros šaltiniai: tarp futurizmo ir paseizmo [Origins of Soviet culture: Between futurism and paseism]. *Darbai ir dienos, 52*, 86–104.
Csíkszentmihályi, M. (1999). Implications of a system perspective for the study of creativity. In R. Sternberg (Ed.), *Handbook of creativity* (pp. 313–335). Cambridge: Cambridge University Press.
Csíkszentmihályi, M. (2016). *The systems model of creativity: The collected works of Mihály Csíkszentmihályi*. Dordrecht, the Netherlands: Springer.
Diržinauskytė, V. (2015). The expression of high school students' creativity through choral singing activity. *Problems in Music Pedagogy, 14*(1), 53–65.

Girdzijauskas, A. (2012). *Aukštesniųjų klasių mokinių dorovinės kultūros ugdymas muzikine veikla* [The development of higher grade students' moral culture through musical activity]. Klaipėda: Klaipėdos Universiteto Leidykla.

Girdzijauskienė, R. (2008). Muzikos mokytojo profesinės kompetencijos ypatumai [The features of music teachers' professional competencies]. *Tiltai, 37*, 5–12.

Girdzijauskienė, R. (2012). The peculiarities of development of creativity of pupils of senior forms while performing, creating, listening to, describing and evaluating music. *The space of creation, 10*, 8–18.

Girdzijauskienė, R. (2013). Educational aspects of pupils' participation in Lithuanian students' song festival. In T. De Baets (Ed.), *The reflective music teacher* (p. 45). Liuven, Belgium: Lemmensinstituut.

Girdzijauskienė, R. (2017). To be creative in music. *The Changing Face of Music and Art Education, 8*, 33–46.

Girdzijauskienė, R. (2018). Singing experiences: Interviews with students. *Fieldnotes*, Klaipėda - Vilnius.

Girdzijauskiene, R. (2020). Singing tradition and perspective. *The Journal of Music Education*, [In press].

Gudelis, R. (2014). Dainų švenčių ištakos ir liuteroniškoji muzikinė tradicija [Origins of song festivals and Lutheran musical tradition]. *Res Humanitariae, 11*, 102–128.

Kramer, O. (2013). Music education between artistic aspiration and the teaching of craftsmanship. In A. de Vugt & I. Malmberg (Eds.), *European perspective on music education artistry* (pp. 31–46). Innsbruk, Austria: Helbling.

Lasauskienė, J. (2013). Būsimų muzikos mokytojų bendrųjų kompetencijų plėtojimo strategijos. [Strategies of Developing General Competencies of Pre-Service Music Teachers]. *Pedagogika, 112*, 41–47.

Maceina, A. (1993). *Liaudies daina – Tautos sielos išraiška [The folk song as the expression of the soul of the nation]* (pp. 145–149). II (IX): Tautosakos darbai.

Martinelli, D. (2015). Dainuojanti revoliucija – viena iš geriausiai (deja) saugomų Lietuvos paslapčių [The singing revolution as one of the best (unfortunately) protected secrets of Lithuania]. *Lietuvos muzikos link*, 18. Retrieved from [30 October, 2018] http://www.mic.lt/lt/diskursai/lietuvos-muzikos-link/nr-18-2015-sausis-gruodis/dainuojanti-revoliucija/

McCarthy, M. (2009). Re-thinking "music" in the context of education. In T.A. Regelski and J.T. Gates (Eds.), *Music Education for Changing Times*, Landscapes: the Arts, Aesthetics, and Education 7 (pp. 29–37). Springer Science+Business Media B.V.

Nakienė, A. (2015). Tradicinės kultūros poslinkiai. Dainos XX–XXI a. didmiestyje [Traditional cultural changes. XX-XXI centuries' songs in a big city]. Tautosakos darbai XLI X, 171–193.

Petrauskaitė, D. (2009). Muzikinio švietimo padėtis bendrojo lavinimo mokyklose [The state of music education in general education schools]. In A. Ambrazas (Ed.), *Lietuvos muzikos istorija: Nepriklausomybės metai 1918–1940* (pp. 272–285). Vilnius: Lietuvos muzikos ir teatro akademija.

Razauskas, D. (2013). Dieviškoji daina [The songs Divine]. *Liaudies kultūra, 3*, 11–17.

Šečkuvienė, H. (2014). Lietuvos muzikinio ugdymo disertacinių tyrimų tematika ugdymo paradigmų virsmo kontekste [Topics of Lithuanian dissertations on music education in the context of a paradigm shift]. In R. Bruzgelevičienė (Ed.), *Ugdymo paradigmų iššūkiai didaktikai* (pp. 362–388). Vilnius, Lithuania: Edukologija.

Sennett, R. (2008). *The craftsman*. New Haven: Yale University Press.

Šmitienė, G. (2010). Dainavimas kaip terpė ir buvimo būdas [Singing as an environment and way of beying]. *Tautosakos darbai, XXXIX*, 80–100.

Trinkūnas, J. (2009). *Lietuvių senosios religijos kelias* [The path of the Lithuanian ancient religion]. Vilnius, Lithuania: Asveja.

Velička, E. (2017). *Lietuvių etninė muzika pradinio muzikinio ugdymo sistemoje* [Lithuanian ethnic music in the system of primary music education]. Vilnius: Lietuvos muzikos ir teatro akademija.

Artistic Citizenship and the Crafting of Mutual Musical Care

Brynjulf Stige

Abstract The notion of *artistic citizenship* is of relevance to both music education and music therapy. I suggest that artistic citizenship needs to be performed with both care and craft and that professional practitioners need to promote mutuality and participation in order to nurture it. The argument challenges the assumption that music educators teach *to music*, while music therapists help people to grow *through music*. This traditional distinction is less than clear, because any person's interest in learning music might give new possibilities for participation in a community. A case example illuminates the social-musical journey of a group of learners with intellectual disabilities in a community music school and introduces discussions of the notions that "everyone is an artist" and that "all forms of music-making and musical interactions can be *artistic*". *Citizenship* is understood as the status bestowed to people as members of a broader community, and the risk of ignoring diversity and of developing a romanticised view of community is elucidated. Artistic citizenship requires care to be realised, and care is intricate, sometimes problematic. Possibilities for developing *mutual musical care* are therefore examined, as well as the need for *zooming in* and *zooming out* on micro and macro dimensions of practice.

> Interdisciplinary work ... is not about confronting already constituted disciplines (none of which, in fact, is willing to let itself go). To do something interdisciplinary it's not enough to choose a "subject" (a theme) and gather around it two or three sciences. Interdisciplinarity consists in creating a new object that belongs to no one. (Roland Barthes in "Jeunes Chercheurs". [Quoted from Clifford & Marcus, 1986, p. 1])

Introduction: Music Education and Music Therapy as Sister Disciplines

Music education and music therapy are both hybrid disciplines, in more than one way. There are artistic and scientific dimensions to both disciplines, for example, and both disciplines take interest in relationships between sound, self, and society.

B. Stige (✉)
University of Bergen, Bergen, Norway
e-mail: brynjulf.stige@uib.no

© Springer Nature Switzerland AG 2021   89
K. Holdhus et al. (eds.), *Music Education as Craft*, Landscapes: the Arts, Aesthetics, and Education 30, https://doi.org/10.1007/978-3-030-67704-6_8

In this chapter I elaborate on the notion of "artistic citizenship", which has become relevant in both disciplines, if in somewhat different ways. I will develop the argument that artistic citizenship requires both care and craft. As we will see, this might involve the craft of being a not-knowing knower, a professional practitioner promoting mutuality and participation.

Music educators teach *to* music (and/or *about* music), while music therapists help people to grow *through* music. The simplicity of the "to-music-versus-through-music" distinction has been appealing in some ways, although the logic behind it has been challenged for decades (Ruud, 1979; Stige, 1995). The claim is perhaps so misleading by now that even its simplicity has lost its appeal. Increasingly, (at least some) scholars argue that music educators should prepare students to put music to work for the benefit of human wellbeing (Elliott, 2012; Elliott, Silverman & Bowman, 2016; Silverman, 2012; Sunderland, Lewandowski, Bendrups, & Bartleet, 2018). And increasingly, (at least some) scholars argue that the human right to music is central to music therapy, so that music therapists take interest in a person's musical development (Aigen, 2005; Kleive & Stige, 1988; Stige & Aarø, 2012). Even the idea that there is a clear division between musical and non-musical goals is challenged (Stige, Ansdell, Elefant & Pavlicevic, 2010).

I am not suggesting that music educators and music therapists now have interchangeable competencies or roles, but intersections and boundaries are changing, both within the professional practices and the academic disciplines. In Norway, there is a tradition for discussing theoretical problems shared by music therapy and music education (Espeland & Stige, 2017; Ruud, 1979, 2000, 2016; Schei, Espeland & Stige, 2013; Stige, 1995), and I argue that contemporary developments in society actualise this in new ways, also at an international level.

I will be making the claim that artistic citizenship requires care to be realised and that care is intricate, potentially problematic. The crafting of careful and caring mutuality enters the discussion. Traditionally, we think of craft as skilled work that requires particular knowledge and dexterity. In educational theory, craft knowledge is often understood as the knowledge that teachers develop when carrying out the demands of their jobs, through processes of practical problem-solving and reflection (Cooper & McIntyre, 1996, p. 76). I will not only be looking into the craft of educators and therapists, but to the craft of students and therapy participants as well. In this context, then, craft is not mainly about creating musical objects (works and performances), but equally or more about relating to musical subjects (agents) in ways that create events and relationships out of which subjectivity and personhood can grow. The etymology of the word craft is interesting here, because the Old English word *cræft* not only referred to skill and art, but to strength and courage as well (Webster's Dictionary & Thesaurus, 2000). It is worth noting that some of the music scholars who have taken interest in the distribution of craft in professional contexts also have taken interest in processes of empowerment (DeNora, 2006, 2007; Rolvsjord, 2010).

Art and Community

Music therapists often challenge the idea that artistic practices are separate from our everyday life in society, as exemplified by this statement:

> One of the basic premises for music therapists is that everyone is an artist. But society dictates that the living, working stuff of art is for 'the artist,' a person removed, specially trained, and usually quite odd. (Kenny, 1979/2006, p. 63)

Some music educators have taken similar perspectives:

> Please note that when I use [the term] *artistic,* I mean *all* forms of music-making and listening and *all* types of formal and informal musical interactions at *all* levels in schools and communities. (Elliott, 2012, pp. 21–22)

Many of the scholars advocating such perspectives have taken inspiration from John Dewey's (1934/1980) seminal work *Art as Experience*, based on a criticism of the splitting of means and ends in modern societies. Undoubtedly, some people will think that ideas such as "everyone is an artist" water down our notions, but there are good reasons to examine notions such as *art*, *artist*, and *artistic* critically and carefully. There is a humanistic dimension to this, suggesting that we should not separate the debates about what defines good music from reflections on what good even means (DeNora, 2013). There is a social dimension to this as well, reminding us about how aesthetic criteria grow out of and are negotiated in the context of specific practices (Stige, 1998). To think about art and community does not necessarily indicate lack of concern about quality, then, but a critical interest in what quality even means, to whom, when, and how.

To acknowledge that the distinction between "to music" and "through music" is less than clear is important in this context, because any person's interest in learning music might give new possibilities for participation in a community. Often we have to work hard over time to get the music right. Our possibilities do not depend upon our own development only, however, but also upon potentials and barriers in the broader community. In an essay about the contextualised effects of musical participation, I have previously discussed such questions in relation to a community music therapy project where music therapists worked collaboratively to help realise people's cultural rights to participation (Stige, 2007). The context was a rural Norwegian community in the early 1980s, at a time when there was no tradition in Norway of including musicians with intellectual disabilities into musical activities in the community, despite the fact that their right to participation was clearly described in national laws and regulations. I was lucky enough to be employed in a government-funded project which was established to try and change this situation.

Here, I will share some excerpts describing experiences of a group called Upbeat. The members of the group were all adults with Down syndrome, and they were invited to become learners in the local community music school. Their interest in music and in community participation was clear from the very first session, but few of the group members had previously had any chance to learn music. In the beginning, therefore, even the task of playing a basic beat together on simple percussion instruments was very, very difficult. Through musical *improvisation*, this gradually changed over the next few months, however, and one day the members of Upbeat had an encounter with Grieg and his music:

> ... the members of this group did not start by asking for Mozart or Grieg. They probably had never even heard of any of them. Their questions in relation to music were about the local marching band ... It took some time before Upbeat discovered Grieg. In fact it just happened by chance. (Excerpt from Stige, 2007)

Perhaps it was a photo of Grieg with a nice moustache that first attracted Upbeat's attention, but we ended up wanting to play music that he had composed:

> As Upbeat's piano-player I had some homework to do. I went home and played through most of Grieg's Lyric Pieces and also Opus 17 and 66, which are collections of Norwegian Folk Tunes arranged by Grieg. I was searching for pieces that could match Upbeat's musical experience and interests. In the improvisations that we had had together, I had experienced Knut's love for splendid strikes on the cymbal, Reidar's interest for the chime bars, Solveig's ability to keep a beat on the drum, etc. Could we find musical pieces that could be arranged so that these musical skills could be honoured?

> The first piece we tried out was Opus 12, No. 2, which is a Waltz with a folk tune feeling. When writing this essay, I have been able to study a video recording made by the Norwegian Broadcasting Corporation NRK in 1986. It is a recording of Upbeat practicing this piece. One of the first things that strikes me when watching this video is the ease with which the musicians play. The group had been practicing for a while before this recording, but there is something more to this; there seems to be a kind of *fit* between the music and the group of musicians here. I have the impression that this music makes sense to them, so that it is natural for them to play what they play. I will try to explain by going into some musical detail.

> The piece starts with two bars of accompaniment only, where the rhythm and the key of A minor is established. That is, Grieg wrote two bars here, but some performers do it differently. The Norwegian jazz pianist Bugge Wesseltoft has made a beautiful recording of this piece, using four bars to get going. ...Upbeat used whatever number of bars it would take Solveig to get going, each particular day. Often two bars would be enough. Sometimes we would have four bars, or eight. ...Then the melody comes in on the piano, accompanied by a harmonic pattern where the first beat of each bar has an A as its base, even though the chords change between A minor, D major and E major seventh. It is all very simple and delicate, and when Upbeat played this, Solveig's beat was the only addition to the piano.

> But then, after eight bars of this there is room for something different. The harmony changes; the next bar starts with a chord in the parallel key C major and ends with a secondary dominant to that key, namely a D seventh chord (with an added ninth). This tension is then resolved; the next bar starts with a G sixth, which after a tripled expression on the first beat is altered to a straightforward G major chord on the second beat. Most musicians play this piece somewhat faster than what Upbeat did, and the sequence from the C to the secondary dominant leading to the G is often played as a light and quick transition, even though the G sixth is usually accented. With Upbeat, the accented G sixth was very important, because it gave Knut such a good possibility to take one of his splendid strikes on the cymbal (and this pattern is repeated several times in this piece, so that he could go for this strike more than once). In order to make this work, however, as pianist I had to play with quite a solid touch and with use of both ritardando and crescendo, so that the secondary dominant creating the tension that could "legitimate" the accented strike on the cymbal

would stand out. This worked well for Knut, and he played with an extraordinary precision in this piece. Grieg's music afforded this, but only as performed in the way described here. A more standard quick and light performance would have been different. (Excerpts from Stige, 2007)

A group of musicians with intellectual disabilities is not usually associated with much craft, but here is a performance with precise and splendid strikes on the cymbal, a delicate chime bar sound, and a solid beat on the drum. Perhaps equally important, here is a performance where the musicians sensitively pay attention to each other and make the piece work as a whole. How much of this depends on the possibilities created by the music selected? How much depends on the craft of the music therapist, for instance, in the conscious use of touch while playing the piano and the use of ritardando and crescendo at the right time? The description above borrows insights from Tia DeNora's (2000) discussion of how different musics afford differently, while the meanings and effects depend upon contextualised appropriations of these affordances. The example indicates that all participants in a context contribute when we put music into action. Later in the chapter I will relate this to the crafting of mutual musical care.

Upbeat decided to put their music to action by going public with their version of Grieg, in response to an invitation to the spring concert of the local community music school. This was exciting, but I also remember being nervous at the time. This piece was different from anything Upbeat had performed publicly before. Usually they played popular music tunes, while Grieg's waltz traditionally is considered a piece of art music, even though it is based on a folk music idiom. As Lubet (2004) and others have demonstrated, Western art music is not an inclusive institution; it is driven by a search for perfection that excludes many people from musical participation. A community music school is an inclusive enclave of this culture, but it was not obvious at all that the local community would welcome Upbeat's unconventional way of playing Grieg.

The audience's reception of the performance ended up being very positive, which was encouraging and heart-warming to the members of Upbeat. I argue that the event was important to the community as well. In a performance like this, the community is not only a surrounding context. People of the local community take active part in creating the event, and as such people and performances constitute each other. In this way we could argue that Upbeat's performance contributed to social change in this community, in allowing for a more wide-ranging understanding of music and of the craft of the people making it. In fact, this event could be considered the beginning of the process of making the Upbeat members' ultimate dream come true, namely, to play in and with the local marching band. This happened 2 years later, after hard work in and with the community. The dream came true, despite the fact that the idea initially was uninvited and considered unrealistic by the marching band members of the community (Stige, 2002).

These excerpts illustrate how our rights to participation in a community need to be performed to be real, in performances that require craft, not only when going public with our music but in the processes leading up an event as well. This will be my point of entry to a discussion of the notion of *artistic citizenship*.

Artistic Citizenship

The notions that everyone is an artist (Kenny, 1979/2006) and that all forms of music-making and musical interactions can be artistic (Elliott, 2012) might be confusing to some readers, and they do warrant some explication. We might explore them in biological as well as sociological perspectives. Using a biological perspective, we can argue that humans' capacity to "artify" is a result of the evolution of our species: in the case of humans, nature chose culture, so to say. All persons have the potential of "making things special" and expressing themselves artistically (Dissanayake, 2000). In applying sociological perspectives, we understand that this universal human capacity of "making things special" is played out very differently from one society to the next. In contemporary societies, some people are more special than others in that they identify as and are acknowledged as artists, in contrast to other professional roles. Such processes of specialised professionalisation characterise modernity, and my errand here is not to question the role of the professional artist as such. I do think, however, that it is important to reflect upon positive and negative aspects of professionalisation of the arts, for instance, when it comes to each person's rights to cultural participation in a community. The arts can be used for exclusion, while they also might open up rich possibilities for participation. To examine the capacity of music educators and music therapists to support inclusive practices is warranted (Stige, 1995).

If we accept that all persons have the potential of expressing themselves artistically in a community, we need to address major philosophical questions about what it means to be a person and a citizen. Some of the aspects of personhood that philosophers typically have discussed are rationality, self-consciousness, command of communication, agency, moral worth, and entitlement to respect (Stige & Strand, 2016). Taylor (1985) is one of many scholars who have challenged such performance criteria to determine who is a person. Who among us would not at times doubt the rationality of our thoughts and the moral worth of our actions? Instead, Taylor advocates for a significance-based view of personhood: what is crucial to persons as agents, Taylor argues, is that things matter to them.

This version of what it means to be a person activates new questions, including questions about our capacity and willingness to see and hear other people, in the context of our vulnerabilities. Some scholars focus upon personhood as a position that is not primarily defined by the individual's performance or experience, but as "a standing or status that is bestowed upon one human being by others in the context of particular social relationships and institutional arrangements" (Kitwood, 1997, p. 7). Personhood – in this perspective – requires collaborative activity in a given context, then.

Citizenship is usually defined as the status bestowed to people as members of a broader community. The notion invites critique of romanticised views of participatory community, which often ignore diversity, social conflict, and political actions. With reference to Fred Twine's (1994) work on the interdependence of self and society, Bartlett and O'Connor (2007, p. 211) argue that "a fundamental difference between personhood and citizenship is that discussions about citizenship are by implication discussions about power, and in particular, the lack of power afforded some citizens in relation to others".

The idea that art and citizenship are related might challenge some well-established ways of thinking about art in modern societies. Many of us are used to think of artists as specialised and highly gifted individuals (and individualists), rather than as group members. Also, many of us tend to think of ordinary group and community members as not being artists. To separate individuals and communities is somewhat artificial, however. They constitute each other, and we need to consider carefully the role of art and aesthetics in relation to power and privilege in society. Informed by the late philosophy of Wittgenstein (1953/1967), I have previously discussed the notion of aesthetic practice in order to highlight the relational and contextual processes that characterise the arts. This suggests a more democratic perception of artistic process, challenging the ideas that art is created by special individuals, that it is autonomous (belongs to another sphere than everyday life), and that it is necessarily technically advanced (Stige, 1998). This does not suggest that craft and skills are not involved, only that we understand our actions and experiences in the context of social practices, bundled "in the middle" between social structures at the macro level and individual agency at the micro level (Stige, 2015).

Lately, ideas about artistic citizenship have created engagement and debate within arts education and related areas of practice and scholarship (Campbell & Martin, 2006; Elliot et al., 2016). Artistry should be linked to social responsibility, and the arts can be put to work towards positive transformation of people's lives in local, regional, and international contexts, these scholars claim. "Artistic" is then no longer an elitist term, but a term referring to people's engagement with the arts, in all walks of life and at any levels of technical accomplishment.

In music education, one of the first publications on artistic citizenship was a paper written by Elliot (2012), where he argued that music should be infused by an ethic of care and be put to work in the community. These are large issues, indeed, and the arguments have been met with criticism. Woodford (2014), for instance, highlights Elliott's avoidance of controversy and lack of attention to the many social obstructions to critical thought and self-reflection in contemporary societies. In short, Woodford argues that there is a "romantic streak" to Elliott's argument, where music's potential to make the world a better place is overemphasised and pitfalls, hindrances, and abuses ignored.

I will return to such critical perspectives, but first we need to examine the idea of citizenship more carefully by considering necessary conditions at an interpersonal level. How – in our everyday interactions – do we prepare ourselves for citizen participation?

Mutual Musical Care

If we take a relational perspective in our understanding of self and society, care for music and care for self and others become interrelated processes (Allsup, 2003; Stige, 2010b). We are invited to acknowledge and highlight our ethical responsibilities when working with persons whose possibilities for citizen participation are not quite yet realised. This is the situation for any child and for people experiencing stigmatisation and exclusion or other limitations to participation.

Care as relational commitment was highlighted by Knud Løgstrup (1956/1991), a Danish philosopher who argued that interdependence is a basic human condition. Consequently, he argued that the ethical demand of caring for others is given; it is not something we choose. The responsibility for the other person is primary; care is not something you do because you feel like it or expect something back. In Løgstrup's philosophy of care, then, our communication with others could not be separated from responsiveness to the other person's needs. For a music therapist or a music educator, such linking of responsiveness and responsibility is central to the role of being professional. This is a secondary description, however. According to Løgstrup, this link is primary for all human beings.

If we follow Løgstrup's argument, care is not (only) a special area of practice for nurses or other health-care workers; it is a quality of human interaction in the everyday life in families, communities, schools, and other institutions. Somewhat similar perspectives were developed by Milton Mayeroff (1971), who also highlighted the notion that care could be described as self-actualisation. In caring for others, in helping them grow, I actualise myself, Mayeroff argued. Writers grow in caring for their ideas, teachers in caring for their students, and so on. As relational process, care puts powers like trust, understanding, courage, and responsibility into play, leading to growth for all partners involved. In other words, when caring, we experience the other person's growth and development as bound up with our own sense of wellbeing.

If the basic perspective developed by philosophers such as Løgstrup and Mayeroff are taken into its ultimate implications, it may become problematic to define any limits on any individual's responsibility. The feminist theories on care that have emerged since the 1980s have paid more attention to this issue. Carol Gilligan's (1982/1993) famous book, *In a Different Voice*, explicitly challenged the image of the caring woman who acts and speaks only for others. Care might be a given, as Løgstrup argued, and a path to self-actualisation, as advocated by Mayeroff. It can also be a burden, however. We need to take into consideration the limits of each person's capacity to contribute and consider how responsibilities could and should be shared and distributed within a community.

This is related to a central problem for care ethics: Could care and justice be combined? We care for the person(s) close to us, with limited possibilities to go beyond the immediate situation, but the needs of someone not so close could be even more severe. This, then, is opposed to the universality implied in most ideals of social justice, and it is sometimes a difficult or impossible conflict to resolve.

Before we examine questions of social justice, we need to go into some more detail about how and why care is a pertinent issue for music therapists and music educators. I will do this by exploring the idea of "musical mutual care".

Christopher Small (1998) argues that through collaborative music-making, we are capable of articulating and shaping human relationships in their multi-layered and multi-ordered complexity and changeability. This perspective has been widely accepted both within music education and music therapy. I do think, however, that we need to specify in some detail the mechanisms that might constitute music's effects in these directions. Unless we are able to do so, we risk ending up celebrating music's positive possibilities and ignore the many pitfalls and problems that characterise professional practices as well as everyday life.

There are some general theories on music's value to human bonding and mutuality, including theories on the psychobiological foundations for musical participation (Dissanayake, 2001; Malloch & Trevarthen, 2009). In professional contexts, we frequently encounter specific challenges that require an extended theoretical elaboration. I will give two examples in this direction, one focusing upon the need for trauma-informed care in some situations and one focusing upon problems of emotional communication related to the stratification that frequently characterise human interaction.

In an interview study where social workers reflected on music therapy in child welfare contexts, Krüger, Nordanger, and Stige (2018) found that the informants' ideas about the benefits circled around four main themes: a) safety and wellbeing, b) relationships and mastery, c) dealing with complex emotions, and d) continuity and stability across situations. The authors discussed these findings in relation to perspectives from trauma-informed care (Bath, 2015), with the three "pillars" of safety, relationship, and sense of mastery. According to Bath, these three dimensions are mutually dependent, with safety as the foundation for the other two. The subtitle of his article is worth noting: "Healing in the other 23 hours". The idea is not that every child who has been traumatised primarily needs individual therapy. The question is more how various professions can collaborate in building the environment that the children need in order to grow. This is directly related to learning. Trauma research shows that children exposed to continuous threats in their environment often live in a state of constant alertness, which orients them towards "guarding themselves", a state that supresses the ability to learn. In neurobiological terms, you could say that the "survival brain" supresses the more advanced "learning brain" (Nordanger & Braarud, 2017). In this perspective, both music educators and music therapists should take interest in how educational contexts can become environments that enhance each child's needs and possibilities to flourish.

Social environments are complex, however, and stratification of human interaction is one of the intricacies, sometimes leading to situations where some participants disempower others. Such challenges were encountered in an ethnographic study of the musical interaction in a group of intellectually disabled musicians (Stige 2010a). The study was informed by Collins's (2004) theory of interaction rituals, and it revealed a broad variety of participatory styles, ranging from non-participation and silent participation to conventional, adventurous, and eccentric participation. In interpreting the findings, I argued that an inclusive space for musical participation allows for low energy as well as high energy inputs and for actions that challenge or support the established focus, respectively. Such processes depend upon high levels of emotionally shared attention, however, based upon successful combination of the various ingredients of an interaction ritual. This does not always happen. In my study, several challenges related to stratification of emotional energy could be observed. Collins (2004, pp. 102–140) uses the term "energy stars" to describe this. In a situation, energy stars might charge their own "batteries" of emotional energy, while participants who find themselves in more secondary or subordinate roles might experience the same situation as an energy drainer. This can be descriptive of the dynamics of the group that the teacher or therapist works with. Sometimes professionals do not regulate their participation sensitively enough either and become energy stars putting participants in unnecessary subordinate roles (Stige, 2010a, pp. 138–141).

Based on these observations, I argue that mutual musical care is often a precondition for the development of artistic citizenship and also that we should think positively about music's potential in the direction of mutual care. We should not take for granted that this potential is realised, however. When we music with other people, there are unique possibilities for experiences of being nurtured emotionally, in ways that create energy and stimulate feelings of togetherness and belonging. There are also many possibilities for experiences of subordination, emotional mismatch, and lack of social space.

The Craft of Zooming In and Zooming Out

The notion of artistic citizenship is helpful in illuminating the social significance of the arts. To some degree, however, there is a "romantic streak" to parts of the existing literature, where music's communal potential is overemphasised and problems and abuses downplayed. In introducing the notion of mutual musical care, I have tried to highlight the craft it usually takes to realise music's potential in a pro-social direction. It requires collaboration, and while music in some ways might ease processes of collaboration, we are talking about processes that take time and effort and that sometimes go wrong (Bolger et al., 2018).

One central problem remains to be discussed. The fact that mutual musical care can be realised does not necessarily suggest betterment beyond the dyad or group. Mutual care is not the same as social justice. Woodford's (2014) critique of Elliott (2012) touches upon this problem. The world would probably be a better place if it was easy to resolve, and I shall make no attempt of outlining fully satisfying solutions. It should be possible to indicate some potentially helpful steps, however. First, it might be fruitful to distinguish between various forms of citizenship that can be related to artistic practices. Second, it might be helpful to develop our capacity to discover and track interactions at various systemic levels.

Turino (2016) discusses music, social change, and alternative forms of citizenship, and he reminds us about the landscape in between music as mere entertainment or pure art on one side and music as a driver of dramatic political change on the other. He takes interest in music and "everyday habit change", as he puts it. His examples are linked to the American Midwest, and relationships between local practices and the broader society vary from country to country and over time. I would argue, however, that the argument that we should take interest in alternative forms of citizenship might be valid across contexts.

Take the group Upbeat that we met in the opening sections of the chapter. The intellectually disabled members of this group performed alternative forms of citizen engagement, leading to social change in the community. The fact that they wanted to play with the prestigious local marching band, for instance, challenged traditional values and practices in the community, where it simply was taken for granted that such a band would not be open for a person with intellectual disabilities. In this case, and in contrast to Turino's examples, opposition to values of the broader society was not the main thing. In fact Upbeat's insistence on the right to participate was supported by national anti-discrimination politics. The members of Upbeat experienced that collaborative local practices have their own biases and limitations. With challenged access to resources such as verbal argumentation, the members of Upbeat were still capable of performing alternative forms of citizen engagement (Stige, 2002, pp. 111–133).

More generally, I argue that music therapists and music educators should not subscribe to grand visions about artistic citizenship without anchoring this in mundane efforts of nurturing participant involvement in local schools, NGOs, health-care institutions, and so on. This might take many different forms, from supporting adolescents who want to write and perform songs about their experience of the Child Welfare System (Krüger, 2012) to building up service user panels that have a voice in the development of research, education, and health-care practices (Stige, 2018). The shared ethos is to support social change as a democratic bottom-up process.

As we saw, Woodford (2014) argues that there is a "romantic streak" to Elliott's (2012) argument about music's many possibilities, and perhaps some readers would have similar thoughts about the contentions and examples above. We do need to examine how our localised everyday efforts might be constrained by structures in the broader society. In my appraisal, "practice turn theories" – inspired by "praxeology" (a branch of philosophy of action) and "practice theory" (a tradition in the social sciences) – offer one way of thinking about this that might be helpful (Stige, 2015). The "practice turn theories" suggest that practices are social and situated by nature, bundled in between social structures at the macro level and agency at the micro level. This seemingly straightforward claim has implications for how we think about artistic citizenship. Naïve assumptions about the power of music as well as resigned thoughts about how we all are products of society are challenged. In this theory tradition, people are understood as practitioners who take part in and contribute to social practices, and these practices form constellations that affect society at large. The societal structures that at times appear unchangeable are not given or given over to the circumstances; they are performed, upheld, or altered by social practices (Hui, Schatzki & Shove, 2017; Nicolini, 2012; Schatzki, 2019; Schatzki, Knorr Cetina & von Savigny, 2001).

These ideas do not necessarily simplify our understanding of society, but they do offer one way of understanding how individual agency and social structures might be connected. Nicolini (2012) offers helpful advice on the value of "zooming in" and "zooming out" on the micro and macro dimensions of practice. In our discussion of artistic citizenship, the micro dimensions include the localised interpersonal processes of mutual musical care that we have discussed. The structures at the macro system level, which include ideology, economy, and various forms of authority, and which Woodford (2014) argues, Elliott (2012) overlooks, are not necessarily changed when we perform music in a local community. Over time, however, it is imaginable that localised practices affect various other practices and that some powerful practices are challenged and changed to some degree. In this perspective, it is relevant to explore the societal impact of the disciplines and professions of music therapy and music education. What stories do we tell about what music could and should be in society, and how do we tell them, to whom?

Concluding Remarks

I have made a case for the pertinence of a vision of music education and music therapy as disciplines and professions nurturing artistic citizenship, and I have argued that this vision invites careful "zooming in" on the intricacies of mutual musical care and prudent "zooming out" on the constellations of social practice that perform the social structures that frame our everyday life.

The assumption that human agency and subjectivity emerges from social practice informs the argument, which leads to a recognition of the relevance of theoretical pluralism. I agree with Nicolini (2012), who argues that the metaphor of "toolkit" is helpful when thinking about how to relate to theory. For disciplines such as music education and music therapy, it is unlikely that any one theory will be satisfactorily equipped both for the activities of "zooming in" and of "zooming out". The metaphor of a "toolkit" suggests that we could use some theories that enable us to zoom in on mutual musical care and others that would serve us in a better way when trying to understand artistic citizenship. In this vision, the "practice turn theories" referred to above might be seen as meta-theoretical tools that enable us to see how practices, participants, and places are mutually constitutive (Stige, 2015).

When zooming in on mutual musical care as practicing music educators or music therapists, our concern is relational-musical. We need a repertoire of ways of interacting musically. This can be put in perspective by a well-known statement made by the Danish philosopher Søren Kierkegaard on the "art of helping":

> If one is truly to succeed in leading a person to a specific place, one must first and foremost take care to find him where he is and begin there. This is the secret in the entire art of helping. Anyone who cannot do this is himself under a delusion if he thinks he is able to help

someone else. In order truly to help someone else, I must understand more than he – but certainly first and foremost understand what he understands. (Kierkegaard, 1859/1998, p. 45)

There is no space here for an exact discussion of Kierkegaard's statement, but I want to use it as a sensitising tool in order to highlight one dimension of the argument made in this chapter. The crafting of mutual musical care usually requires both resourcefulness and sensitivity, but not only from the teacher or therapist, but from the student and therapy participant as well. As professionals, we need to "find them" where they are as persons and musicians and to listen to and respond to their contributions.

The relational-musical craft we are talking about could be described as that of a "not-knowing knower", a professional practitioner promoting mutuality and participation. I use the term not-knowing with reference to Anderson and Goolishian's (1992) critique of practices that define humans as information processing machines. If we respect humans as meaning-generating beings, the need for a not-knowing attitude becomes clear. As professionals with this perspective, we take real interest in the world of the people we work with, and we are willing and able to enter a dialogue based upon this starting point. This is not to suggest that our own competencies become unimportant. A "not-knowing" approach is not an excuse for abdication of professional responsibility. It has more to do with openness than anything else, and it requires considerable knowledge and craft. The point here is to acknowledge the contributions of all participants in a situation, where the role of the teacher or therapist is that of a qualified and qualifying partner who works to create a space where all participants can grow.

The crafting of mutual musical care requires flexible musical skills, then. We remember that collaborative improvisation was key to Upbeat's process, and I do think that the interest in improvisation that we see both in music therapy and music education is of relevance to this discussion. Because the crafting of mutual musical care is as much about relating to musical subjects as about creating musical objects, dialogic improvisation (Aadland et al., 2017) is of particular relevance here. I have previously argued that the relational practice of improvisational music therapy (Nordoff & Robbins, 1977) could inform attempts of developing inclusive and participatory music education practices (Stige, 1995) and in my appraisal that the current interest in improvisation in education and teacher education bears promise for innovative developments (Espeland & Stige, 2017; Holdhus et al. 2016; Sawyer, 2011). Many of the scholars exploring these possibilities have taken inspiration from the practices of performing artists such as jazz musicians. I can see the relevance of this, especially if we supplement our interest in these artists' resourceful use of rhythms, chords, and scales with an interest in the responsive and creative interpersonal interaction that usually characterise artists who improvise (Schogler, 1998).

Music education and music therapy are two different disciplines and professions. What the practitioners – with Kierkegaard's words – "understand more" than the people they work with will differ. The tools and the repertoire each profession and professional brings to the process of building possibilities for mutual musical care will differ as well. We do, however, share an object (a purpose), if we acknowledge that artistic citizenship requires care to be realised.

References

Aadland, H., Espeland, M., & Arnesen, T. H. (2017). Towards a typology of improvisation as a professional teaching skill: Implications for pre-service teacher education programmes. *Cogent Education, 4*(1). https://doi.org/10.1080/2331186X.2017.1295835

Aigen, K. (2005). *Music-centered music therapy*. Gilsum, NH: Barcelona Publishers.

Allsup, R. E. (2003). Mutual learning and democratic action in instrumental music education. *Journal of Research in Music Education, 51*(1), 24–37. https://doi.org/10.2307/3345646

Anderson, H., & Goolishian, H. (1992). The client is the expert: A not-knowing approach to therapy. In S. McNamee & K. J. Gergen (Eds.), *Therapy as social construction*. London: Sage Publications.

Bartlett, R., & O' Connor, D. (2007). From personhood to citizenship: Broadening the lens for dementia practice and research. *Journal of Aging Studies, 21*, 107–118.

Bath, H. (2015). The three pillars of traumawise care: Healing in the other 23 hours. *Reclaiming Children and Youth, 23*, 44–46.

Bolger, L., McFerran, K., & Stige, B. (2018). Hanging out and buying in: Rethinking relationship building to avoid tokenism when striving for collaboration in music therapy. *Music Therapy Perspectives, 36*(2), 257–266. https://doi.org/10.1093/mtp/miy002

Campbell, M. S., & Martin, R. (Eds.). (2006). *Artistic citizenship: A public voice for the arts*. New York: Routledge.

Clifford, J., & Marcus, G. E. (1986). *Writing culture: The poetics and politics of ethnography*. Berkeley: University of California Press.

Collins, R. (2004). *Interaction ritual chains*. Princeton, NJ: Princeton University Press.

Cooper, P., & McIntyre, D. (1996). *Effective teaching and learning: Teachers' and students' perspectives*. Buckingham, UK: Open University Press.

DeNora, T. (2000). *Music in everyday life*. Cambridge, UK: Cambridge University Press.

DeNora, T. (2006). Evidence and effectiveness in music therapy. Problems, power, possibilities, and performances in health contexts (a discussion paper). *British Journal of Music Therapy, 20*(2), 81–93.

DeNora, T. (2007). Health and music in everyday life: A theory of practice. *Psyke & Logos, 28*, 271–287.

DeNora, T. (2013). *Music asylums: Wellbeing through music in everyday life*. Farnham, UK: Ashgate.

Dewey, J. (1934/1980). *Art as experience*. New York: Perigee Books.

Dissanayake, E. (2000). *Art and intimacy: How the arts began*. Seattle, WA: University of Washington Press.

Dissanayake, E. (2001). An ethological view of music and its relevance to music therapy. *Nordic Journal of Music Therapy, 10*(2), 159–175.

Elliott, D. (2012). Another perspective: Music education as/for artistic citizenship. *Music Educators Journal, 99*, 21–27.

Elliott, D., Silverman, M., & Bowman, W. (Eds.). (2016). *Artistic citizenship: Artistry, social responsibility, and ethical praxis*. New York: Oxford University Press.

Espeland, Å., & Stige, B. (2017). The teacher as co-musician: Exploring practices in music teaching. *International Journal of Education & the Arts, 18*(22) Retrieved from http://www.ijea.org/v18n22/

Gilligan, C. (1982/1993). *In a different voice: Psychological theory and women's development*. Cambridge, MA: Harvard University Press.

Holdhus, K., Høisæter, S., Mæland, K., Vangsnes, V., Engelsen, K. S., Espeland, M., et al. (2016). Improvisation in teacher education – Roots and implications: A review of relevant literature. *Cogent Education, Teacher Education & Development.* https://doi.org/10.108 0/2331186X.2016.1204142

Hui, A., Schatzki, T., & Shove, E. (2017). *The nexus of practices: Connections, constellations, practitioners.* London: Routledge.

Kenny, C. (1979/2006). *Music & life in the field of play: An anthology.* Gilsum, NH: Barcelona Publishers.

Kierkegaard, S. (1859/1998). *The point of view (Writings, Volume 22).* [Translated by Hong, H.V & Hong, E.H., with introduction and notes]. Princeton University Press.

Kitwood, T. (1997). *Dementia reconsidered: The person comes first.* Buckingham, UK: Open University Press.

Kleive, M. & Stige, B. (1988). Med lengting, liv og song. Prøveordning med musikktilbod til funksjonshemma i Sogn og Fjordane. Samlaget.

Krüger, V. (2012). Musikk – Fortelling – Fellesskap. En kvalitativ undersøkelse av ungdommers perspektiver på deltagelse i samfunnsmusikkterapeutisk praksis i barnevernsarbeid [Music – Stories – Community. A qualitative investigation of young people's experience of community music therapy in the context of Child Welfare]. Unpublished PhD dissertation. Bergen, Norway: The Grieg Academy, University of Bergen.

Krüger, V., Nordanger, D., & Stige, B. (2018). Music therapy: Building bridges between a participatory approach and trauma-informed care in a child welfare setting. *Voices: A World Forum for Music Therapy, 18*(4) Retrieved from https://voices.no/index.php/voices/article/view/2593

Lubet, A. J. (2004). Tunes of impairment: An ethnomusicology of disability. *Review of Disability Studies, 1*(1), 133–155.

Løgstrup, K.E. (1956/1991). *Den etiske fordring* [The Ethical Demand]. Gyldendal.

Malloch, S., & Trevarthen, C. (Eds.). (2009). *Communicative musicality.* Oxford, UK: Oxford University Press.

Mayeroff, M. (1971). *On caring.* New York: Harper and Row.

Nicolini, D. (2012). *Practice theory, work, and organization: An introduction.* Oxford, UK: Oxford University Press.

Nordanger, D., & Braarud, H.C. (2017). *Utviklingstraumer: Regulering som nøkkelbegrep i en ny traumepsykologi* [Development trauma: Regulation as key concept in a new trauma psychology]. Fagbokforlaget.

Nordoff, P., & Robbins, C. (1977). *Creative music therapy.* New York: John Day.

Rolvsjord, R. (2010). *Resource-oriented music therapy in mental health care.* Gilsum, NH: Barcelona Publishers.

Ruud, E. (1979). *Musikkpedagogisk teori* [Theory in Music Education]. Norsk musikkforlag.

Ruud, E. (2000). 'New musicology,' music education and music therapy. Keynote presentation at the Thirteenth Nordic Congress for Music Researchers, Århus, August 2000.

Ruud, E. (2016). *Musikkvitenskap* [Musicology]. Universitetsforlaget.

Sawyer, R. K. (Ed.). (2011). *Structure and improvisation in creative teaching.* Cambridge: Cambridge University Press.

Schatzki, T. R. (2019). *Social change in a material world.* London: Routledge.

Schatzki, T. R., Knorr Cetina, K., & von Savigny, E. (Eds.). (2001). *The practice turn in contemporary theory.* London: Routledge.

Schei, T.B, Espeland, M. & Stige, B. (2013). Research and research education in music – Disciplinary or interdisciplinary approach? *Nordic Research in Music Education.* Yearbook Vol. 14 2012, 27–45. https://brage.bibsys.no/xmlui/handle/11250/172323

Schogler, B. (1998). Music as a tool in communications research. *Nordic Journal of Music Therapy, 7,* 40–49.

Silverman, M. (2012). Virtue ethics, care ethics, and "The good life of teaching". Action, criticism, and theory for music education, 11(2), pp. 96–122. http://act.maydaygroup.org/articles/Silverman11_2.pdf

Small, C. (1998). *Musicking: The meanings of performing and listening*. Hanover, NH: Wesleyan University Press.

Stige, B. (1995). Samspel og relasjon. Perspektiv på ein inkluderande musikkpedagogikk. Samlaget.

Stige, B. (1998). Aesthetic practices in music therapy. *Nordic Journal of Music Therapy, 7*(2), 121–134.

Stige, B. (2002). *Culture-centered music therapy*. Gilsum, NH: Barcelona Publishers.

Stige, B. (2007). The Grieg effect: On the contextualized effects of music in music therapy. *Voices: A World Forum for Music Therapy, 7*(3). https://doi.org/10.15845/voices.v7i3.548

Stige, B. (2010a). Musical participation, social space, and everyday ritual. In B. Stige, G. Ansdell, C. Elefant, & M. Pavlicevic (Eds.), *Where music helps: Community music therapy in action and reflection* (pp. 125–150). Surrey, UK: Ashgate.

Stige, B. (2010b). Practicing music as mutual care. In B. Stige, G. Ansdell, C. Elefant, & M. Pavlicevic (Eds.), *Where music helps. Community music therapy in action and reflection* (pp. 254–275). Surrey, UK: Ashgate.

Stige, B. (2015). The practice turn in music therapy theory. *Music Therapy Perspectives, 33*(1), 3–11. https://doi.org/10.1093/mtp/miu050

Stige, B. (2018). Partnerships for health musicking: A case for connecting music therapy and public health practices. In L. O. Bonde & T. Theorell (Eds.), *Music and public health. A Nordic perspective* (pp. 115–128). Berlin, Germany: Springer.

Stige, B., & Aarø, L. E. (2012). *Invitation to community music therapy*. New York: Routledge.

Stige, B., Ansdell, G., Elefant, C., & Pavlicevic, M. (2010). When things take shape in relation to music: Towards an ecological perspective on music's help. In B. Stige, G. Ansdell, C. Elefant, & M. Pavlicevic (Eds.), *Where music helps: Community music therapy in action and reflection* (pp. 277–308). Surrey, UK: Ashgate.

Stige, B., & Strand, R. (2016). Philosophy and music therapy research. In *Music therapy research* (3rd ed.). Dallas, TX: Barcelona Publishers.

Sunderland, N., Lewandowski, N., Bendrups, D., & Bartleet, B.-L. (Eds.). (2018). *Music, health and wellbeing: Exploring music for health equity and social justice*. London: Palgrave Macmillan.

Taylor, C. (1985). The concept of a person. In C. Taylor (Ed.), *Philosophical papers, Volume 1* (pp. 98–102). Cambridge, UK: Cambridge University Press.

Turino, T. (2016). Music, social change, and alternative forms of citizenship. In D. Elliott, M. Silverman, & W. Bowman (Eds.), *Artistic citizenship: Artistry, social responsibility, and ethical praxis* (pp. 297–312). New York: Oxford University Press.

Twine, F. (1994). *Citizenship and social rights: The interdependence of self and society*. London: Sage.

Webster's Dictionary & Thesaurus (encyclopedic edition). (2000). New York: Trident Press International.

Wittgenstein, L. (1953/1967). *Philosophical investigations*. Oxford, UK: Blackwell.

Woodford, P. (2014). The eclipse of the public: A response to David Elliott's "Music education as/ for artistic citizenship.". *Philosophy of Music Education Review, 22*(1), 22–37.

Music Listening: An Evolution of Craft

Jody L. Kerchner

Abstract The purpose of this chapter is to consider contemporary theoretical, neuroscientific, and pedagogical shifts in thinking about music listening and how these understandings might affect teachers' pedagogical craft and the processes by which students develop their personal music listening craft. Responsive listening, deep listening, and creative music listening definitions will be explored, along with rationales for using multisensory pedagogical tools that have the potential to increase listeners' awareness of their perceptual and affective responses to music. The sonic events of music, pedagogical strategies for facilitating music listening, and individuals' personal attributes are the primary materials with which students and teachers might co-create—craft—deep access into music. Pedagogical craft involves the development and use of observational tools with which teachers learn from students about their prior music listening experiences and with which they subsequently scaffold students' new music listening experiences. If we understand how, why, and what students are listening to outside of school, then perhaps music teachers can come closer to crafting pedagogical strategies for enhancing music listening skill development in schools. With the assistance of skilled and insightful instructional materials and strategies, then, students can develop their own music listening craft.

"We are all apprentices in a craft where no one ever becomes a master."
(Ernest Hemingway, 1962, *Hemingway: The Wild Years*)

Introduction

Hemingway's quotation comes from his autobiographical collection of short stories that, published posthumously, recounts his youthful travel adventures as a budding journalist in Europe. His book is a retrospective that sheds light on the evolution of his writing craft, professional life, and mystery he embodied. One might interpret

J. L. Kerchner (✉)
Oberlin College & Conservatory of Music, Oberlin, OH, USA
e-mail: jody.kerchner@oberlin.edu

© Springer Nature Switzerland AG 2021
K. Holdhus et al. (eds.), *Music Education as Craft*, Landscapes: the Arts, Aesthetics, and Education 30, https://doi.org/10.1007/978-3-030-67704-6_9

this quotation as Hemingway's morose surrender to the elusive state of mastery and perfection. Hemingway's sentiment might even seem rather inappropriate for inclusion in a monograph celebrating Magne Espeland's masterful contributions to the music education profession. However, I selected this quotation specifically because the evolution of craft is a pervasive theme historically in thinking critically about music listening research and pedagogy—topics near and dear to Magne's own professional evolution as music educator and scholar.

The purpose of this chapter is to consider contemporary theoretical, neuroscientific, and pedagogical shifts in thinking about music listening and how these new understandings might affect teachers' pedagogical craft and the processes by which students develop their personal music listening craft. If we understand how, why, and what students are listening to outside of school, then perhaps music teachers can come closer to crafting pedagogical strategies for enhancing music listening skill development in schools. The sonic events of music, pedagogical strategies for facilitating music listening, and individuals' personal attributes are the primary materials with which students and teachers might co-create—craft—deep access into music. Pedagogical craft involves the development and use of observational tools with which teachers learn from students about their prior music listening experiences and with which they subsequently scaffold students' new music listening experiences. With the assistance of skilled and insightful instructional materials and strategies, then, students can develop their own music listening craft by implementing refined music listening skills that enable them to encounter new and familiar musics in fresh, creative ways.

Tools and Ideology for Crafting Music Listening

Before turning to contemporary understandings of the nature of music listening, let us journey back to Espeland's (2011) centenary review of the evolution of music listening pedagogical craft from the perspective of cultural psychology. After describing the gramophone as the technological innovation that forever changed how people accessed and listened to music, Espeland discusses the impact of historical debates regarding how music listening (i.e., music appreciation) should be taught in schools and the materials students would encounter (i.e., aural skills, musical "masterpieces," and the focus on musical elements) as they learned to craft their music listening skills and experiences.

Looking at curricular documents and declarations, Espeland classifies music listening practices in schools as representing the principles of rationalification (i.e., listening to and discerning formal, psycho-acoustical phenomena), narratification (i.e., encountering culturally prescribed programs or creating personal, referential programs associated with music), and artification (i.e., using artistic objects in an effort to learn about the listening process). At the heart of his chapter is a challenge for music education professionals to use a variety of pedagogical strategies that bring "music listening as *living learning processes* in classrooms" (p. 165). To that end, he called for teachers to craft music listening experiences in the schools that are both participatory and relevant to students' lives in and outside of music classrooms.

I also wrote an historical overview (Kerchner, 2014b) of music listening research that influenced our professional thinking about music listening experiences in music classrooms and ensemble rehearsal spaces. My writing traces the evolution of music listening research and teaching from behaviorist to constructivist ideology, from atomistic investigations of people's perception of discrete musical elements to holistic considerations of music listening processes and experiences, from quantitative to qualitative research explorations, and the impact of the cognitive science revolution on music listening pedagogical craft. I questioned how an "old" and "traditional" behavior—music listening—might be transplanted afresh into modern research agendas and school cultures. Similar to Holdhus and Espeland (2017), I wondered if "it is therefore possible for this part of school music [music listening] to be beyond the possibility of transformative renewal" (p. 102).

There have been countless research studies related to music listening craft— pedagogical best practices and students' music listening responses and behaviors demonstrated during music listening. As a profession, we might consider ourselves enlightened about the pedagogical craft we use to engage students in guided music listening and our knowledge about music listening processes, music perception and cognition, students' focused attention during music listening, music listening preferences, music listening relative to identity development, and music listening in a variety of cultural contexts. Yet, there are questions the music education profession continues to pose about music listening that closely resemble those raised over the past hundred or so years. Indeed, professional music educators and researchers remain apprentices in terms of how to assist students in crafting their music listening experiences. Additionally, we remain at a loss in capitalizing on our past research, compiling that acquired knowledge into a comprehensive and cogent body of literature about music listening, and translating that knowledge into relevant classroom praxis. The world spins quickly, technologies change by the minute, and our students participate in creating cultural shifts that might seem foreign to many music educators. It is not surprising that the chasm between pedagogical practices, research, and vernacular (i.e., out-of-school, personal) music listening continues to expand and confound our pedagogical music listening craft.

Evolving Pedagogical Craft

To begin the discussion of pedagogical craft, I survey the evolution of the profession's definitions that undergird our understanding of the essence of music listening itself. Furthermore, I explore the goal toward which music educators develop their music listening pedagogical (and research) craft—enhanced music listening experiences for students.

Responsive Music Listening

Espeland (1987) uses the term "responsive listening" as a model of auditive impression (music heard and processed) and expression (overt verbal, visual, and kinesthetic responses to music). He suggests five stages of a process that leads to responsiveness while listening to music. By "activating" children's minds and bodies to which they are listening, they can become aware of and responsive to music in formalistic and referential ways. These processes, in turn, have the potential to lead students toward music appreciation and evaluation.

On a personal note, it was Espeland's 1987 publication which caught my attention as a doctoral student at Northwestern University. My dissertation research was a qualitative investigation of children's verbal, visual, and kinesthetic responses to music. When I found Magne's article, I was relieved to know that my practitioner instincts coincided with aspects of his report on the *Music in Use* project. His article was seminal in supporting my dissertation research design. I took his notion of responsive music listening and created space in my own research craft for its evolution. Ultimately, I found patterns related to age and musical training in what children attended to musically in their verbal, visual, and kinesthetic reports (Kerchner, 1996). Additionally, my research corroborated Magne's theory: through repeated listenings, students responded to both the perceptual (related to music structure/elements) and the affective and associative (related to stories, images) elements of the music (Kerchner, 1996, 2000).

Deep Listening

Shehan Campbell (2005) provides pedagogical steps toward "deep listening"— focused attention on music, guided by a teacher in order to lead the students' ears and minds toward developing beyond "their surround-sound selves" (p. 30). The final stage of her listening pedagogy (i.e., "the enactive stage") involves listening analysis with the aim of preparing students to perform music they had previously listened to in deep, intensive ways. I value bringing students closer to the point of deep or "close" listening to music. However, the act of music listening need not lead to anything other than the music listening experience itself. Certainly, music listening can be the springboard for engaging other musical behaviors (Espeland, 1987; Kerchner, 2014a): composition, improvisation, and moving, for example. Music listening might even become a tool for crafting empathy among students, social justice and democracy in the classroom (Silverman, 2013, 2015), or physical and social skills among students with disabilities in the classroom. However, music listening must remain valued for its own worth. As the cornerstone of all musicking behaviors, the music listening experience itself, and one's personal and communal responsiveness during music listening, must become a priority in our instruction and investigations.

Creative Music Listening

The term "music creativity" typically refers to a person or group of people engaged in music composition, improvisation, or performance. These musical behaviors enlist processes and products that are observable, tangible, and measurable. In recent years, researchers have also sought to include music listening among that list of creative musical behaviors.

Kratus (2017) suggests means of teaching for creative music listening and thinking, moving pedagogies beyond those that lead to conceptual musical thinking. He takes Guilford's (1959) and Torrance's (1979) frameworks for creativity and superimposes dimensions of creativity—fluency, flexibility, originality, and elaboration—onto his model of creative music listening. He states that each of these dimensions of creativity reflects four types of creativities relevant to music listening. Kratus encourages teachers to pose questions that engage students' higher-order thinking skills and subsequently demonstrate information about their internal music listening processes in externalized forms.

While having students' reflect on and respond to questions in observable, multisensory ways is not objectionable pedagogically, Kratus' rationale for music listening as a creative behavior seems dependent on students' overt responses for the sake of fitting traditional definitions of creativity. Tangible products, a traditional hallmark of creativity, inherently contain evidence of covert music listening processes, and music educators often rely on this information, albeit incomplete, to bolster their understanding of students' music listening experiences. What is missing from this model is the integration of the dimensions of creativity into a symbiotic system of convergent and divergent thinking processes and affective responses, all of which are internal, that occur during music listening.

Dunn (1997) describes the creative product resulting from music listening as a "holistic, inner perceptual structure of the music" (p. 45). Later the basis of his model for "intuitive music listening," Dunn (2006) states that music listening is predicated on the intersections of a person's past experiences, extra-musical associations, and physical, cognitive, imaginative, and affective responses that occur relative to expectations for what could be experienced musically during listening (p. 35). His notion of "intuitive listening" aligns with the non-conscious corporeal engagement and knowing brought to the fore by neuroscientific research that will be discussed later in this chapter. Dunn also acknowledges contextual, sociocultural influences inherent to the music listening experience.

Peterson (2006) provides a compelling argument for music listening as a creative experience. She maintains that music listening is a creative act despite the fact that the products of music listening are not necessarily tangible. Peterson, along with Dunn (2006) and Kratus (2017), considers music listening to involve novel ways of thinking, making connections, and refining perceptions. With each repeated listening, for example, listeners might find new discoveries about the music and its inherent elemental relationships. Furthermore, these "aha" moments while listening to music are based on students' discovering, investigating, and problem-solving in order to create unique mental models of the music they encounter. Peterson posits that the quality of music listening experience depends on listeners' memory, the flexibility of their mental models, and their ability to create new music listening models upon each encounter with a piece of music.

Finally, Rinsema (2017) provides her own definition of musical creativity: It "is acting with sound for the purpose of creating some product that is new for the creator" (p. 128). Her definition also combines facets of music perception (i.e., action and understanding), the ecological understanding that "acting" embraces physical and mental operations engaged during music listening, individuals' personal characteristics, and their prior experiences that intersect as one listens to music. This definition arises from Rinsema's plea to validate people's natural music listening craft: the meaning people ascribe to everyday music listening experiences, wherever and whenever they may occur and to whichever musics they may choose to listen, without the guidance of teacher or the use of pedagogical tools used to prompt attentive, structural listening.

From my perspective, creative music listening involves the process of exercising musical and mental flexibility as one encounters musical sounds in whatever space they occupy. Creative music listening is marked by those external, observable responses *and* internal cognitive and affective processes and products that remain intangible, even ineffable. They are crafted as one develops new meanings that move a person beyond their currently held mental models and brain mappings. These integrated body-mind-spirit-feelingful processes and products are inherently linked to one's memory of prior musical and non-musical experiences and the imagination employed during the creation (production) of personally novel music listening experiences.

Evolving Neuroscientific Understandings

The expansion and sophistication of neuroscientific research continues to illuminate brain and body functioning as people listen to (perceive) and process musical sound. Similarly, this information has the potential to confirm, challenge, and expand music educators' pedagogical craft—the music listening methods and materials that teachers use to facilitate students' deep and creative listening experiences.

During the cognitive science revolution, the brain was likened to a machine that perceived auditory and visual stimuli and subsequently stored these sound bytes and images as exact replications in the brain. Following that time, scientific theorists suggested that brain processing of musical sound involved localized processing of rhythmic and pitch patterns (van der Schyff and Schiavio, 2017). With the use of magnetic resonance imaging (MRI) devices, however, scientists have found neural mappings of the ever-changing brain to be resilient and capable of recreating itself throughout a lifetime (Doidge, 2007). MRI images have debunked the previously held notion that auditory processing is relegated to a single portion or hemisphere of the brain (Anderson, 2007). Instead, images demonstrate the brain as an integrated and interactive system, showing increased volume of blood flow through-out areas of the musically stimulated brain.

Neuroscientific research has also facilitated the evolution of understanding regarding affective (e.g., the emotional and feelingful) responses one might encounter during music listening experiences. In their investigation of biological origins of emotional and feelingful states while listening to music, Habibi and Demasio (2014) suggest that any change in body stasis, including musical stimuli, result in auto-matic body responses in order to return the body to balance. "Music-related affects are accompanied by physiological and behavioral changes" (p. 93). These changes occur at the single-cell level and involve neural systems. The authors clearly dif-ferentiate between "feelings," responses related to changes in one's internal body environment (i.e., thirst, hunger, pleasure), and "emotions," responses to one's envi-ronment. Johnson (2007) further theorizes that by the time one feels an emotion, the unconscious body adjustments relative to the environment have already occurred. This means that the body-in-motion via neuronal, chemical, and behavioral action provides the genesis of affect, not the conscious "mind."

Research suggests that perceiving sound events during music listening involves dopamine cells and cortical regions of the brain, in relation to areas of the brain that store information from prior music listening experiences (Menon and Levitin 2005; Salimpoor, Zald, Zattore, Dagher & McIntosh 2015). If a person's expectations for a piece of music coincide with what is actually perceived in the music, then the more pleasurable the experience will be because of the body's increased release of dopamine. Neural patterns, or "mental images," in the body hold expectations for events (i.e., sounds) in one's environment and anticipates responding in non-conscious, corporeal manners (Johnson, 2007). These scientific findings hearken back to Leonard Meyer's (1956) "absolute expressionist" construct for musical meaning that involves processes such as anticipation, expectation, experience, and emotional responsiveness to music.

Habibi and Demasio (2014) boldly state that music listening triggers drives and emotions that can lead to feelings. Their notion of the integrated body-mind-feelingful-spirit self (Kerchner, 2014b; Kreutz et al., 2008) impugns Descartes' position in which affective responses (including emotions and feelings) are separate from perceptual responses. Additionally, their brain research indicates that when the body engages with music, its neural systems are those feelingful body systems related to sensing the well-being and social benefits of a person. Therefore, research-ers consider music a part of our natural biological system in relation to its environ-ment (Cross, 2001; van der Schyff & Schiavo, 2017).

Given these research findings, it will be interesting to see how current music listening practices change our musical brain processing mechanisms and how our brain processing systems will inform and transform the means by which we listen to music in our evolving environments. How might instantaneous access to music via digital technologies ultimately change our music processing capabilities? How might the spaces in which we listen to music change our processing, preferences, and attitudes toward music (Rodriguez, 2014)? How will this drive music perfor-mance and production?

Neuroscientific Implications for Pedagogical Craft

The question "So what?" now comes to mind. How do these research findings transform music educators' and students' music listening craft? Perhaps the greatest shift in developing our pedagogical craft must be our renewed recognition that students bring richly diverse musical (listening) experiences into our classrooms. Music of all styles and genres are immediately accessible to our students who seem to constantly engage with it. Traditionally, a music teacher's role included exposing students to music for the purposes of "expanding students' musical horizons." In an age when music was primarily relegated to concert venues or limited by access to musical recording resources, this role might have been essential. With each technological innovation (i.e., gramophone, Internet), however, music has become increasingly accessible and diverse beyond what they would experience in music classrooms.

It is still important for our pedagogical craft to expose students to diverse musics, but for the purpose of challenging their notion of what music is or can be. But it is equally important for our pedagogical craft to be musically and culturally inclusive (i.e., bringing students' musical choices into the classroom), provoking critical thinking and reflection on music and helping students become sensitive to how they are perceptually and affectively responding to the music to which they are listening and musics that they have yet to encounter. Mindful music listening refers to pedagogical strategies that help prepare students to become open to novelty, alert to distinct elements of music, sensitive to different musical contexts, implicitly and explicitly aware of multiple perspectives of music, and be present in the moment (Anderson, 2012-2013, p. 13).

Awareness during music listening is the result of focusing one's attention on musical elements and their relationships, patterns, mood, and one's own emotional transformations as they might occur. In other words, mindful music listening invites listeners to bring into their consciousness "what they are thinking, feeling, and hearing" (Kerchner, 2014a). But focusing only on elemental aspects of music is only a portion of music listening experience. People are drawn to music because it makes them feel something.

Neuroscientific research points to the coalesced nature of affect and perception during music listening. Yet, self-reports obtained from listeners suggest that they are not necessarily aware of emotional and feelingful responses that accompany listening to music and that aesthetic responses were not a conscious (or necessary) component of listening to music in their everyday lives (Juslin, 2013). Consequently, music listening pedagogies must create space for students in which they explore both music elemental relationships and the potential emotional provocations and programmatic associations that can be a part of music listening. Further, teachers must implement pedagogies that help students craft verbal and non-verbal ways to articulate what they experience.

Given the neuroplasticity of the human brain and its natural capability to remap itself, any new exposure to musics changes that mapping, especially when it occurs at an early age (i.e., the "critical period") or when we are intent on paying attention to something in which we are interested and/or wish to learn (Doidge, 2007). Therefore, providing intentional means for developing students' attention throughout the lifespan seems potentially beneficial to student learners. Neuroscientific understanding calls on music educators to re-craft guided music listening pedagogies suited for diverse age groups of listeners.

Guided music listening pedagogical tools like mapping, movement, and verbal reporting (among other methods) can serve the purpose of focusing attention and bringing awareness of musical features, programmatic associations, and emotional responses to students as they listen to music (Espeland, 1987; Kerchner, 2000, 2009, 2014a). Rinsema (2017), however, takes issue with these types of strategies, because, she argues, they tend to prioritize formalistic thinking by imposing on students what teachers wish for them to hear in the music. Furthermore, she suggests that having students focus only on formal musical elements is reminiscent of the bygone "music appreciation" era and thus rarefies concert hall listening. *Maybe*. But, what if students encountered an array of musics while using these tools, maybe even experiencing them in a new ways and in a variety of spaces? What if these tools fostered students' choice and voice in the classroom? What if students choose what to (and what not to) represent relative to what they were thinking, feeling, and hearing as they engage with music and these (or any other constructivist) pedagogical tools? What if multisensory music listening tools have the potential to share responsibility with students by encouraging them to become informants of their music listening experiences?

I also think it is the *intent* with which these pedagogical tools and strategies are used, rather than the tools themselves, that give or deprive learner agency in crafting their music listening skill development. Teachers might spend too much time using multisensory tools in classrooms, in ways that intellectualize the music listening experience and strip it of emotional impact and awareness. When used as tools for students to discover music elemental relationships, student-generated maps, movements, and verbal reports have the potential to help teachers understand facets of the students' music listening experiences. As with any methodological strategy, multisensory tools should not accompany all classroom music listening experiences. Rather, these are mere tools that can facilitate crafting students' awareness and responsiveness to what they are "thinking, feeling, and hearing" during music listening, in purposeful, mindful ways. For students, these tools might serve as "training wheels" in crafting their listening skills, until they developmentally no longer need or want to use them. Students should also have the opportunity to listen to an array of musics holistically, uninterrupted by any mediating pedagogical tool.

By experiencing music along various felt (i.e., cognitive and affective) pathways (Blair, 2008), students might build metaphoric (verbal, visual, kinesthetic) frames for accessing, knowing, and crafting personal meaning as they listen to music. These pedagogical strategies seem to be in line with Cox's (2016) "mimetic hypothesis" in which music experience—recalling, planning, and otherwise thinking of music—is metaphoric and experienced as motor imagery. While he describes kinesthetic empathy with musical sounds as listeners experience them, Cox also acknowledges other types of multisensory metaphors that comprise a person's understanding of musical sounds.

Therefore, pedagogical strategies implemented in their music classrooms should emulate the multimodal nature of the brain's processing of musical sound. Music listening is not just an aural experience. Instead, it is a multisensory experience, in which we use our senses to perceive aspects of music as it exists in our environment. We experience music through our aural networks and throughout our bodies, in conjunction with visual contexts in which the music is performed or images the music evokes in our minds. As research indicates, there is a strong kinesthetic (body) connection during music listening. Therefore, pedagogical strategies that incorporate kinesthetic, Dalcrozian expressions of what is seen, heard, and felt during music listening seem important in facilitating the development of students' music listening craft.

Finally, neuroscientists and theorists suggest that music cognition is dependent on the coevolution of people and their environments. Since music listening is culturally situated, music educators are called on to understand the cultures in which they teach, in order to create opportunities for relational music listening experiences—those music listening experiences that authentically connect a listener to other listeners in a variety of communities and across generations. To that end, educators and researchers might seek to craft pedagogies that incorporate and honor community music resources and student music engagement as it occurs outside of the classroom. Pedagogies that provoke students to articulate their definition of music, and why unfamiliar musics challenge that notion, seek to expand and build students' neural mappings.

Continuing Evolutions

An important evolution in our pedagogical craft is the scientific affirmation that music listening, frankly *any* musical behavior, is a body-mind-feelingful experience. Because of the holistic nature of music listening, research purports that it *does* involve "living learning processes" (Espeland, 2011, p. 165) and that these processes are part of every human's evolutionary autobiography. This in and of itself seems a compelling case for including intentional music listening as a prime component of music curricula for all children.

It is the *experience* that individuals have with the music during music listening that our pedagogical craft seeks to enhance. Music listening experience is an individually defined, ever-changing relationship that can evolve with (and even without) guidance. Evidence suggests that informed pedagogical craft can facilitate the enrichment of students' relationships with repeated encounters with music to which they listen. Regardless of the pedagogical tools that are utilized in the classroom, it is the *experience* that we must focus on with intentionality as the primary educational goal. After all, it is the music experience that is the means for fully experiencing our own humanity and connection to others.

Our pedagogical craft is called on to find ways of bringing listeners' awareness to the multifarious and complex relationships listeners might possibly engage in with music. Whether leading students to become aware of musical elements, mood, affect, or preferences, we do so in order to deepen the relationship with the music so the students can locate themselves in relation to the music they listen to. The tools we employ are used in order to give agency to students so they can craft lifelong musical responsiveness and relationships across a span of musical genres and styles, per their own choosing.

Teachers and researchers seek to sharpen their craft—designing and implementing pedagogies and research methodologies—in order to explore, understand, and facilitate students' music listening skill development and music experience itself. At the same time, students engage in crafting co-constructed meanings of the music they encounter as they listen and respond to musical sounds. That the music education profession continues to find more and more questions, even as we address some of its prior wonderments, points to the complexity of brain functioning, music listening, and the nature of learning. The development of our craft is evident when we ask questions that push us beyond our current knowledge and practice, never settling for the status quo. The questions we generate reflect the complexity of the mind-body-feelingful-spirit selves that we call humankind in concert with music and our environs.

References

Anderson, M. (2007). Massive redeployment, exaptation, and the functional integration of cognitive operations. *Synthese, 159*(3), 329–345.

Anderson, W. T. (2012-2013). Mindful listening instruction: Does it make a difference? *Contributions to Music Education, 39*, 13–30.

Blair, D.V. (2008). Do you hear what I hear? Musical maps and felt pathways of musical understanding. *Visions of Research in Music Education, 11*. Retrieved from http://www-usr.rider.edu/~vrme/v11n1/vision/D.Blair.VRME.pdf

Cox, A. (2016). *Music and embodied cognition: Listening, moving, thinking, and feeling.* Bloomington: Indiana University Press.

Cross, I. (2001). Music, mind, and evolution. *Psychology of Music, 29*, 95–102.

Doidge, N. (2007). *The brain that changes itself.* New York: Penguin Group.

Dunn, R. E. (1997). Creative thinking and music listening. *Research Studies in Music Education, 8*, 42–55.

Dunn, R. E. (2006). Teaching for lifelong, intuitive listening. *Arts Education Policy Review, 107*(3), 33–38.

Espeland, M. (1987). Music in use: Responsive music listening in the primary school. *British Journal of Music Education, 4*(3), 283–297.

Espeland, M. (2011). A century of music listening in schools: Toward practices resonating with cultural psychology? In M. Barrett (Ed.), *A cultural psychology of music education* (pp. 143–178). Oxford, UK: Oxford University Press.

Guilford, J. P. (1959). Three faces of intellect. *American Psychologist, 14*(8), 469–479.

Habibi, A., & Demasio, A. (2014). Music, feelings, and the human brain. *Psychomusicology, 24*(1), 92–102.

Holdhus, K., & Espeland, M. (2017). Music in future Nordic schooling: The potential of the relational turn. *European Journal of Philosophy in Arts Education, 2*, 84–117.

Johnson, M. (2007). *The meaning of the body: Aesthetics of human understanding.* Chicago: University of Chicago Press.

Juslin, P. N. (2013). From everyday emotions to aesthetic emotions: Towards a unified theory of musical emotions. *Physical Life Reviews, 10*, 235–266.

Kerchner, J. L. (1996). *Perceptual and affective components of the music listening experience as manifested in children's verbal, visual, and kinesthetic representations* (Unpublished doctoral dissertation). Evanston, IL: Northwestern University.

Kerchner, J. L. (2000). Children's verbal, visual, and kinesthetic responses: Insight into their music listening experience. *Bulletin of the Council for Research in Music Education, 146*, 31–50.

Kerchner, J. L. (2009). Drawing middle-schoolers' attention to music. In J. Kerchner & C. Abril (Eds.), *Musical experience in our lives: Things we learn and meanings we make* (pp. 183–198). Lanham, MD: Rowman & Littlefield.

Kerchner, J. L. (2014a). *Music across the senses: Listening, learning, making meaning.* Oxford, UK: Oxford University Press.

Kerchner, J. L. (2014b). Music listening: Vistas, visions, and vim. In J. Barrett & P. Webster (Eds.), *The musical experience: Rethinking music teaching and learning* (pp. 45–62). New York: Oxford University Press.

Kratus, J. (2017). Music listening is creative. *Music Educators Journal, 103*(3), 46–51.

Kreutz, G., Schubert, E., & Mitchell, L. (2008). Cognitive styles of music listening. *Music Perception, 27*(1), 57–73.

Menon, V., & Leviton, D. J. (2005). The rewards of music listening: Response and physiological connectivity of the mesolimbic system. *NeuroImage, 28*, 175–184.

Meyer, L. (1956). *Emotion and meaning in music.* Chicago: University of Chicago Press.

Peterson, E. M. (2006). Creativity in music listening. *Arts Education Policy Review, 107*(3), 15–21.

Rinsema, R. M. (2017). *Listening in action: Teaching music in the digital age.* New York: Routledge.

Rodriguez, C. (2014). Music listening spaces. In J. Barrett & P. Webster (Eds.), *The musical experience: Rethinking music teaching and learning* (pp. 88–102). New York: Oxford University Press.

Salimpoor, V., Zald, D., Zattore, R., Dagher, A., & McIntosh, A. R. (2015). Predictions and the brain: How musical sounds become rewarding. *Trends in Cognitive Science, 19*(2), 86–91.

Shehan Campbell, P. (2005). Deep listening to the musical world. *Music Educators Journal, 92*(1), 30–36.

Silverman, M. (2013). A critical ethnography of democratic music listening. *British Journal of Music Education, 30*(1), 7–25.

Silverman, M. (2015). Listening-for social justice. In L. C. DeLorenzo (Ed.), *Routledge studies in music education: Giving voice to democracy in music education* (pp. 157–175). New York: Routledge.

Torrance, E. P. (1979). *The search for satori and creativity.* Buffalo, NY: Creative Education Foundation.

van der Schyff, D., & Schiavio, A. (2017). Evolutionary musicology meets embodied cognition: Biocultural coevolution and the enactive origins of human musicality. *Frontiers in Neuroscience, 11*, 519–537.

The Craft of (Re-)Presenting Musical Works

Randi Margrethe Eidsaa

Abstract In this chapter, I explore the encounters between music and participants in learning environments. The encounters I refer to are situations when a teacher or instructor presents music intending to involve participants in responsive activities. The activities can be dialogues about music and meaning, creative music-making or construction of performances, the writing of poems or narratives inspired by the music, creating dances based on the music or singing or playing a selected repertoire. The discussion is primarily related to music listening as a curriculum element in schools and higher music teacher education, and the chapter seeks to analyse strategies and competencies which may be defined as the craft of re-presenting musical works. The choice of the topic is motivated by Holdhus and Espeland Music in the Future Nordic Schooling: The Potential of the Relational Turn. In European Journal of Philosophy in Arts Education 2(02), 2017) who discuss general school music in the light of relationality in their article "Music in Future Nordic Schooling: The Relational Turn". From their perspective, music educators need to achieve a greater awareness of the cultural and critical aspects of listening. They call for "a stronger focus on personal as well as aesthetic, artistic and critical listening so that pupils can relate to, interact with and discuss music in and across cultures" (Holdhus & Espeland, 2017, p. 102). This chapter seeks to investigate various perspectives on music listening by asking the following questions: (i) How can teachers relate to present day thinking about music and music education when presenting "musical works" in educational contexts? (ii) What aesthetic, musical, relational, ethical or social choices should be considered when selecting repertoires for different target groups? The questions will be discussed by referring to empirical and theoretical perspectives on the craft (or crafts) of presenting musical repertoires for various participant groups. The theoretical approach is based on research in music education and music performance. The empirical perspective draws on several examples from my practice as a music educator, primarily in higher education.

R. M. Eidsaa (✉)
University of Agder, Kristiansand, Norway
e-mail: randi.m.eidsaa@uia.no

Prelude

> Yesterday I played "The Hunting of The Snark" to a group of 5-year-old children in kinder-
> garten. The children were enthusiastic about the piece. One girl commented that the music
> was "cosy". She asked if she could borrow the CD until the next day. I played the piece
> several times while the children were drawing "snarks", a kind of fantasy animal. They cre-
> ated their drawings without questioning the existence of "snarks", and nobody commented
> on the musical style. This was interesting because I found the music strange. (Kindergarten
> teacher Helena, 15.11.1998)

The vignette referred to a situation when a group of children listened to "The
Hunting of the Snark", a modern piece for solo trombone by the Norwegian composer Arne Nordheim (1931–2010). The teacher organised an exhibition and invited
the parents to watch the children's drawings, and this is one example (Fig. 1).

The Hunting of the Snark is one of 51 music excerpts presented in Music in Use
1 by Magne Espeland (1991). In this volume, Espeland introduced strategies for
music listening in the classroom. The strategies are linked to selected instrumental
classical and folk music.

Background

As a teacher in Norwegian primary schools, and later in higher music education, I
have repeatedly presented music and listening activities from Espeland's Music in
Use 1 (1991) and Music in Use 2 (1998) for children, music students and teachers.

Fig. 1 The Snark. Created by Ingvild (5) when listening to Arne Nordheim's music. Workshop
12.11.1998

The practical examples in this chapter are in various ways connected to method-ological approaches to music listening described by Espeland. The examples are collected mainly during performance projects connected to the research network *Art in Context* at University of Agder, Norway. The *Art in Context* researchers are mainly concerned with intersection points – where art meets other contexts, for example, social, cultural, didactic and historical contexts and the development of interdisciplinary artistic concepts. The tenets of the research network have influenced the artistic practices described in the chapter.[1]

Merriam-Webster dictionary defines *to re-present* "to present again or anew". In this chapter, to *re-present* means presenting music which already exists and adds dimensions or details which creates meaning to those involved. It could be considered as a new presentation of facts stated. Dahl (2011) and Espeland (1987) have developed respectively analysis theory and methodological principles aiming at in-depth knowledge about music and meaningful, practical engagement with music. My definition of *musical works* is based on Dahl (2011), who explains that an analytic approach to music is "to start with the music itself rather than external factors". A *musical work* in this context, therefore, refers to a wide variety of genres in various practices where the centre of attention is the music itself. When introducing the principles behind *Music in Use*, Espeland refers to the emphasis on the selection of music, but underlines that the pupils' *involvement* with the music is crucial:

> To introduce the concept 'use' at the centre of the project by *using* sounds/pieces of music as a basis not only for learning in music, but also for learning and activities in other expressive subjects. In this way, we hoped to be able to put music on to a more equal footing with pictures and texts in the daily life of the classrooms. (Espeland, 1987, p. 287)

Dahl (2011) and Espeland (1987) are sources of inspiration for my work with music listening in educational contexts. With this chapter, I intend to shed light upon various aspects of music listening, starting with the music itself. In the next section, I will present theoretical aspects and practical examples and discuss the craft of re-presenting musical works.

Examples and Discussion

This section starts by identifying four categories or dimensions which, from my perspective, characterises present-day thinking about music and may serve as thematic strands for musical practices: the ubiquity of music, post-performance artistic concepts, relational and cultural aspects and relevance, empathy and uniqueness.

---

[1] University of Agder: Art in Context www.uia.no

The Ubiquity of Music

When Ruud (1996) describes the cultural life in Norway at the turn of the century, he refers to issues such as multiculturalism and globalisation, the development of music technology, the creation of crossover musical concepts and interest in inter-disciplinarity and multimodality (Ruud, 1996, p. 164). Ruud also presents an in-depth description of how music influences individuals' everyday lives, and he points towards the ubiquity of music as one of the significant changes in the second half of the 1900s (Ruud, 2005). For example, concerts and music performances take place outside, in natural surroundings or in buildings considered unconventional for artistic presentations. In addition, new arenas for music experiences have been developed, such as music listening in the car or listening to music through headphones. Wherever you go, you may listen to music, a phenomenon Ruud calls "nomadic listening". Espeland (2011) also comments on the ubiquity of music and compares the changes modern technology has created in music education to those created by the gramophone and the radio during the first decade of the twentieth century. There is:

> ...a global situation with unlimited access to music of all sorts...A technology-based society has created a new situation for music education in general and for music listening in particular. Future practices have to deal with this situation on the basis of priorities in cultural values as well as in theories of learning and an effective listening education for all. (Espeland, 2011, p. 160)

Espeland's reflections correspond with Thibeault (2018). In his article, "Music education in the post-performance world", Thibeault describes how teachers' attitudes to technology in education have changed since the early 1900s when they felt that new technology was threatening the school from outside. At that time, teachers should strive to create "a stance towards commercialism" (Thibeault, 2018, p. 206). However, several decades later, technology is celebrated for expanding the possibilities for getting to know new music, new music cultures and new practices in a few seconds. Teachers can interpret traditional expressions of art in unconventional ways and develop new artistic concepts. According to Thibeault, this has changed the way we learn:

> In essence, the process of learning and the products of learning are rapidly merging into ubiquitous knowledge engagement. The implication for this profound transformation—for formal schooling, for online communities, for evolving definitions of public knowledge, and global interconnectedness and economic development—cannot be underestimated. (Thibeault, 2018, p. 212)

Thibeault underlines that *ubiquitous knowledge engagement* is typical for learning environments today. Children and young people interact with friends, teachers and even parents and grandparents in social media. Barriers between the young and the older or even elderly listeners seem weakened, and contrasts between "outside school music" and "inside school music" are less distinct. A group of teachers who attended a course in music technology at the University of Agder recently discussed the issue. One of them said:

> I recently read about the anthropologist Ruth Finnegan who defines music as "a pathway into society". However, I do not believe that young people today use music in this way. Now they are more open-minded and listen to a wide variety of musical genres, even music played by their parents. Categories such as "high" and "low" culture are less noticeable. From my point of view, Finnegan's perspective is outdated. (Music teacher, University of Agder, 20th September 2018)

The teacher's opinion needs further investigation for credibility. However, Beech, Broad, Cunliffe, Duffy and Gilmore (2015) who studied audiences' approach to concert hall events refer to corresponding perspectives:

> The audience of today and tomorrow may tend to be more stylistically promiscuous and enthusiastic to sample different musical experiences, and less concerned with the conventions and formalities of traditionally conceived musical events today and tomorrow. Rather than restrict themselves to favourite forms, the most avid consumers of art and culture increasingly tend to engage with a broad spectrum of experiences as possible, cutting across old categories such as "high" and "popular". (Beech et al., 2015, p. 5)

Even if music still is categorised as different genres and stylistic concepts, there is no doubt that the easy access to YouTube, Spotify and iTunes has provided learners of all ages with endless opportunities to experience music. As a result, children as well as music students appear to be more open-minded when exposed to "new" music. Easy access to newly produced recordings and videos facilitates our work with music listening activities in the classroom and inspires performances and creative adaptions of all kinds. This is fundamental to developing the craft of (re-)presenting musical works in learning contexts, such as described in the following production note.

Example 1

> One of the music students puts on a black wig and gazes towards the audience with an unfriendly expression. Then an excerpt from the movie *Le Roi Danse* (Corbiau, 2000) is presented on widescreen. Twenty-five sixth-graders watch a dance ceremony, featuring King Louis XIV and the aristocrat's companion, the composer Jean-Baptiste Lully. They appear in a ballroom packed with people dressed in extravagant costumes. When the composer shouts "Le Roi Danse", the king dances with slow and strange movements on an oval-shaped stage. Arrogance beams from his face. Lully appears as a conductor in front of a chamber ensemble. Other actors are seen in small groups, whispering to each other. Any teenager or adult spectator would notice the tense atmosphere on the screen while the actors' faces radiate with suspicion. Four music students in baroque costumes imitate Louis XIV. The children attentively watch the performance while the soundtrack powerfully presents *Idylle sur la paix: Air pour Madame la Dauphine* by Lully. At a feedback session after the concert, one of the visiting teachers suggested that for the next concert the students should try to involve the children in the movement part. (Pluvinel's Academy workshop, 11 November 2017)

This example shows how the *ubiquity of music* gives educators numerous possibilities in presenting musical works. In this case, French late baroque music was made accessible for a young audience by a spectacular movie. The film sequence also calls for critical reflections on King Louis' and the aristocrats' position, power and

Fig. 2 Students imitate the movie *Le Roi Danse*: Slow dance sequence to music by J. B. Lully (1632–1687)

extravagance. For teachers who work with older pupils, themes related to music, society and politics may easily be delineated from ***Le Roi danse*** or similar movies based on historical events (Fig. 2).

Post-performance Artistic Concepts

Thibeault (2018) uses the term "post-performance time" since nowadays, experiences with music for the majority primarily come through recordings rather than by attending live performances. Due to technology, it is possible to create music in a studio, which could not have been possible to perform live. High-quality recordings can be produced almost anywhere once technical equipment is available and the participants have sufficient skills in digital tools. Instead of worrying about the fact that most young people have their encounters with music primarily through digital media, Thibeault argues that teachers should "recognise this world" which means:

> …to acknowledge new practices, new opportunities and new meanings for traditional activities…Media also offers expanded notions of learning, inviting educators to participate in the wider nets cast by those who are interested in music in everyday life, in traditionally excluded music, in the uses and purposes of music, and in understanding music as a cultural practice embedded in multiple discourses. (Thibeault, 2018, p. 213)

From Thibeault's point of view, it is by enhancing our knowledge about the "post-performance" concept that we will understand the values of live performances. The next example describes how recorded music and live music, recorded narratives and dance were blended in the performance *Pluvinel's Academy*.

Example 2

> The students recorded five songs in the studio yesterday, and now they are checking the sound. The acoustics in the hall is challenging, but due to the use of pre-recorded music and narratives, they will be able to move freely on stage during the performance. They have spent hours of rehearsing, recording, mixing and mastering and are pleased with the result. The balance between music and words is excellent, and transitions between the recorded music and the band's live presentation are almost seamless. After a few seconds, the recorded music fades away, and *Hedwig's Theme* begins. Seven children run as fast as they can across the arena with fluttering costumes imitating owl. The children discuss the group's choreography with one of the music students. "Let us just run around when the music is like this", one of the girls says while she hums *Hedwig's Theme*. "But when the melody changes, let's make a circle together". "And after that", another girl interrupts, we can stand in a row, one by one after each other". "And", suggested the student, when Adrian plays the glissandi, let's run as fast as we can and behind the curtain. All of you who are owls should carry an envelope in your mouth". "Yes, that's exactly how it is in the Harry Potter movie", one of the girls comments. (Notes, Pluvinel's Academy, rehearsal 9 November 2017)

The use of technology should not be considered an easy way to prepare listening activities or artistic performances. No time was saved during the work process, but in their evaluation reports, the students commented that they felt more relaxed; they could move freely on stage and did not need to worry about pitch or acoustics. Moreover, they were able to concentrate on the children who were involved in their project. The performance repertoire for this project was *Air on the G-string*, *Ave Maria*, *Badinerie and Gavotte* from *Suite No. 3 in D BWV 1068* (Bach), the duet *Let Us Wander* (Purcell) and *Idylle sur la paix* (Lully). The students added *Hymn for the Fallen* and *Hedwig's Theme* by John Williams, *The Rehearsal* from the movie *The King's Speech* by the French composer Alexandre Desplat and *Dame Tartine* and *En passant par La Lorraine*, two French folk songs. Some of the pieces were performed live, while others were pre-recorded, and in some cases, the participants duplicated the recorded music live on stage.

This project was included in the module *Concert Production and Music Mediation* in the Bachelor in Music Performance Programme at University of Agder.[2] The first step was to rehearse the repertoire, and the second step was to develop movements which corresponded with the music. Finally, the students developed a narrative for the music performance, re-telling the story about Pluvinel's Academy, an educational institution in Paris in 1595[3] (Fig. 3).

---

[2] https://www.uia.no/en/studieplaner/topic/MUK164

[3] The academy is described in Kate van Orden (2005): *Music, Discipline, and Arms in Early Modern France*.

Fig. 3 Student and children, inspired by Harry Potter, in the performance *Pluvinel's Academy* 2

Guidelines for *Pluvinel's Academy* corresponded with *Music in Use* principles; the students worked creatively to modify, rearrange, reshape, identify, define and reconstruct the music (Reimer, cited in Espeland, 1987, p. 290). Besides, the group also created narratives by connecting words and music, which is one way of expressing responses to music, described by Espeland as *associative listening* (p. 291). Since the ensemble reshaped already published, recorded music and presented "new" compositions at the performance, the students needed to take questions about copyright laws and regulations into consideration. The students concluded in their reports that live performing combined with pre-recorded music and narratives provided them with more energy for the relational dimension in the ensemble. One student commented that the post-performance concept enhanced his aesthetic experience with the music.

Relational and Cultural Aspects

In their article "Youth Culture and Secondary Education", Allsup, Westerlund and Shieh (2012) claim that the days are gone when one kind of music has more inherent worth in education than another. The authors argue that the aim of music educators should be "...to bring authentic musical practices, judiciously selected both for their familiarity and unfamiliarity, to young people" (Allsup et al., p. 469). They challenge music teachers not only to assist the pupils in performing a song they enjoy. They go on to say that music teachers should "help them to become co-authors of that song, metaphorically or literally". All genres or stylistic concepts could be relevant for classroom use if the teacher succeeds in sharing which *meaning* could be connected to the music. Allsup et al. (2012, p. 461) quote John Dewey (1920) who underlined that each component in the curriculum should, "… speak for itself. Any idea, principle, or cultural form must present its birth certificate, it must show under just what conditions or human experience it was generated, and it must justify itself by its works, present and potential".

According to the three authors a meaningful approach when working with young people, in particular, is to ask: (1) What is the music doing in this or that context, (2) In which way is the music valuable in this particular context, or (3) How can we use this music to get more familiar with it?

Elsewhere, Warren (2014) criticises music education for not having included ethics as an in-depth topic. From his point of view, ethical aspects in music education are strongly related to connections between society and music. He lists various perspectives on music and society and emphasises the ethical dimensions in all musical activities in saying: "Music experiences involve encounters with others and the ethical responsibility that arise from those encounters – being part of society – in turn, shape society… Music activities take places in relationship with other people and thus involve ethical relationship" (Warren, 2014, p. 24). The definition of ethics in this context does not correspond to *morality*. Warren refers to the responsibility that arises when two individuals meet. His approach is inspired by the French philosopher Emmanuel Levinas' doctrine on each person's responsibility for "the other". Here, an experience from the international school project, *Bridges* (2011), may serve as an example.

Example 3

> "Why are none on these songs composed in an Arabic scale?" A 17-year-old boy asked the question when I presented the Norwegian music students' pop melodies for the upcoming collaborative musical "Bridges". The pupil politely listened when I played a couple of songs the students had recorded. These were traditional Western pop-style songs, easy to remember, with catchy melodic lines and traditional chord progressions. After having listened for a while, the boy said: "European music is dull. Because you never use microintervals. Arabic music is full of quartertones. In my opinion, your music is a bit flat. I am going to choose an Arabic piece of music from Youtube, and we can include that piece in our performance. And by the way; what is a *musical*?" (Eidsaa, 2015a, p. 222–223)

The conversation took place at a bilingual Arab-Jewish school in Jerusalem. The ensemble included pupils, music students and teachers from Switzerland, Israel, Palestine and Norway. The 1-week workshop aimed for a stage presentation of a musical. As project leaders coming from Western Europe, we took it for granted that *a musical* will be a comprehensive didactic framework for a collaborative project. However, it did not take long until I felt uncomfortable. A primary objection was that a musical as a stylistic concept or *work* is complex. Songs and dialogues demand hours of rehearsing. Costumes, props, light and technical equipment request significant involvement from a large ensemble as well as substantial financial support. The expressive style usually preferred by musical performers, such as intense emotions in dialogues and songs, did not seem to suit the European-Middle-Eastern ensemble. Folk music would have been a better choice for this ensemble. The example illustrates that a lack of cultural knowledge may result in misunderstandings and prevent meaningful creative processes. In this case, a professional musician who played the Arabian string instrument *oud* was invited into the ensemble. His ability to combine improvisations in Arabic scales *makam*, with the students' traditional songs, re-shaped the musical into a meaningful fusion of European and Arabic (Eidsaa, 2015a, p. 226).

O'Neill (2011) claims that to take part in music performances opens up the possibility for new relationships. By being involved in music-making together with participants from diverse music cultures, all involved will get closer to each other's understanding of life (O'Neill, 2011). In international collaborative projects, cultural diversity can be a tool for social action and used to inform, challenge and expand the conceptualisation and representation of self and others.

Relevance, Empathy and Uniqueness

The American music professor Gerald Klickstein, who has worked extensively with concert production and musical entrepreneurship, summed up a lecture on communication between musicians and audiences in three concepts: *relevance*, *empathy* and *uniqueness* (Klickstein, 2015). According to Klickstein, *relevance* refers to participants' or audiences' identification with an aesthetic expression, a topic or a particular repertoire. The music teacher may ask questions such as "how can the pupils (or audience) connect with this music?" or "in what ways may this music encourage the listeners' critical thinking?" Klickstein explains *empathy* as *reaching out to audiences' or participants' emotions*, while *uniqueness* means that there are dimensions or aspects in the music or performance which are recognised as "exceptional", "different" or "noticeable". Example 4 and Example 5 mirror Klickstein's concept of communication.

Example 4

The airport manager had invited music students and children to participate in the opening ceremony of a new departure hall at the local airport. After four rehearsals, the pupils were enthusiastic. There were no comments on the repertoire which included the two songs: *You can fly* from the movie *Peter Pan* (1953) and *Fly me to the moon* (1954). Neither did anyone complain about dancing. The teacher decided that all the boys and girls should join in on a dance sequence parallel with *Fly me to the moon* (Fig. 4):

Fig. 4 Students, pupils and teacher Lisa Haaland perform at Kristiansand Lufthavn Kjevik, 15 June 2015

It is ten o'clock in the morning on 15th June 2015 at Kristiansand Airport Kjevik. The departure hall is crowded. The majority are passengers, but there is a TV-team is present, officials from the airport are there, the mayor and a group of journalists. Immediately after the mayor has declared the new departure hall for opened, a lady raises up from her chair and starts playing *You can fly*. After a few seconds, a girl with a microphone joins in and *You can fly* sounds in the departure hall. Conversations end, passengers and visitors watch the singer and put up their mobile phones to record the event. Two girls join the soloist while moving towards one of the gates.

At this stage, a roll-up poster is removed from a corner, and a guitarist, a double bass player and a percussionist appear. For a short while, they accompany the girls and the flautist, but then make a sudden break and continue with a jazzy introduction to *Fly me to the moon*. Behind one of the café counters, a music student turns up and sings in a Frank Sinatra-like style. A soon as the chorus begins, twenty-eight seventh-graders dance with high energy in front of Gate 11 in the departure hall.

Greig and Nicolini (2015) define a flash mob as a new artistic concept with "audience participation by interrupting the flow of day-to-day life" and describe the concept as an example of co-configuration, which means that "several groups come together as a relational grouping for the final product to emerge" (Greig & Nicolini, p. 190). In this case, what emerged was an encounter between the music, airport management, children, the band and the interrupted passengers. The flash mob is a *site-specific performance*, closely connected to the performance arena, which often is a place for transitions such as a railway station, an airport or a shopping mall. From my point of view, the dimension *uniqueness* (Klickstein, 2015) characterises the flash mob, regardless of the repertoire.

In 2011, the American cellist Dale Henderson founded *Bach in the Subways*. The network rapidly expanded, and in 2015, *Bach in the Subways* events were presented in 150 cities in 40 countries. Henderson's vision is "to present Bach's music to all, it is an invitation to the audience, most importantly to the multitudes who never otherwise encounter live classical music" (Henderson: Bach in the Subways. Webpage). All *Bach in the Subways* performances are free for audiences, and the performers will not get paid. The concept is unique in its originality and based on empathy. A large number of concerts and performances give the network relevance and connection in everyday life, which next example mirrors.

Example 5

> During the last two months, music students and teachers at University of Agder have developed a series of Bach concerts. The music will be presented in a recital hall, at a school concert, in a flash mob in Kristiansand Zoo and as a collaborative project with pupils in Year 5 from Ytre Torridal School. The repertoire will be performed in a traditional way, but the use of costumes, video projection and site-specific arenas are untraditional. The project is included in the international movement Bach in the Subways and the celebration of the composer Johan Sebastian Bach's 330th birthday all over the world. The purpose of Bach in the Subways is to bring live Bach concerts to as many people around the world as possible (Except from programme notes, 20th March, 2015).
>
> Seven music teacher students dressed in baroque costumes brought their instruments to Kristiansand Zoo and performed music by Bach in four different locations. There were no formal presentations, comments or programmes given to visitors passing by. The idea was to create a kind of "tableaux" with music, costumes, animals and everyday life in the zoo, showing colours, shapes, emotions, movement and sound. To perform the Bach repertoire technically perfect was not the primary intention since the students found it challenging to play when the animals were so close. The photos and video clips will be used during the upcoming school project with fifth-graders. (Field notes, 9th March, 2015)

The flash mob-like presentation in the zoo reflects Klickstein's three dimensions: *relevance*, because this was a worldwide celebration of a famous composer whose music is documented to have reached out all over the world; *empathy*, since people all over the world have become emotionally touched by Bach's music; and *uniqueness* because music by Bach is unique, the ensemble which presented the flash mob was organised for this project only and further that the ensemble played Bach in the zoo on this particular morning (Fig. 5).

Conclusion

In this chapter, I have discussed approaches to music listening in educational contexts. From my perspective, the craft to re-present musical works in educational contexts is based on insight into the music cultural life in society, skills in communication, and deep knowledge about repertoires and teaching strategies. To identify categories referred to in the discussion, such as *the ubiquity of music*, the concept of *"post-performance performing" cultural and relational considerations,* and the three dimensions, *relevance, empathy* and *uniqueness*, may serve as tools for developing the craft of re-presenting musical works. Such competence will emerge from thorough explorations of musical repertoires and performance concepts in addition to the categories mentioned above. However, even if the music educator is well prepared for teaching, there is no guarantee that he or she always will succeed. The paragraph "Purpose" in the National Norwegian Curriculum for music reminds us that:

Fig. 5 Students playing *Air on the G-string* in the lemur habitat in Kristiansand Zoo

> The perception of music is unpredictable, but it is still informed. This is an acknowledgement that the experience of music is not only intuitive, but rather that familiarity with music, knowledge about music, development of musical skills and reflection on music inform our perception of music, understood as both an aesthetic and existential experience. In working with music, the interaction between us and music is important. (The Norwegian Directorate for Education and Training, 2006)

I remember a stack of vinyl records on a table in the classroom when I was a primary school pupil in the 1960s. My music teacher played one piece from the record collection *Adventures in Music* (1961) almost every week. Espeland (2011) mentions *Adventures in Music* in his thorough presentation of listening practices in schools during the twentieth century. He quotes the producers Gladys and Eleanor Tipton, who argue that teachers should be aware that an intellectual encounter with music is not sufficient for the children:

> In order to take music into their hearts, children must have ample opportunity to find out for themselves what the music has to *say* to them. For only through a process of gradual, interested 'discovery' of the music itself, on their own terms, the children will remember and treasure it. From this time on, I found music listening meaningful. Later as a music teacher student, I became curious about which competencies I would need to involve others in meaningful activities with music (Tipton & Tipton, 1961, cited in Espeland, 2011, p. 163)

Espeland's *Music in Use* (1991) was my first encounter with a research-based approach to music listening in educational contexts. I found the collection of music highly valuable and the methodology inspired my further research in music education.

Postlude

In 1998, I presented Espeland's *Music in Use 1* to a group of kindergarten teachers during a seminar at the local Teacher Training College. Afterwards one of the participants did a small-scale research project on the adaption of *Music in Use* – principles in kindergarten. In the introduction section of this chapter, I presented a vignette, which referred to a music listening project in kindergarten. This was the teacher who came to the seminar.

As a conclusion to this discussion on the craft of (re-)presenting musical works in educational contexts, I have included another fantasy animal drawing inspired by *The Hunting of the Snark*, the modernistic solo trombone piece by Arne Nordheim, a well-known Norwegian composer. The young artist, six-year-old Kristina, described the fantasy animal as "a rabbit with chicken legs…".

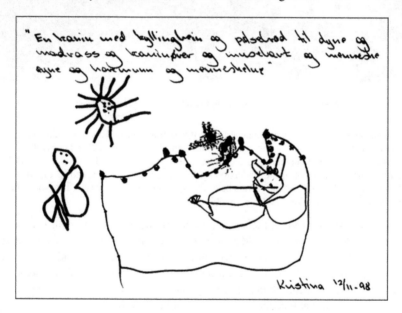

References

Allsup, R. E., Westerlund, H., & Shieh, E. (2012). Youth culture and secondary education. In G. McPherson & G. Welch (Eds.), *Oxford handbook of music education* (Vol. 2, pp. 460–475). Oxford, UK: Oxford University Press.

Beech, N., Broad, S., Cunliffe, A., Duffy, C., & Gilmore, C. (2015). Developments in organisational theory and organising music. In N. Beech & C. Gilmore (Eds.), *Organising music: Theory, practice and performance* (pp. 5–24). Cambridge, UK: Cambridge University Press.

Corbiau, G. (2000). *Le roi danse: Idylle sur la paix. Air pour la Madame Daphine* (03:25–05:30). Retrieved from https://www.youtube.com/watch?v=BMvpvDjFvHA

Dahl, P. (2011). *Verkanalysen som fortolkningsarena*. Oslo: Unipub forlag.

Eidsaa, R. M. (2015a). *Med musikal i bagasjen: Erfaringer fra et internasjonalt musikkprosjekt. I Engebretsen: Det tredje språket. Multimodale studier av interkulturell kommunikasjon i kunst, skole og samfunnsliv.* [With musical luggage: Experience from an international music project. In Engebretsen: The third language. Multimodal studies of intercultural communication in art, school and social life.] (pp. 12–229). Kristiansand, Norway: Portal forlag.

Eidsaa, R. M. (2017). Epona ryttersenter: Pluvinels Akademi 1 og 2 [Epona Equestrian Centre: Pluvinel's Academy 1 & 2] [https://www.youtube.com/watch?v=xrdx7OvXo6I&t=27s

Eidsaa, R.M, Martinsen, A., & Olsen, F. O. (2015). *Bach reflections at the zoo; Bach in the subways day, 2015.* Retrieved from https://www.youtube.com/watch?v=3p7OvxaVdz0

Espeland, M. (1987). Music in use: Responsive music listening in the primary school. *British Journal of Music Education, 4*(3), 283–297. https://doi.org/10.1017/S026505170000615X

Espeland, M. (1991). *Musikk i bruk 1* [Music in use 1]. Bergen, Norway: Fagbokforlaget.

Espeland, M. (1998). *Musikk i bruk 2* [Music in use 2]. Bergen, Norway: Fagbokforlaget.

Espeland, M. (2011). Towards a cultural psychology of music education. In M. Barrett (Ed.), *A cultural psychology in music education* (pp. 143–178). Oxford, UK: Oxford University Press.

Greig, G., & Nicolini, D. (2015). Managing artistic work in the real world. In N. Beech & C. Gilmore (Eds.), *Organising music. Theory, practise, performance* (pp. 188–201). Cambridge, UK: Cambridge University Press.

Holdhus, K., & Espeland, M. (2017). Music in the future nordic schooling: The potential of the relational turn. *In European Journal of Philosophy in Arts Education, 2*(02)

Klickstein, G. (2015). *Lecture in music production.* Washington, DC: Philips Collection.

O'Neill, S. (2011). Learning in and through music performance: Understanding cultural diversity via inquiry and dialogue. In M. S. Barrett (Ed.), *A cultural psychology of music education* (pp. 179–197). Oxford, UK: Oxford University Press.

Ruud, E. (1996). Musikk og verdier. [Music and values]. Universitetsforlaget.

Ruud, E. (2005). *Lydlandskap. Om bruk og misbruk av musikk.* [Soundscapes: On use and abuse of music]. Bergen, Norway: Fagbokforlaget.

Thibeault, M. (2018). Music education in the post-performance world. In G. M. Pherson & G. Welch (Eds.), *Oxford handbook of music education* (pp. 517–529). Oxford, UK: Oxford University Press.

Van Orden, K. (2005). *Music, discipline and arms in early modern France.* Chicago: Chicago University Press.

Warren, J. R. (2014). *Music and ethical responsibility.* Cambridge, UK: Cambridge University Press.

Developing Craftsmanship in Music Education in a Palestinian Refugee Camp and Lebanese Schools

Signe Kalsnes

Abstract For several years, music teacher students at the Norwegian Academy of Music have participated in a collaborative music project with a Palestinian refugee camp and in school concert performances in Lebanese friendship schools. The refugee camp music project offers weekly music and dance education for children and youth aged 6–20. During an internship period in Lebanon, Norwegian students teach music to 50–60 children and youth for 3–4 days in the refugee camp and play concerts for Lebanese pupils in three primary schools, as well as in one high school. The empirical basis for this article is the reflective logs of 23 students from their internship period in Lebanon. Through the logs, the students express their thoughts and experiences on the concert and music communication praxis, and my analysis of the logs is based on the research question: *What kind of experience does the Lebanon Project give students and what is the impact of this experience with regard to their subsequent professional life as music teachers and musicians?* The Lebanon Project, and this specific study, provides a basis for a more general reflection on the concept of music education as a "craft".

Introduction

This chapter is informed by my experiences, reflections and research relating to a music education project in the Palestinian refugee camp, Rashidieh, in South Lebanon and a school concert collaboration with Lebanese schools in the same region. For several years, music education students and teachers from the Norwegian Academy of Music (NMH) have been involved in the so-called Lebanon Project, which involves teaching Palestinian children and young people, as well as music outreach and concerts for and with Palestinian and Lebanese pupils. Many of the NMH students have described the Lebanon Project as the single most significant event in their teacher training, and the outcomes they report go far beyond the

S. Kalsnes (✉)
Norwegian Academy of Music, Oslo, Norway
e-mail: Signe.kalsnes@nmh.no

© Springer Nature Switzerland AG 2021
K. Holdhus et al. (eds.), *Music Education as Craft*, Landscapes: the Arts, Aesthetics, and Education 30, https://doi.org/10.1007/978-3-030-67704-6_11

academic aspect. They describe a project that has allowed them to mature as people; given them a deeper understanding of society, insights into music outreach work with vulnerable and marginalised groups; and prepared them for working as music teachers in a multicultural Norway (Brøske−Danielsen, 2013; Norwegian Academy of Music, 2011).

Central to this chapter are the results of a study looking at the experiences of the student music teachers from their concert and outreach practice in Lebanon. The Lebanon Project and the results of this study provide the basis for a more general reflection on the concept of music education as a "craft", such as music education for all rather than the few, sharing in different ways, respect for the learner and reflecting on one's own practice. I also reflect on the future potential of music as a discipline for school music and for children and young people in relation to the perspective of participation. These reflections are related to challenges encountered by musicians and music educators in a Norwegian context in response to the dilemmas that may arise when the role of the musician must be balanced against that of the music teacher.

To provide some background to this discussion I will first describe the Lebanon Project, various challenges surrounding the use of music in a Muslim culture and the impact of the project on the children and young people who participated. Next I will introduce the above-mentioned study on the student music teachers' practice in Lebanon and discuss the findings in light of the concept of music education as a "craft".

The Lebanon Project

The music project in the Rashidieh refugee camp offers music and dance tuition to children and young people aged 6–20. The project was launched in the 2000s by Norwegian music teachers in partnership with the Palestinian aid organisation Beit Atfal Assumoud, which works to help and develop Palestinian society in Lebanon through education, healthcare and arts. The project has its roots in NORWAC's mental health programme for Palestinian refugee children in Lebanon[1] and is run on a weekly basis by 3–5 Palestinian teachers. The main focus is on all participants performing in a large group, and the training now includes tuition on a range of instruments such as violin, keyboard, band instruments, voice, sax and darbuka (Arabic hand drum). The Palestinian teachers also teach traditional Palestinian folk dance (dabke). One important part of the project is the cultural exchange that occurs when the Palestinian children, young people and teachers visit their twin schools in Norway and also when the students and teachers from the NMH travelled to Lebanon in the period 2005–2013 until the war in Syria put a stop to the students'

---

[1] NORWAC is a Norwegian humanitarian organisation funded by the Norwegian government. The organisation has been training healthcare workers in Lebanon since 1983 following the Israeli invasion.

participation. Even though the students have not been part of the project in recent years, the music activities in the refugee camp continue unabated with regular visits by teachers from Norway. The plan is to resume the practice in Lebanon for the music education students.

According to the UNRWA,[2] around 300,000 Palestinians fled to Lebanon in 1948 as a result of *al-Nakba* (the catastrophe), the Arab-Israeli war and the establishment of the state of Israel. There they live segregated from civil society in permanent refugee camps. The Palestinian children and young people participating in the music project are growing up as third and fourth generation refugees in Lebanon. Many of them have lost one or both parents or have parents who are disabled or out of work. Their childhoods are affected by the plight of the Palestinians in Lebanon: poverty, health issues, oppression and little prospect of a better future. This is because the Palestinians in Lebanon do not have ordinary citizens' rights such as citizenship, suffrage, the right to own property and the freedom to choose a profession (Chaaban et al., 2010).

During their practice period in Lebanon, the music education students would spend 3–4 days teaching 50–60 children and young people in the refugee camp.[3] At the same time, the students themselves were taught Palestinian dance and Arabic music by the Palestinian teachers and oldest students on the project. Every year this music and dance collaboration would culminate in a joint concert where the Palestinian children and young people and the Norwegian students participate and where friends, family and invited guests made up the audience. Because these concerts are deemed to be important events, some of them were held outside the camp – in concert venues in Tyre or Beirut – in connection with major Palestinian celebrations.

In addition to the teaching and concerts in the refugee camp the music education students performed school concerts in three Lebanese primary schools and one secondary school in South Lebanon. The Lebanon Project at the Norwegian Academy of Music includes both the school concerts at these twin schools and the music activities in the Palestinian refugee camp.[4]

Music Outreach on the Lebanon Project

The Rashidieh refugee camp:

> The concert starts with the national anthems – that is, the Palestinian, Lebanese and Norwegian anthems – and the Palestinian pupils sing all of the lyrics at the top of their

---

[2] The UNRWA is a UN agency working to improve living conditions for Palestinian refugees in Jordan, Lebanon, Syria, the West Bank and the Gaza Strip – https://www.unrwa.org.

[3] Many of the pupils would be part of the project for several years, but there was also some turnover which meant that there were always a few beginners in the group.

[4] A video from the project can be viewed here: https://nmh.no/om_musikkhogskolen/fagmiljo/musikkpedagogikk.

voices. The stage, which has been decorated with Norwegian, Lebanese and Palestinian flags, is full of instruments, children, teenagers and students, and in the hall sits an expectant and noisy audience. For four days the Norwegian students have been teaching the Palestinian children and young people partly in small groups according to instrument and partly as a full ensemble. The orchestra is now ready to perform "Reodor's Ballade"[5] – a song from the Norwegian film "Flåklypa". It starts with a low note on the synth and chime bells before the tune is introduced on a melodica. Next follows a section where everyone plays the theme under the guidance of a steady accompaniment. Then the saxophones pick up the melody, before everyone joins in the next section again. The beautiful tune continues to flow back and forth across the orchestra, paying a visit to the xylophones, keyboards, violins, guitars and glockenspiel before climaxing in a magnificent tutti section in which everyone takes part. The song is followed by several other items. When the students and the Palestinian pupils – all dressed in Palestinian costumes – conclude the concert with a Palestinian dance and an Arabic song, the applause raises the roof.

The music outreach activities in the refugee camp have always been an integral part of the students' teaching practice. Every day the students would perform individually and in groups to enable the children and young people to experience and familiarise themselves with different types of music, and the children and young people have performed both music and Palestinian dances for the Norwegian guests. Over the years an extensive collection of intercultural musical repertoire and CD recordings has been developed for use in teaching and concerts. It includes folk music from all over the world, pop and rock songs, ballads and singing games created for educational use – all collected and edited by teachers and students at the Norwegian Academy of Music and other partners on the project. Key to this collection are the *multi-use arrangements* which, with their numerous parts for every song, can be used with large and small ensembles with varying ability levels and instrumentation with a view to enabling all of the participants to experience meaningful musical participation, fulfilment and recognition. The music project and multi-use arrangements could be seen in the context of community music-making in which performance is a key aspect and where the participants' social and personal well-being are as important as the learning that takes place (Brøske-Danielsen & Storsve, 2016; Storsve, Westby & Ruud, 2009; Veblen & Olsson, 2002). There are also obvious parallels to Christopher Small's (1998) concept of *musicking*, which indicates both that music is not a thing but an action and that the meaning of musical action can be found in the interrelationships between people.

Observing and studying this music activity in Rashidieh, I keep wondering about what it takes to be a successful student teacher in these situations. In other words, what teaching skills are necessary or the most important? Is it the ability to organise the whole situation and exercise good classroom management in this big group of children and youth of different ages? Is it the ability to utilise the music arrangements in the best possible way, or is it a community music attitude where participation is more important than proficiency and musical results?

School concerts in Lebanese twin schools:

---

[5] https://www.youtube.com/watch?v=eFhyev9G_Pg

The big hall at the Imam Sadr Foundation School has been fitted out with colourful decorations for the occasion. This is not the first time we are visiting this school. On previous occasions the pupils have prepared several musical items for the concerts. We are excited about today's concert, and the school's music teacher suggests that the students and a group of her pupils prepare a joint performance for the concert finale. They begin to practise.

Pupils and teachers fill the hall, and you can feel the anticipation in the air. The arrival of the school leadership together with key leaders from the Imam Sadr Foundation signals that the concert is an important event. After the national anthems the Norwegian students take to the stage to perform a selection of their varied programme: an arrangement of The Pink Panther, a clarinet duo, a pop song with full band, a Norwegian folk tune, and finally an Arabic song the students have learnt in Rashidieh. The excitement is palpable. Next it is the Lebanese pupils' turn, and a large choir with children from years 4, 5 and 6 file onto the stage to perform Offenbach. After that there is a performance of "Kitchen Rhythm" by year 4 and the special class in which they use pots and various kitchen utensils as instruments. This is followed by several other items before the concert concludes with a joint performance of a popular Arabic song. I think the fact that the concert is seen as an important event is just as much down to increasing pupil participation as to the Norwegian visitors. The applause is resounding, and there are smiles and laughter both on stage and in the audience.

Music outreach is an increasingly important part of the Lebanon Project thanks to increasing concert activity in the Lebanese twin schools. The original idea was for the students to visit the schools with their prepared programme to perform a traditional school concert. But very quickly – and to the Norwegians' surprise – the Lebanese pupils began to perform their own pieces, first a little hesitantly, as a thank you, but eventually as a proud manifestation of the regular and expanding music tuition that was taking place in the schools. In all of the twin schools, the concerts have turned into a kind of partnership project in which the students and the Lebanese pupils perform their respective programmes but with a joint final performance where everyone performs Arabic music prepared in situ ahead of the concert. The experience gained by the students through the school concerts therefore challenges traditional roles often seen in school concerts, whereby the pupils are (passive) recipients of the music being performed by the (professional) musicians. In terms of craftsmanship, these experiences help the students to reflect on and perhaps develop more flexible concert and outreach formats aimed at children and young people.

Music Outreach in a Muslim Cultural Tradition

There are both cultural and religious challenges surrounding music education and outreach in Muslim cultures. This is partly because music in general – or rather certain types of music, musical instruments or lyrics – are seen by some as *haram* (forbidden) and partly because there are restrictions on girls and women performing music, especially solo singing and performing in public. In many Muslim cultures musicians do not enjoy high status; on the contrary, they are often seen as shallow and frivolous entertainers (Storsve & Danielsen, 2013). Yet we have encountered very divergent views on music, on who should be allowed to perform music and on which instruments, types and genres of music are deemed *haram* or not in the communities we have been working with. The long-standing partnership has also resulted in more positive attitudes towards music and music performance amongst the participants, including when it comes to developing music as a school subject (Storsve & Danielsen, 2013).

As well as cultural and religious challenges, there are also issues around language. English skills are lacking both in the refugee camp and in the twin schools, especially amongst the youngest pupils. The children and young people and the Norwegian students generally have few shared musical points of reference. For many of the pupils on the Lebanon Project, the Norwegian students' school concerts are their first concert experience (Kalsnes, 2013).

In this cultural context, the skills required of the teacher or musician are primarily about openness and tolerance of cultural diversity combined with the professional musician's wish to build good relationships in which the connections between music, humanity and society can generate mutual growth and development (Nerland, 2004). In this particular setting, it can be difficult to approach diversity in a way that balances respect for the local culture with the desire to challenge it (e.g. in relation to girls' participation in musical activity). Acknowledging that a teacher or musician can never be value-neutral is essential. Craftsmanship in this context is also about how to specifically teach and promote music to and with children and young people without a shared language or musical references. I also hold that craftsmanship is always context-dependent and susceptible to relational factors. For the music education students, their craftsmanship must be seen in relation to the Palestinian and Lebanese pupils' experiences on the music project and the relationships that develop when the students and pupils make music together.

The Impact of the Lebanon Project

In this section I will briefly cite key findings from studies on the impact of the Lebanon Project on the participating pupils and their communities. The findings complement the picture of the practice setting the music education students encounter in Lebanon, forming a backdrop that allows us to look more closely at how the practice helps the students develop their craft as music teachers and musicians.

An evaluation based on information about participation and activities on the project in the period 2005–2011 in which interviews with staff in the Rashidieh refugee camp and written evaluations from the partner organisations in Lebanon formed part of the empirical evidence concludes that the Lebanon Project is seen as highly significant by all stakeholders (Norwegian Academy of Music, 2011). For the people in Lebanon, the project has brought about considerable change: 700–800 children are now receiving weekly music tuition in Lebanon and in Palestinian refugee camps, and the Palestinian and Lebanese music teachers feel they are learning a great deal by observing how the Norwegian students teach. The partner organisations in Lebanon see the school concerts given by the students together with their pupils as something that gives direction to the tuition during the year. They state that the children gain self-confidence by being on stage and that the concerts have made them proud of their own music and culture because students are coming all the way from Norway to learn from them.

In an article based on experiences and observations surrounding the music activities in Rashidieh, Storsve, Westby and Ruud (2009) assert that the music project gives the Palestinian children and young people access to a repertoire of roles that challenge traditional boundaries and perceptions and which create possibilities and a hope that the world can be changed: "Girls can play the guitar, the adults can "play" and "fool around"; good humour and laughter are important ingredients in a learning situation" (p. 195). Drawing on Wenger's (2004) perspectives on identity formation and learning through participation in a community of practice in which different participant pathways enable varied forms of affiliation, the authors point out that the music project has generated results in the form of musical learning, a fundamental feeling of being seen and acknowledged by the wider community and experiences that have had a positive effect on the children and young people's self-efficacy.

In an ethnographic follow-up study, Ruud (2011) investigates young Palestinians' experiences of being part of a musical ensemble. He was looking for possible correlations between cultural participation and "perceived health" – that is to say, the subjective perception of increased well-being and improved quality of life. In interviews with a number of the youngsters participating in the music project in Rashidieh, he links "perceived health" to vitality and self-perception, sense of belonging, achievement and recognition as well as to meaning – in the sense of affiliation to tradition – and hope. Ruud concludes:

> If we assume, then, that there is a link between health and a subjectivity mode in which we are able to open up to the world, to live the music, to conceptualise and express our emotions or to have an aesthetic experience, we can see a correlation between music and health, and we can assert that participating in the orchestra has an effect on health. (Ruud, 2011, p. 73)

In his doctoral thesis Boeskov opts for an anthropological approach when he investigates how the participants in the music project in Rashidieh negotiate their social (refugee) and cultural (Palestinian) identity through the music activities (2013, 2017, 2018). Looking at the cultural exchange taking place on the project, Boeskov (2013) uses the term *communitas* to describe an existential experience and a feeling of coherence and integration between the individual and the world. Boeskov sees the cultural exchange activities as ritual acts that recreate balance in life and make it meaningful, and he claims that the activities have the potential to create moments of *communitas* for the participants and therefore also a feeling of meaning, equality and togetherness. This can make the participants feel respected and valued rather than excluded and marginalised (Boeskov, 2018). In group interviews with Palestinian youths who are long-standing participants in the cultural exchanges on the Lebanon Project both in Norway and in Rashidieh, Boeskov found three clear tendencies: the participants describe the cultural exchange as an opportunity to *see themselves in new ways*, as an opportunity to *experience togetherness and recognition* and as a way of *fighting the Palestinian cause* (2013 p. 137). Both the relational experiences and the music and musical activities themselves are interpreted in the same way – *as symbols of friendship and recognition*.

In an interview study with music teachers and leaders from the Lebanese twin schools and the music project in Rashidieh as informants, I looked at the impact of the active participation in the concerts on the children and young people on the music project (Kalsnes, 2013). Key findings from the study include the *recognition* gained by the Lebanese children and young people through their participation in the concerts and the positive impact that the collaboration between them and the Norwegian students appears to have had on their *self-esteem and self-confidence* but also on their *all-round development and learning*. In particular, the teachers in the refugee camp highlight how the concerts help instil pride and create a *heightened sense of identity* in that the learning and communication go both ways: the children get to learn Norwegian and Western music, while the students learn Palestinian songs and dances which they then perform alongside the children and young people:

> It's very important to play with the kids – we are playing with our colleagues – the students. The kids feel proud, and their goal is to play together. They also feel proud when the Norwegian students dance Palestinian dances and sing Palestinian music – that really means a lot to us, it's our identity. (From an interview with a Palestinian music teacher)

Against this backdrop I will now look more closely at the music education students' experiences during their Lebanon practice and at how their reflections shine a light on and help inform their craftsmanship as music teachers and musicians.

In What Way Does the Lebanon Project Frame and Shape the Students' Craftsmanship as Music Teachers and Musicians?

The study on which this section is based is part of a broader study looking at experiences from the music outreach activities on the Lebanon Project. The methodological framework is ethnographic and is based on interviews, analyses of student diaries, participant observation, extensive video material and field notes from 8 years of teaching and supervising students on the project.

The study draws on 23 student diaries describing the Lebanon practice in 2010, 2011 and 2012 in which the students give an account of their own experiences of the outreach/concert practice. The main intention behind the decision to include the students in the Lebanon Project was to give them an experience that would be important for them in their subsequent careers as music teachers and musicians. The research question in this part of my study was therefore as follows: *What kind of experience does the Lebanon Project give the students, and what is the impact of this experience with regard to their subsequent professional careers as music teachers and musicians?* Or in other words, in what way does the Lebanon project frame and shape their craftsmanship as music teachers and musicians?

The Lebanon practice took place in the students' third year of the 4-year bachelor's programme in music education at the Norwegian Academy of Music.[6] The programme provides a range of practice settings in several types of schools along with numerous concert opportunities, albeit largely for adult audiences with an interest in music. The Lebanon Project therefore represents an important platform for school concert collaborations and music outreach practice involving children and young people. To prepare for their practice in Lebanon, the groups of students[7] put together varied concert programmes with flexible content that could be used in a variety of contexts. The programmes have consisted of a cappella pieces – performed by the entire group of students – a few jazz/pop/rock songs, a couple of Norwegian folk tunes, some classical pieces for various instruments and a couple of humorous and playful musical items, often with audience participation. This way the concert programmes have been wide-reaching in terms of genres and instrumentation, and they have reflected the students' different specialisms and musical diversity.

I will now present the key findings from the study. By analysing the practice diaries, I identified four overarching themes that are descriptive of the students' experiences and reflections: *(1) perspectives on music and meaningfulness, (2) cultural exchange as a quality in music outreach involving children and young people, (3) the roles of the musician and the audience in music outreach involving children and young people and (4) professional development and dilemmas.*

Perspectives on Music and Meaningfulness

Many of the students' reflections concern their perspectives on music and meaningfulness, with particular focus on the significance of music in a (multi-)cultural context to children and young people living in difficult circumstances and as an element in communication between individuals. To musicians and music teachers, their understanding of the potential significance and functions of music in people's lives is a fundamental factor in both justifying and motivating their professional practice (Kalsnes, 2004; Nerland, 2004). Such perspectives can therefore help give meaning to their professional practice and have an impact on the music education students' professional development. In particular, the students highlight the joy of music and of life itself that comes with music-making and relate this to the Palestinian children and young people's difficult circumstances:

> Student 1: *Participating in this concert and seeing the children enjoying themselves and giving a very good concert/performance was a powerful experience. It was touching to see a high-spirited crowd who just loved playing, singing and dancing. In a way this just confirms to me why I want to become a teacher, and it's just wonderful.*

---

[6] https://nmh.no/en/study/undergraduate/bachelor-music-education
[7] Every year an average of 10–12 students would participate, but the cohorts have ranged from 5 to 18 participants from year to year.

Student 2: *Bringing joy and making music is valuable, even if it doesn't solve any conflicts [...] I think you can express a lot through music and that it can be good for the soul. If people in the refugee camps are able to express some of the hopelessness, fear and trepidation through music, then I think it can serve as therapy and be an important thing.*

The contribution of music to communication and shared experiences was mentioned by several students. The reflections concern the potential impact of such experiences both for the pupils and for themselves as teachers and musicians. The experiences help raise awareness of both the significance and the legitimacy of music education for all, as opposed to the few, and of which values can be associated with music-making.

Student 3: *I don't mean to disparage the other aspects of our training but to highlight a view on music that could disappear if the musical training is too specialised and technical. It's about creating and sharing human musical experiences irrespective of genre, language, culture and technical quality and to guide each other in a landscape of expressions that everyone can be part of.*

Student 4: *It's because of concerts like those we did in Lebanon that I want to be involved in music. In my opinion, music is something that acquires value when it's shared between people, and in my case it was incredibly important to be reminded of that miles away from the practice rooms at the NMH [...] The project gives self-centred, practice-driven musicians a reminder of what music outreach can be.*

Craftsmanship in music education is unthinkable without an awareness of what it means. When we see the results of craftsmanship in the shape of joy and artistic and aesthetic expression, we can be touched, especially in a refugee setting where hopelessness and resignation often dominate everyday life. Viewed this way, the craft of meaningful music teaching becomes something beautiful that not only appeals to us as learning, but as an achievement for everyone involved.

Cultural Exchange as a Quality in Music Outreach Involving Children and Young People

In many of the diaries, the students focus on the cultural exchange and the mutual acknowledgement and respect for the participants' different cultural expressions:

Student 1: *It was also emotional to discover how important it is to exchange music both ways. The way in which we the students and these youngsters were proud to show each other aspects of our respective music and dance cultures made a deep impression on me. I think such cultural exchanges and the opportunity to learn how to communicate music is hugely important for my self-esteem.*
    Student 2: *This cultural exchange where we perform both Western and Eastern music means that we can create and use a more universal musical language [...] I've always been keen to promote music to children and young people. This desire has been strengthened after Lebanon, and I've also gained a new and greater focus on ethnic minority cultures.*

The statements indicate that the students see their experience of the pupils' active participation as being especially positive. In terms of craftsmanship, this challenges not only traditional views on formats and roles in music outreach and school concerts for children and young people but also the musician's and the music teacher's ideas about quality – *what* creates quality and *which quality criteria* should apply when you make music with children and young people. Central to this theme is a strong focus on the target group:

> Student 3: *The concerts have given me greater insights into how to create a concert programme that reaches out to target groups that are seemingly very different to me. Both during the planning and at the concerts themselves I felt that the focus on the target group was central. Music outreach involving children and young people means other quality criteria that I'm used to when preparing concert programmes based on my own preferences and ideals.*

The Roles of the Musician and the Audience in Music Outreach Involving Children and Young People

A clear focus on the target group can have consequences for how the students interpret and evaluate their own role as musicians. Although this issue may exist with other target groups, too, music outreach with children and young people may be conducive to raising awareness of the musician's potential roles and focus. The potential roles of the musician, and consequently of the audience, is a key issue when it comes to school concerts and when considering which competencies a musician needs (Borgen, 2006; Christophersen, 2013; Holdhus, Waade, Romme, Almås, & Espeland, 2019; Kalsnes, 2004, 2012;). Should the pupils assume a traditional audience role, or can we envisage some form of participation? What role expectations are there in a potential collaboration between the musician and the teacher in a school concert setting? How can we best create a good musical experience and a positive concert experience for the pupils? Many of the students touch upon these issues, and their reflections indicate that the monologic concert format and the traditional and partly hierarchical performer and audience roles are being challenged on the Lebanon Project:

> Student 1: *The concerts in Lebanon have helped me confirm or reject many of the ideas I've had about concerts for children and young people. One of the most important discoveries I made was the value of engaging the audience. In light of the project I'd say that active involvement is one of the best ways of giving the youngest children a positive musical experience.*

> Student 2: *After these concerts I've become even more determined to do school concerts. They've made me realise the importance of audience activity and of working with the location you're visiting – something many schools have said they want to see. I also see the importance of not turning up with a ready-made solution, but to adapt your programme to the school in question. The main thing is to have a good and large repertoire that you can mix and match as required. When I teach my own pupils I've always emphasised the outreach aspect, but thanks to this project I've had new ideas about performance spaces for them.*

Student 3: *My experience of the final concert in Rashidieh was especially good because we'd been working on the material together for three days. So for that reason it was amazing to reach our goal with our jointly prepared material and be able to show it to parents and others.*

Professional Development and Dilemmas

The students' experiences and reflections can broadly be seen as a contribution to their professional development, to the development of their professional identities as teachers and musicians and to skills development. They describe a range of issues and problems: what can be perceived as legitimate or not in light of different roles as musicians and teachers, linguistic challenges, their own (lack of or new-found) ability to deal with the challenges of the practice and what makes the students better musicians and teachers. In particular, many of the issues they raise suggest that their readiness to engage in pedagogical improvisation is key to a musician's and music teacher's craftsmanship. Mastering pedagogical improvisation requires experience but also flexibility, openness and a willingness to analyse the situations that arise with a view to finding solutions while also acquiring suitable professional and didactic tools. Perhaps craftsmanship in this context also means not taking yourself too seriously and daring to take on challenges you feel unsure of and where there is a risk of failure:

Student 1: *The best thing about the concerts in Lebanon was that we always had to be prepared for the unexpected [...] We learnt to let go of our self-censorship [...] to let our hair down a bit. It did us good.*

Student 2: *Another important experience for me in this concert setting was that I had to do things I wasn't exactly comfortable about doing. However! I then realised that these things aren't really that important when you look at the bigger picture. So for me it was nice to learn how to grin and bear it and to focus on the audience and on the joy of performing something so varied and fun for people from a completely different background to ours.*

Student 3: *Textual content became less important in Lebanon because the children and young people didn't speak English or Norwegian. I therefore found that I had to rely more on body language and mimicry in order to convey the mood and feeling I wanted to express. This was an adjustment I've not had to make before and which I learnt a lot from.*

The students' experiences and reflections clearly show that there are certain difficult professional dilemmas associated with the school concerts. These dilemmas are often linked to the students' dual role as both teachers and musicians, and they concern choice of repertoire, the objective of the concerts, quality assessment, role identities and who the students want to be as musicians and teachers (Angelo & Kalsnes, 2014). The following statements illustrating the students' preparations for the Lebanon Project reflect these dilemmas:

Student 4: *I learnt a lot from working with the class on the concerts across genres and preferences. In particular, I think we realised that our ideas of what is "valid" and "non-*

*valid" music has to be discarded when it comes to concerts with children and young people
[...] That was important learning to take home with me.*

Student 5: *Another interesting thing was how our planned repertoire changed between the
time of planning and when we got there. When we talked about the programme in advance
it was more about showing what we could do. [...] That changed along the way, and once
we got there it was no longer about showing off. It was about giving the audience a good
musical experience!*

We can see the students' perspectives change as they find themselves in the practice
setting and their focus shifts away from themselves as musicians and onto the audience. Many of the statements also shine a light on what in teacher training is considered a key competency – *capacity for change and development*. Thus,
craftsmanship will also involve reflecting critically on one's own practice, interacting within a professional collective and evaluating the benefits and drawbacks of
change and development (White Paper no. 11).

The students' reflections also show their different stances on dilemmas that occur
as a result of multiple considerations and quality criteria vying for space as they
plan and execute their concert programmes. For some the dilemmas resulted in frus-
tration but also a conscious assessment of different courses of action and decisions,
as demonstrated in the following statement:

Student 6: *The programme comprised a number of different items with considerable variation and diversity as a key factor. [...] My role was therefore more that of an entertainer
than a musician, and I found that the musical quality suffered as a result. With low-quality
instruments and difficult acoustics, the good, musical experience of my own performance
was also absent. I therefore felt that the concerts we held in Lebanon did not give me much
musical fulfilment. Our main focus was primarily to give the children a good experience
with enjoyment and entertainment as the obvious priority. Still, I wish we could have combined that with higher musical quality. To me that would be an important ambition for
subsequent tours.*

Discussion and Conclusion

In this text – and against the backdrop of the Lebanon Project and the music education students' reflections – I will now reflect on the music teacher's competencies
and actions that can form the basis for a "craft of meaningful music teaching". The
word "craft" can hold a number of meanings and can be interpreted both narrowly
and broadly. The narrow interpretation of a craft in this context would be the ability
to create and use multi-use arrangements, to perform on and teach an instrument
and to organise and lead ensemble play in large classes and groups. A broader definition of a craft contains all those interpretations but also attitudes, values, professional reasoning and the ability to see the music and music teaching profession in a
wider social context.

The impact of the Lebanon Project; the experiences, learning and development
of the Palestinian children and young people; and the students' practice experiences

all help illuminate the concept of music education as a "craft" and perspectives that include music education for all, rather than the few, sharing in different ways, respect for the learner and reflection on one's own practice. The *participant perspective* is particularly conspicuous in the students' accounts of the project. As we have seen in this text, participation has allowed the children, young people and music education students to experience meaning, identity and togetherness. The participant perspective can be investigated and legitimised in a variety of ways.

Participation can be seen in the context of theories on learning, health and quality of life in which learning is viewed as a social practice and the learning process as a gradual qualification for competent participation in a given community (Stige, 2005). Here, music serves as a condition of possibility for growth and development in which participation denotes a relationship between a musical situation and a relevant person or group. In light of the students' practice, this could be the relationship between the concert, the students and the children and young people as active participants. Stige's assertion is that when we use music as a means of participation, the musical perspective cannot be the sole perspective but must be balanced with taking an interest in both the individual and the situation. In terms of the discussion on a music teacher's or musician's craft, this could relate to the musician's and music teacher's reflections on the concept of quality and what that concept contains. In a community perspective – on which the Lebanon Project can be said to be founded – we must adopt a broad quality concept which, in addition to musical and artistic qualities, also includes the quality of the interpersonal relationships and the relevance of the music and the musical activities to the participating children and young people, as well as to the audience generally. The perspective can easily be broadened to apply to music education for all children in Norwegian schools through *The Cultural Schoolbag*[8] and more generally in music outreach *for* and *together with* children and youth (Kalsnes, 2012).

In Norwegian music education today, there are several areas and trends that challenge the roles and duties of musicians and music teachers as well as the purpose and goals of music education and outreach (Kalsnes, 2014a, 2014b). At the time of writing, a reform process is underway to create new curricula in all subjects in Norwegian primary and secondary education by 2020. One key objective is that the tuition should result in *deep learning* for the pupils. According to Dahl and Østern (2019), deep learning can be seen as relational, corporeal, affective, creative and cognitive learning that involves the whole pupil and which is both sense-making and involves identity construction. It is difficult to imagine that such profound experiences of music can be had without the participant perspective playing a prominent role in the tuition.

The participant perspective is also raised in discussions on how best to realise the goals for The Cultural Schoolbag which involve "[giving] pupils and schools the chance to experience, become familiar with and develop an understanding of all

[8] The Cultural Schoolbag is a national collaborative project, launched in 2001, by the Ministry of Culture and the Ministry of Education and Research designed to ensure that all pupils (aged 6–19) in Norway can experience professional art and culture of all kinds.

kinds of professional artistic and cultural output" (TCS). Most research concludes that there is a need for more pupil participation and closer co-operation between schools, teachers, pupils and artists on The Cultural Schoolbag (Borgen & Brandt, 2006; Breivik & Christophersen, 2013; NIFU STEP, 2010). The trialing of dialogic school concert formats with the aim of giving ownership to all the parties involved shows that important success criteria are the pupils' co-determination, creative and musical activities, a pro-active teacher and musicians who are willing to balance artistic criteria against the interests of the pupils and the school context (Holdhus et al., 2019).

This book raises questions about how the long traditions of music education respond to a rapidly changing environment in society and in education, and how music education could contribute to creative and sustainable solutions to societal and educational challenges created by multiculturalism, globalisation, technology and accountability. This is the basis on which Peter Renshaw (2003, p. 1) states that "higher arts education institutions might well consider taking the three Cs – connections, context and conversations – as their mantra" and that no one remains unaffected by the rapidly advancing social, economic and technological developments that are leading to growing uncertainty, anxiety and fear. With that in mind, Renshaw wants the arts to open doors, cut across boundaries, create meaning and togetherness in life and help us find our voice in a fragmented world. All humans should therefore be able to actively express themselves through artistic activity: "One of the greatest strengths of the arts is that they can enhance the quality and meaning of people's lives" (Renshaw, 2003, p. 3). According to Renshaw's thinking, music teachers and musicians need skill, self-confidence and vision to help different groups of people find fellowship, meaning and participation with the consequence that both their professional identity and expertise must be in constant development to prevent professional stagnation.

The dual role as a teacher *and* a musician, which awaits the music education students in their future careers, offers both challenging professional dilemmas and rich opportunities for development and innovation as a result of the broad-based skills they are acquiring. The students are in the middle of a process in which the challenge is to identify themselves with a musician/teacher profession in flux in which they must find themselves as professional practitioners. One central theme is developing a professional identity – one linked to how we practise our profession – where the skills, attitudes, knowledge, abilities and values that make up the teacher and musician in us are key (Heggen, 2008; Kalsnes, 2014b).

My concluding assertion is that a central dimension in the concept of music education as a craft is the music teacher's and the musician's readiness to both refine and redefine their responsibilities and roles in step with changes in wider society. For music education students, this means reflecting on and gaining an awareness of their professional role both now and in the future. It also means continuing to work on their identity both as a *teacher* and as a *musician* – if not various identi*ties* in both these roles.

References

Angelo, E., & Kalsnes, S. (2014). *Kunstner eller lærer? Profesjonsdilemmaer i musikk- og kunstpedagogisk utdanning.* Oslo, Norway: Cappelen Damm Akademisk.

Boeskov, K. (2013). Meningsfyldte møder – om norskpalæstinensisk kulturudveksling. In V. R. Storsve & B. Å. B. Danielsen (Eds.), *Løft blikket – gjør en forskjell. Erfaringer og ringvirkninger fra et musikkprosjekt i Libanon* (NMH Research Publications 2013(9)) (pp. 127–148). Norwegian Academy of Music: Oslo, Norway.

Boeskov, K. (2017). The community music practice as cultural performance: Foundations for a community music theory of social transformation. *International Journal of Community Music, 10*(1), 85–99.

Boeskov, K. (2018). Moving beyond orthodoxy: Reconsidering notions of music and social transformation. *Action, Criticism, and Theory for Music Education, 17*(2), 92–117.

Borgen, J. S. (2006). Asymmetri mellom det «kunstneriske» og det «pedagogiske» i den kulturelle skolesekken. In E. Angelo & S. Kalsnes (Eds.), *Kunstner eller lærer? Profesjonsdilemmaer i musikk – og kunstpedagogisk utdanning* (pp. 138–154). Oslo, Norway: Cappelen Damm Akademisk.

Borgen, J. S., & Brandt, S. S. (2006). *Ekstraordinært eller selvfølgelig? Evaluering av den kulturelle skolesekken i grunnskolen.* Oslo, Norway: NIFU STEP.

Breivik, J.-K., & Christophersen, C. (2013). *Den kulturelle skolesekken.* Oslo, Norway: Arts Council Norway.

Brøske-Danielsen, B. Å. (2013). Community music activity in a refugee camp: Student music teachers' practicum experiences. *Music Education Research, 15*(3), 304–316.

Brøske-Danielsen, B. Å., & Storsve, V. (2016). Musikkarbeid med palestinske flyktningbarn i Libanon. Et community music perspektiv. In K. Stensæth, V. Krüger, & S. Fuglestad (Eds.), *I transitt – mellom til og fra. Om musikk og deltagelse i barnevern* (pp. 173–190). Oslo, Norway: NMH Research Publications.

Chaaban, J., Ghattas, H., Habib, R., Hanafi, S., Sahyoun, N., Salti, N., et al. (2010). *Socioeconomic survey of Palestinian refugees in Lebanon.* Beirut, Lebanon: American University of Beirut (AUB) and the United Nations Relief and Works Agency for Palestine Refugees in the Near East (UNRWA).

Christophersen, C. (2013). "Jeg bare tegnet et kunstverk": Om elevene og Den kulturelle skolesekken. In J.-K. Breivik & C. Christophersen (Eds.), *Den kulturelle skolesekken* (pp. 61–84). Oslo, Norway: Arts Council Norway.

Dahl, T., & Østern, T. P. (2019). Dybde//læring med overflate og dybde. In T. P. Østern, T. Dahl, A. Strømme, J. A. Petersen, A.-L. Østern, & S. Selander (Eds.), *Dybde//læring – en flerfaglig, relasjonell og skapende tilnærming* (pp. 39–56). Oslo, Norway: Universitetsforlaget.

Heggen, K. (2008). Profesjon og identitet. In A. Molander & L. I. Terum (red.), *Profesjonsstudier* (pp. 321–332). Oslo, Norway: Universitetsforlaget.

Holdhus, K., Waade, R., Romme, J. C., Almås, R. & Espeland, M. (2019). Skole og konsert – fra formidling til dialog (DiSko). Erfaringsrapport 2019. Høgskulen på Vestlandet.

Kalsnes, S. (2004). Musikkformidling i musikkutdanningen – mellom kunst, pedagogikk og politikk. In G. Johansen, S. Kalsnes, & Ø. Varkøy (Eds.), *Musikkpedagogiske utfordringer. Artikler om musikkpedagogisk teori og praksis* (pp. 92–110). Oslo, Norway, Cappelen Akademisk Forlag.

Kalsnes, S. (2012). *OASE. Om kulturskoleutvikling og lokal forankring av Den kulturelle skolesekken. Rapport fra et samarbeidsprosjekt mellom grunnskole, kulturskole og musikklærerutdanning* (NMH Research Publications 2012: 6). Oslo, Norway: Norwegian Academy of Music.

Kalsnes, S. (2013). Music outreach in Lebanon. In V. Storsve & B. Å. B. Danielsen (Eds.), *Løft blikket – gjør en forskjell. Erfaringer og ringvirkninger fra et musikkprosjekt i Libanon* (NMH Research Publications 2013: 9) (pp. 149–168). Oslo, Norway: Norwegian Academy of Music.

Kalsnes, S. (2014a). Kunstnerlærerens yrkesfelt. In E. Angelo & S. Kalsnes (Eds.), *Kunstner eller lærer? Profesjonsdilemmaer i musikk- og kunstpedagogisk utdanning* (pp. 42–63). Cappelen Damm Akademisk: Oslo, Norway.

Kalsnes, S. (2014b). Kulturskolen som ressurssenter – konsekvenser for kulturskolelærerrollen? In E. Angelo & S. Kalsnes (Eds.), *Kunstner eller lærer? Profesjonsdilemmaer i musikk- og kunstpedagogisk utdanning* (pp. 109–124). Cappelen Damm Akademisk: Oslo, Norway.

Nerland, M. (2004). Musikkpedagogikken og det musikkulturelle mangfoldet. In G. Johansen, S. Kalsnes, & Ø. Varkøy (Eds.), *Musikkpedagogiske utfordringer. Artikler om musikkpedagogisk teori og praksis* (pp. 135–148). Oslo, Norway, Cappelen Akademisk Forlag.

NIFU STEP. (2010). *Spørsmål til Skole-Norge spring 2010* (Report 14/2010). Oslo, Norway: NIFU STEP.

Norwegian Academy of Music. (2011). *Evaluering av Libanon-prosjektet basert på tilbakemeldinger fra involverte lærere ved NMH, studenter ved NMH og samarbeidspartnere i Libanon.*

Renshaw, P. (2003). *Connecting conversations: The changing voice of the artist. European league of institutes of arts teachers' academy.* Barcelona, Spain: Institut del Teatre avd Escola Massana.

Ruud, E. (2011). Musikk med helsekonsekvenser. Et musikkpedagogisk prosjekt for ungdommer i en palestinsk flyktningleir. *Nordic Network for Research in Music Education. Yearbook 12* (NMH Research Publications 2011:2) (pp. 59–80). Oslo, Norway: Norwegian Academy of Music.

Small, C. (1998). *Musicking: The meanings of performance and listening.* London: Wesleyan University Press.

Stige, B. (2005). Musikk som tilbud om deltakelse. In R. Säfvenbom (Ed.), *Fritid og aktiviteter i moderne oppvekst – grunnbok i aktivitetsfag* (pp. 121–146). Oslo, Norway: Universitetsforlaget.

Storsve, V., & Danielsen, B.Å.B. (2013). *Løft blikket – gjør en forskjell. Erfaringer og ring-virkninger fra et musikkprosjekt i Libanon.* NMH Research Publications 2013(9). Oslo, Norway Norwegian Academy of Music.

Storsve, V., Westby, I. A., & Ruud, E. (2009). Håp og anerkjennelse: Om et musikkprosjekt blant ungdommer i en palestinsk flyktningleir. In E. Ruud (Ed.), *Musikk i psykisk helsearbeid med barn og unge* (NMH Research Publications 2009(5)) (pp. 192–204). Oslo, Norway: Norwegian Academy of Music.

TCS: *The cultural schoolbag.* Retrieved from https://www.artsforyoungaudiences.no/

Veblen, K., & Olsson, B. (2002). Community music: Toward an in international overview. In R. Colwell & C. P. Richarson (Eds.), *The new handbook of research on music teaching and learning* (pp. 730–753). Oxford, UK: Oxford University Press.

Wenger, E. (2004). *Praksisfællesskaber – Læring, mening og identitet.* Copenhagen, Denmark: Hanz Reitzlers Forlag.

White Paper no. 11. (2008–2009). *Læreren Rollen og utdanningen.* Ministry of Education and Research, Norway.

A Creative Global Science Classroom: Crafting the Global Science Opera

Kathryn Urbaniak, Vivek Venkatesh, and Oded Ben-Horin

Abstract This paper details a narrative case study of the Global Science Opera (GSO) – the first opera initiative in history to produce and perform operas as a global community. During GSO productions, teams in up to 30 countries collaborate to create and perform a single science opera, thus exemplifying a global classroom. The research questions framed within this paper are twofold. Firstly, they focus on the pedagogical principles and teaching crafts that are potentially involved in an international complex multisite project of the kind GSO represents. Secondly, they focus on the relationship between what can be called arts-based pedagogic elements and science education-based elements. The chapter examines what aspects of such crafts are most important for a successful implementation of GSO productions. The study uses an exploratory approach, based on grounded theory methodology and principles, so as to provide an opportunity to gain a deeper understanding of 15 adult participants' perceptions of the learning and transfer experiences occurring within the GSO creation and performance for 3 successive annual opera productions. Findings are discussed in relation to the arts-based and inquiry-based pedagogical approaches favoured by the creators of GSO and reified by its practitioner community.

Introduction

Global Science Opera (GSO) is the first opera initiative in history to produce and perform operas as a global community. This creative education initiative is made possible through digital interactions and live-streaming involving a network of scientists, art institutions, schools and universities in all of the inhabited continents. GSO

K. Urbaniak · V. Venkatesh
Concordia University, Montreal, QC, Canada
e-mail: kathryn.urbaniak@concordia.ca; vivek.venkatesh@concordia.ca

O. Ben-Horin (✉)
Western Norway University of Applied Sciences, Bergen, Norway
e-mail: oded.ben@hvl.no

© Springer Nature Switzerland AG 2021
K. Holdhus et al. (eds.), *Music Education as Craft*, Landscapes: the Arts, Aesthetics, and Education 30, https://doi.org/10.1007/978-3-030-67704-6_12

exists at the meeting point of science and art, of pupils and scientists, of human cultures and of research and practice. GSO produces annual productions during which a global community explores interwoven science, art and technology within a creative and democratic inquiry process (Global Science Opera, 2017). During productions, teams in up to 30 countries each year collaborate to create and perform a single opera. This is achieved by dividing the opera's preliminary script (libretto) into a number of scenes equal to the number of participating countries early in the calendar year. Then, a team in each country develops an arts education performance (typically 2 min long). Performed in sequence, these various scenes combine to make a global opera production. The teams may choose to perform by live-streaming or pre-recorded video. The result is streamed on television as a complete educational opera.

Research Questions

The research questions framing this chapter are manifold. First, they focus on the pedagogical principles and teaching crafts that might be involved in an international complex multisite project. Second, they focus on the relationship between what can be called arts-based pedagogic elements and science education-based elements.

- To investigate what arts-based pedagogical principles can be gleaned from STEAM contexts, e.g. astrophysics and particle physics education, and discuss aspects of what teaching crafts could be involved
- To examine how a complex multisite international project – the GSO – can communicate scientific principles and possibly affect knowledge transfer and how different education crafts linked to arts and science can interact in such contexts

Summary of Context

The collaborators of the Global Science Opera (GSO) are an international group of scientists, artists, educators as well as students from elementary to university level who take part in the production and performance of the operas with the intent of stimulating curiosity about both science and the arts. Since 2014, schools and universities from 27 to 30 countries participate in both local and international activities which culminate in the live-streaming of an annual, three-act opera based on a scientific topic, grounded in a message of peace and collaboration.

The GSO approach is, in part, based on "Write An Opera" which was originally developed by the education department at the Royal Opera House in London and was later adapted and re-developed into Write a Science Opera (WASO) (Ben-Horin, Chappell, Halstead, & Espeland, 2017). The GSO workshops and materials similarly are founded in an inquiry-based science education (IBSE) approach with the goal of giving equal emphasis to both science and the arts, all the while working in an international context. The collaborative creative process is intended to be democratic and aims to be respectful of the different cultures of those involved (Robberstad, 2017). These pedagogical methods possess complexity as a common denominator – complexity in terms of people and participants involved, subjects and teaching items involved, challenges in timing and planning and a number of other factors very different from the idea of schooling as a relationship between one teacher and a group of students or between a specific part of a school subject and an accompanying learning trajectory for students. The GSO initiative might be considered even more complex than its forerunners given the participation across continents and its reliance on technology and various communication forms. Consequently, the kind of educational crafting involved in initiatives of this kind and what aspects of such crafts are the most important ones for successful implementation are interesting discussion questions.

Art-Based Pedagogies in Science Education

Empirically based research of the GSO process and product has thus far been scarce, a fact which put forth the need for the research described here. Science opera activities limited to single-school implementations in which school classrooms take part in simultaneous and intertwined art and science inquiry, however, have received more attention and enable a point of departure with regard to our understanding of the larger, global versions. Wise Humanizing Creativity (Chappell, Pender, Swinford, & Ford, 2016) is an approach to creativity in which co-creators (students and teachers) must consider ethical consequences of their creations and their own collaborative identity development as central in the creative process: individuals contribute while negotiating the needs of others, resulting in shared ownership. Taking this point of view of the creative process, Ben-Horin et al. (2017) found that interdisciplinary art/science educational environments of the type represented by science operas exemplify learning which directly relates to students' emotions and that it is precisely those emotions which drive the creative learning process. In other words, the "carrying over" of knowledge and information across disciplinary boundaries requires emotional engagement as a driving force. Furthermore, science operas can have the potential to increase student engagement in the educational process (this occurs by the educational design's creation of a continuous dependency (on the part of the student) on elements of one discipline in order to complete a task in another). Finally, the science opera environment may encourage students to value that which matters for the community, as they are constantly aware that the result of their creative process will be presented to the local community by means of a school performance.[1]

---

[1] Families and the local community were invited to observe the performances reported.

Researchers have asked if schools should be adopting an "arts across the curriculum" pedagogy, meaning that arts activities are taught for their intrinsic value but also employed in meaningful ways to teach other subjects. The successful implementation of arts across the curriculum often requires funding or a specific focus. Therefore, programmes may only run during periods when funding is available or rely on sympathetic school leaderships who value the role of the arts. But the arts can be used to raise the profile of a school at specific times of the year or aid recruitment (Buck & Snook, 2016). While some of the teachers and schools participating in GSO are implementing arts across the curriculum, it is not the norm for the majority of schools, and in some cases the teachers were working with extracurricular groups rather than as part of the curriculum.

Creativity is at the heart of culture, design and innovation, and students deserve an opportunity to take advantage of their creative talent within classroom and extracurricular settings (c.f., Craft et al., 2016). Students' understanding, perceptions and experiences of science can be strengthened through seeing it as a creative field (Gershon & Ben-Horin, 2014). Creative drama-based instruction involving spontaneous and unscripted learning with improvisation and role-play around real-life situations and experiences can increase the science achievements and scientific process skills of students (Taşkın-Can, 2013). Furthermore, creative drama-based instruction can lead students to better understand scientific concepts and also increase positive attitudes towards science (Cokadar & Cihan-Yılmaz, 2010).

Gershon and Ben-Horin (2014) have investigated the effects of using music in classrooms and as a means of conveying scientific ideas. They posit that inquiry-based science education (IBSE) and music – even if restricted by rules – are both crucial and creative activities. In their research, scientific education came forth as scientific inquiry and research processes, while music appeared restricted by genre, form, emotion and expression (Gershon & Ben-Horin, 2014). Gershon and Ben-Horin (2014) also indicated that producing science-inspired music (e.g. writing songs) and music-inspired science are effective for teaching IBSE, because they create an opportunity for students, teachers and scientists to examine scientific concepts and procedures from a more complete viewpoint.

Creative and innovative thinking in science, technology, engineering and mathematics (STEM) disciplines requires moving beyond a siloed separation between the traditionally logical STEM subjects and the creative arts. Research suggests that STEAM (STEM plus Art) education is able to cultivate the criticality and creativity necessary for learners' authentic engagement in both the science and artistic domains (Radziwill, Benton, & Moellers, 2015). However, educators face numerous challenges in implementing a STEAM approach. Zimmerman (2016) posits that novice teachers lack confidence in their abilities to teach lessons based in either inquiry- or art-based pedagogies, both of which are central to the success of a STEAM approach, in part because they require a high level of content knowledge but also the confidence to tolerate uncertainty in the classroom.

The CREAT-IT (Implementing Creative Strategies into Science Teaching) project (2013–2015) is an example of practitioner-led change in Europe that puts the emphasis on creativity and the incorporation of social media tools into science education (Craft et al., 2016). This project linked science education with engagement activities for students and teachers and also partially funded the first GSO activities, for example, teacher-student collaborative and dialogue activities (Science Cafes); cultural, artistic and role-playing activities (Science Theaters); training laboratories; mobility activities; and CREAT-IT project workshops (Craft et al., 2016). Teachers in primary and secondary science education were encouraged to participate in training seminars offered in the partner universities including the above-mentioned Write a Science Opera (WASO) methodology training course. Teaching kits provided teachers with the materials and opportunity to conduct experiments and laboratory-like activities, always grounded in inquiry-based teaching.

Methodology

We used an exploratory approach, based on grounded theory methodology and principles (Strauss & Corbin, 1990) to provide the opportunity to gain a deeper understanding of participants' perceptions of the learning and transfer experiences occurring within the GSO creation and performance. Specifically, we adopt a constructivist grounded theory approach (Charmaz, 2008) in analysing and interpreting the data. Such a methodology allows us to (i) refer to existing theoretical frameworks; (ii) account for and use themes already discussed in existing literature; and (iii) allow theoretical presuppositions and empirical evidence discussed in the literature to interact with the emergent codes and themes from the data collected for the present study. Using open "in vivo" coding and subsequent categorisation of codes into themes, we used a constant comparative method (Spiggle, 1994) of analysis to ensure that only codes that repeated themselves across multiple sources of data were used to construct themes discussed in the results, thereby enabling an approximation of theoretical saturation. In addition to rigorous analyses of interviews and opera performances, we applied qualitative content analysis (Bryman, 2008) as we searched for key themes from the data.

This qualitative research began by obtaining ethics approval from the Norwegian Centre for Research Data (NSD). Ethics approval was then also obtained at Concordia University in Canada, whose researchers undertook the analysis. Participating individuals' signed consent was then gained from selected opera participants who were all adults. These were the organisers, creators, classroom educators, scientific advisors/experts and theatre experts. No students aged under 18 years participated in the research due to ethics restraints.

All GSO's are publicly available on YouTube for viewing. We conducted blind reviews of the three operas. The first opera, Skylight, lasts 1 h 41 min and consists of 3 acts with 18 scenes and 3 additional sequences. The second opera, Ghost Particles, lasts 1 h and consists of 3 acts with 18 scenes, a scene at CERN and 3 additional sequences. The third opera, Moon Village, which was performed in December 2017, lasts 1 h 38 min with 3 acts, 31 scenes and 2 additional scenes.

We conducted 15 individual, semi-structured interviews (Kvale, 2007) with the adult participants, allowing us to gain an in-depth understanding of their experiences, understanding their perceptions of the learning and transfer experiences occurring within the GSO creation and performance, along with the supporting teaching. They also reported on their student participants' reactions and other reactions from parents and the wider community.

The semi-structured interview format afforded us the opportunity to probe more deeply into participants' responses and to ask follow-up questions leading to richer, more robust data (Kvale, 2007). Participants from all of the scenes and all three operas were invited to participate in the research, and anyone who responded positively was interviewed in person during the Global Hands-On Universe conference in Norway in 2016, by Skype or by email. The semi-structured interview protocol covered themes of the differences between the different operas, the co-creation process, the performances and the opera products themselves, as well as challenges faced and recommendations for future iterations of the GSO initiative.

How Has Light Pollution Been Addressed for Primary- and Secondary School-Aged Learners?

Light pollution is the theme of the first Global Science Opera. Currently, industrialisation and the broad use of natural environmental resources have become global challenges (Aydin, 2015). Light pollution, also known as an inappropriate or intrusive way of using light that disturbs living things, has become a central environmental concern worldwide and has made environment education a priority in the twenty-first century (Aydin, 2015). Studies have revealed that students have limited knowledge on the interdisciplinary nature of light pollution (Sadık, Çakan, & Artut, 2011; Shariff et al., 2016). The United Nations designated 2015 as the "International Year of Light (IYL)" which signified an opportunity for the global astronomical community to highlight the importance and preservation of dark skies for the natural environment through citizen science and public outreach (Walker, 2015; Walker, Buxner, & Montmerle, 2012; Walker & Pompea, 2011). The International Year of Light brought attention to projects including Dark Skies Rangers and Globe at Night, as well as Global Hands-On Universe (GHOU) and GSO.

How Has Particle Physics Been Addressed for Primary- and Secondary School-Aged Learners?

Particle physics, the topic of the second Global Science Opera, is rarely part of high school curricula, but the basic notions in physics are included in school syllabus in most countries (Kourkoumelis & Vourakis, 2016). Physics teachers face challenges in the development of an appropriate learning process for learners of particle physics. The challenges include the abstract nature of the material and the limited number of practical experiments that are suitable for school students (Wiener, Schmeling, & Hopf, 2015, 2017).

Some members of the particle physics educational community have generated classroom exercises and materials to aid the development of science education in schools and convey enthusiasm for new research to students and teachers (Bardeen, Johansson, & Jean Young, 2011). Activities like The Quark Puzzle (Gettrust, 2010) present a promising learning activity that can be used to teach particle physics to a wider audience. Gettrust (2010) introduced this hands-on project that helps physics students to understand quarks and their role in forming composite particles. In addition, the realisation that school children develop preferences about the subjects they like in primary school means various academic establishments are now focusing some of their public engagement activities towards the younger ages, including primary schools, such as games about CERN (The European Organisation for Nuclear Research), CERN's ATLAS resources (Barnett et al., 2012) and science content such as atoms and particles (Pavlidou & Lazzeroni, 2016).

Findings from Analysis of Opera Scenes

If the objective of participation in the opera is for students to explore learning through different media, then it has been achieved. However, the educational merit is skewed more on the side of producing the opera than on viewing the final products. In other words, participation in the development of a Global Science Opera is in itself a major learning experience for the students involved in the production. In the words of one of the instructor participants: "… [a]s a teacher, I would show this to fellow teachers in terms of what can be achieved with a creative and intricately planned project such as this".

Each year the viewing experience improves with supplementary materials, subtitles, explanations and signposting. The subjects are taught more explicitly, and the overall quality of the contributions is higher based on blind review by researchers as well as feedback from participants. If broken down scene by scene, some scenes could be used with supporting materials as distinct lessons. If the objective of viewing is to entertain the viewer, then this is often achieved. If the objective of viewing is to educate the viewer, then again this is often achieved depending on the viewer's prior knowledge and understanding of the scientific content knowledge. It is interesting to see how different schools placed emphasis on different elements (i.e. content, visuals, music, coherence, etc.) – possibly indicative of within which subject they were originally working.

It would be impossible to describe all of the scenes, the creative elements they focus on and the science that each scene communicates but the following provides some highlights. The visit to CERN in Switzerland in the second opera gives context to the scientific knowledge content presented in the opera and brings everything together with a scientist explaining the experiments conducted at CERN while also explaining why and how the experiments are conducted. Similarly, the final Dutch scene in the third opera, which brings together the opera characters in the future in a talk show format, serves as both a summary of the plot, including themes of repatriation, but also situates the science of Moon Village because it is filmed at the European Space Agency Technology Centre. This allowed the children, more than half of whom were refugees, to visit the Agency during the making of the scene.

Scenery and eco-scenography are seen throughout, in addition to the use of props. In the Chilean scene in the third opera, umbrellas are used as props to represent the movement of satellite dishes being used to gather data. The Slovakian scene in the third opera contains a lesson explaining gravity in which the moon children wear headphones as a prop to explain how sound waves need a medium to spread.

The Chilean scene in the second opera included high school students doing interpretive dance with text on screen to explain how dancers' movements represent the workings of the Large Hadronic Collider. This scaffolded the students as to what they are seeing. Other music-based pieces include choral scenes from many countries including England, Wales, Sweden, Brazil, Argentina and Germany, as well as a rock music video from Romania, folk pop from Ireland and a pop video from the USA.

Findings from Analysis of Interviews

In interviewing adult participants involved in the science operas, it is clear that the roles, backgrounds and expertise vary greatly, as one would expect with an international endeavour such as GSO. The scope of involvement also varied with some participants working only on one scene, some on multiple scenes or larger themes such as musical motifs or the libretto. In some cases, due to language, geography or polymath participants, the scenes are developed more in isolation. Sometimes many people are involved in building a single scene such as an American scene with contributions from the UK, Norway and Greece. But throughout, interviewees mentioned that the relationships and trust between participants are of paramount importance. The GSO community itself endeavours to be an accepting, cross-cultural community of passionate people, mostly educators of some variety. Some people in the community identify strongly as either a scientist or an artist, but most embrace both sides, and all of whom are committed to bring science, arts and creativity to a wider audience, often with themes of peace and environmentalism. Members provide each other support both virtually and in person. For example, more artistic members draw on the expertise of scientists to validate their materials as well as the explanations they are using with the students. The more scientific members experience support and encouragement as they learn to embrace new kinds of creative processes. These relationships create a collective educational craftsmanship which would not be possible with a single teacher in isolation.

Challenges faced included that as students get older from one opera to the next, thereby moving up a grade (or graduating) necessitated a fresh start from one year to the next. The flip side of this is that new students were involved each year. Another issue was choosing which schools to include within a country for a particular year. Two participants in different countries spoke of the challenge of choosing the school for the next opera because the school from the previous opera wanted to participate again, but the decision had been made to give a new school an opportunity to participate each year in order to broaden the GSO community and due to the limited number of scenes available each year. The potential to scale up to multiple operas is limited by time and resources, but as a process would theoretically be possible given the network of support within the community. Multiple participants spoke of the important encouragement, recognition and support they received from their ministries of education, and school administration, as well as the science and arts experts within the GSO community which allows them the opportunity to participate year after year. The local communities participated with local musicians coming into schools to participate and perform. Parental involvement was viewed as positive, and for some schools, the opera has become a watershed moment where parents talk about the school before and after the opera as a defining point in time for the children and school as a whole. Educators also described the children translating and explaining the science to their parents while watching the opera performances streamed.

Findings Related Specifically to Engagement with Scientific Concepts

Some of the instructors talked specifically about the use of IBSE in creating their opera scenes, "… but you can't use only one methodology… you do need to do lots of background and build it up… help the students make the links". In terms of presenting the scientific content, approaches included talks in classes, experiments, demonstrations, guest speakers from local universities or scientific associations and online visits. Some classrooms such as Spain focused on a project-based approach. Some participants were in regular contact with science experts, while others used Google rather than using experts from GSO or availed of in-house expertise. When asked how much of the science the children grasped one participant replied "probably about as much as me… a lot". Another participant said, "Some of the kids really understood the science and explained it well to the teacher... and others didn't grasp as much".

Findings Related to Perceptions of Art and Opportunities for Differential Abilities

Science operas in general, and GSO specifically, are based on inquiry-based science education, implying student-led participation. This approach varied with some scenes emphasising student-led development of music, costume, scenography and performance/acting rather than the development of the opera design, libretto and characters. Given the lack of classroom time and the age constraints of the children participating, there is a limit to the types of student involvement in areas such as composition. However, in scenes where university students were involved such as Serbia and Spain, the creative approach was observed to be more democratic, and the students led the composition of the music and songs. In Chile the dance choreography was also developed democratically; interviews with the Chilean instructor revealed that "[the opera and plot] gave me a new look at music, ... and how to define a scientific motif using a melody... the spirit of the story also had a great influence".

All of the interviewees agreed that participants learned more from participating than observing the opera as a final result. Participation in the opera is perceived to be open and democratic. In fact, as was related to use by the Dutch instructor, the deaf and differently abled schools in the Netherlands were chosen in part "to show that anyone can participate".

The quality of the pedagogic, scientific and artistic product of each scene varied greatly, as one would expect when the resources, infrastructure and opportunities varied so much between countries and participants. As one artist stated, "the scenes themselves are creative... but the aesthetic challenge is to find unity when the scenes are so different". By instilling standards, the opera would lose the flat, democratic and welcoming culture which is core to its existence, and therefore this variance has remained in the operas. "If you want a better product you have to be prepared to say 'It's not good enough'", and the creators have decided that participation and openness are prioritised over the aesthetic quality of the final product, at least at this stage of the opera development. The opera as it is has a "strong message and the opera is a catalyst". How unity is found in future iterations of the opera is an ongoing challenge and process.

Art/Science Tension

A tension between art and science might have been expected. However, the sentiment expressed by many participants was that of this educator: "there is no art and science barrier... but I know my experience is not normal". An artist states, "The science and art – everyone is eager to have this combination, so that is not the problem. Art is always saying something, trying to communicate something, and in our case, it is science. It never competes. Art is a communication form". Another participant said, "A show is always about a subject, doesn't matter what (subject) it is – both science and art have their role. They (the scientists) don't see their science as the end point. They see their science as a way to improve the world".

If anything, the scale of the project appeared more challenging than the possible art-science divide. Another educator said, "Most people involved are already combining art and science, and done small things, but nothing this big". The other obvious tension is between "wanting to let the kids guide versus a product you can actually show people".

Discussion

The Global Science Opera (GSO) is in its early phases. Our findings point at a variety of advantages as well as areas of potential improvement. There is evidence of the positive impact of opening doors for pupils and their teachers to cross (at least) two kinds of boundaries: the one between the classroom and the world outside it on a global scale and the one between art and science. It is from here that we return to this book's overarching theme of the craftsmanship of music (and in the case of GSO, STEAM) education. An important part of the teacher's craftsmanship needed to implement the GSO relates to the building of relationships and trust between participants in a rapidly changing, multicultural, globalised society in which technological applications provide a continuous flow of new opportunities. We understand GSO, based on our findings, to be a creative framework for the teacher's craftsmanship based largely on the context which it provides: viewed from the perspective of Wise Humanising Creativity and its affordances in science opera (Ben-Horin et al., 2017), the GSO allows pupils to potentially experience a common identity development with people in other areas of the world and who adhere to different cultural, religious and educational traditions than they themselves do. Opening the doors between art and science teaching also has potential in this context, and the collaboration with internationally acclaimed scientific institutions such as CERN seems to have provided ample inspiration for artistic productions worldwide while encouraging new questions amongst pupils. However, there is still room for improvement with regard to how the art and science interact. For example, the research provided here does not account for how different scientific topics (e.g. astronomy and particle physics) could interact differently with the arts due to the characteristics of both the exploration processes and equipment employed in those respective scientific fields. An important principle which we may base on our analysis, however, is that science and art should and can be placed on equal grounds and that it is not necessary to view the one discipline as a "tool" in the learning of the other. Negotiating that complexity within a globalised classroom is an aspect of STEAM education's craftsmanship that will consequently require further development in the future.

Acknowledgements This research was funded by the Norwegian Research Council's project "Integrating Science of Oceans, Physics and Education (iSCOPE)" 2015-2019. The authors would like to thank the pupils, teachers, scientists and artists who took part in the Global Science Opera productions reported in this text. Furthermore, we thank the European Commission's Horizon 2020 project "Developing an Engaging Science Classroom (CREATIONS)" for its support in the implementation of GSO's in 2016 and 2017, which to a large extent enabled the research conducted here.

References

Aydin, G. (2015). The effects of computer-aided concept cartoons and outdoor science activities on light pollution. *International Electronic Journal of Elementary Education, 7*(2), 142.

Bardeen, M. G., Johansson, E. K., & Jean Young, M. (2011). Particle physics outreach to secondary education. *Annual Review of Nuclear and Particle Science, 61,* 149–170.

Barnett, R. M., Johansson, K. E., Kourkoumelis, C., Long, L., Pequenao, J., Reimers, C., et al. (2012). *Learning with the ATLAS experiment at CERN. Philadelphia: Institute of Physics Publishing.*

Ben-Horin, O., Chappell, K. A., Halstead, J. & Espeland, M. (2017). Designing creative interdisciplinary science and art interventions in schools: The case of Write a Science Opera (WASO). *Cogent Education, 4*(1). Available at http://www.tandfonline.com/doi/abs/10.108 0/2331186X.2017.1376926

Bryman, A. (2008). *Social research methods*. Oxford, UK: Oxford University Press.

Buck, R., & Snook, B. (2016). Teaching the arts across the curriculum: Meanings, policy and practice. *International Journal of Education & the Arts, 17*(29). Retrieved from http://www.ijea.org/v17n29/

Chappell, K., Pender, T., Swinford, E., & Ford, K. (2016). Making and being made: Wise humanising creativity in interdisciplinary early years arts education. *International Journal of Early Years Education, 24*(3), 254–278.

Charmaz, K. (2008). Grounded theory as an emergent method. In S. N. Hesse-Biber & P. Leav (Eds.), *The handbook of emergent methods* (pp. 155–170). New York: Guilford.

Cokadar, H., & Cihan-Yılmaz, G. (2010). Teaching ecosystems and matter cycles with creative drama activities. *Journal of Science Educational Technology, 19,* 80–89.

Craft, A., Ben Horin, O., Sotiriou, M., Stergiopoulos, P., Sotiriou, S., Hennessy, S., et al. (2016). CREAT-IT: Implementing creative strategies into science teaching. In *New developments in science and technology education* (pp. 163–179). New York: Springer.

Gershon, W. S., & Ben-Horin, O. (2014). Deepening inquiry: What processes of making music can teach us about creativity and ontology for inquiry based science education. *International Journal of Education & the Arts, 15*(19), 1–37.

Gettrust, E. (2010). The quark puzzle: A novel approach to visualizing the color symmetries of quarks. *The Physics Teacher, 48*(5), 312–315.

Global Science Opera. (2017). Website. www.globalscienceopera.com

Kourkoumelis, C., Vourakis, S., & ATLAS Collaboration. (2016). How the HYPATIA analysis tool is used as a hands-on experience to introduce HEP to high schools. *Nuclear and Particle Physics Proceedings, 273,* 1244–1249.

Kvale, S. (2007). *Doing interviews*. Los Angeles: Sage.

Pavlidou, M., & Lazzeroni, C. (2016). Particle physics for primary schools—Enthusing future physicists. *Physics Education, 51*(5), 054003.

Radziwill, N. M., Benton, M. C., & Moellers, C. (2015). From STEM to STEAM: Reframing what it means to learn. *The STEAM Journal, 2*(1), 1. https://doi.org/10.5642/steam.20150201.3

Robberstad, J. (2017). *Creativity and ecoscenography in the Global Science Opera. How the integration of ecoscenography unto the Global Science Opera affects the creative process.* Master's thesis. Western Norway University College of Applied Sciences.

Sadık, F., Çakan, H., & Artut, K. (2011). Analysis of the environmental problems pictures of children from different socio-economical level. *Elementary Education Online, 10*(3), 1066–1080.

Shariff, N. N. M., Osman, M. R., Faid, M. S., Hamidi, Z. S., Sabri, S. N. U., Zainol, N. H., & Husien, N. (2016). Creating awareness on light pollution (CALP) project: Essential requirement for school-university collaboration. In *Industrial Engineering, Management Science and Application (ICIMSA), 2016 International Conference on IEEE* (pp. 1–4).

Spiggle, S. (1994). Analysis and interpretation of qualitative data in consumer research. *Journal of Consumer Research, 21*, 491–503.

Strauss, A. L., & Corbin, J. (1990). *Basics of qualitative research: Grounded theory procedures and techniques.* Thousand Oaks, CA: Sage.

Taşkın-Can, B. (2013). The effects of using creative drama in science education on students' achievements and scientific process skills. *İlköğretim Online, 12*(1), 120–131.

Walker, C. E. (2015). Session 21.7–education programs promoting light pollution awareness and IYL2015. *Proceedings of the International Astronomical Union, 11*(A29A), 490–499.

Walker, C. E., Buxner, S., & Montmerle, T. (2012). The impact of light pollution education through a global star-hunting campaign & classroom curricula. *International Astronomical Union. Proceedings of the International Astronomical Union, 10*(H16), 732.

Walker, C. E., & Pompea, S. M. (2011). National education program for energy efficient illumination engineering. In *Proceedings of SPIE*, 8065, 80650Q-1

Wiener, G. J., Schmeling, S. M., & Hopf, M. (2015). Can grade-6 students understand quarks? Probing acceptance of the subatomic structure of matter with 12-year-olds. *European Journal of Science and Mathematics Education, 3*(4), 313–322.

Wiener, G. J., Schmeling, S. M., & Hopf, M. (2017). Introducing 12-year-olds to elementary particles. *Physics Education, 52*(4), 044001.

Zimmerman, A. S. (2016). Developing confidence in STEAM: Exploring the challenges that novice elementary teachers face. *The STEAM Journal, 2*(2). https://doi.org/10.5642/steam.20160202.15

The Craft of Teaching Musical Improvisation Improvisationally: Towards a Theoretical Framework

Nick Sorensen

Abstract This chapter explores a specific and unique aspect of the craft of music education by addressing the particular pedagogical challenge of: how do we teach musical improvisation improvisationally? The response offered to this question is in two parts: the first is concerned with *what* we are trying to teach when we teach musical improvisation, and the second is concerned with *how* we should teach musical improvisation. A greater understanding of the *what* and the *how* provides us with knowledge about the craft of teaching musical improvisation improvisationally, a unique craft that is of special significance to the discourse of music educators. A theoretical framework that views teaching musical improvisation improvisationally as a hybrid craft enriches this discourse. The framework unites the theory and craft of musical improvisation with the findings of empirical research into the improvisational craft of teacher expertise (Sorensen, Improvisation and teacher expertise: a comparative case study. PhD thesis. Bath Spa University, 2014). These two crafts are brought together by a third dimension of metacognitive self-reflection, characterised by the ability to transfer knowledge between these two domains and to critically reflect on this process. The chapter concludes with some examples of how the theory is put into practice drawing on a case study of an innovative programme of improvisation workshops offered at the British and Irish Modern Music Institute (BIMM) in Bristol, UK, and offers suggestions for the further professional development of music educators.

Introduction

This chapter explores a specific and unique aspect of the craft of music education by addressing the particular pedagogical challenge of "how do we teach musical improvisation improvisationally?" The response I offer to this question is in two parts: the first is concerned with *what* we are trying to teach when we teach musical

N. Sorensen (✉)
Bath Spa University, Bath, UK
e-mail: improvisingschool@yahoo.co.uk

© Springer Nature Switzerland AG 2021
K. Holdhus et al. (eds.), *Music Education as Craft*, Landscapes: the Arts, Aesthetics, and Education 30, https://doi.org/10.1007/978-3-030-67704-6_13

improvisation, and the second is concerned with *how* we should teach musical improvisation. My argument is that this greater understanding of the *what* and the *how* provides us with knowledge about the craft of teaching musical improvisation improvisationally, a unique craft that is of special significance to the discourse of music educators.

What do we mean when we talk about an activity as a craft? The Cambridge English Dictionary defines craft as "skill and experience, especially in relation to making objects; a job or activity that needs skill and experience, or something produced using skill and experience". These ideas, which date back to the Middle Ages, emphasise the practical activity of making objects (a wheel, a pot or a tapestry) with expertise: one progressed through the stages of apprentice and journeyman to become a master craftsman. The development of craftsmanship is gained through experience over a long period of time.

However, as Richard Sennett (2008) points out, the notion of craft is poorly understood if it is only equated to manual skills and that activities are improved when they are seen as a skilled craft. The notion of craft can therefore be applied to a wide range of practices (to which can be included teaching and musical improvisation), characterised by taking a pride in one's work, a pride that is rewarded through the level of skill and commitment brought to the work and by wanting to do things well for their own sake. Sennett also talks about "slow craft time", the process through which skills mature beyond imitation through an evolution that promotes reflection and imagination.

Michael Eraut (1994) conceptualises reflection and imagination as the interplay between theory and practice. This dynamic relationship generates craft knowledge, sometimes referred to as practical knowledge. This interpretative form of knowledge, which requires the demonstration of professional judgement, is expressed only in practice and learned only through the experience of practice. This is a form of knowledge that is essentially non-verbal, in that it cannot be reduced to simple technical descriptions, which is not sufficiently supported by what we call propositional knowledge or *knowing that*. The knowledge that is embedded in craft knowledge is *knowing how*.

When we talk about a craft, we are talking about activity that is value driven; practice that is informed by pride, wisdom and experience and is shaped by professional judgement and which has an intrinsic worth. When we apply these to the craft of teaching musical improvisation improvisationally, I would argue that we are talking about a special and unique craft characterised by hybridity. This is a craft formed by uniting craft skills and knowledge from two different domains: the craft of teaching and the craft of musical improvisation. However, there is also a third dimension, the metacognitive craft of transferring knowledge, skills and understanding from one domain to another. Exploring this complex interrelationship is the purpose of this chapter that, hopefully, will have a significant impact on the discourse of music educators.

The question of *what* we are teaching when we are teaching musical improvisation raises a number of important issues; for example, can musical improvisation actually be taught? Derek Bailey (1980) makes the oft-quoted point that "improvisation enjoys the curious distinction of being the most widely practised of all musical activities and the least acknowledged and understood" (p. 1). Being able to improvise therefore privileges the craft knowledge of *knowing how* over propositional knowledge (knowing that something is improvised) which leads to the claim that the craft of musical education is best learnt through the experience of improvising. Consequently, it is of fundamental importance to acknowledge that *how* we teach needs to be grounded in an understanding of the nature and craft of improvisation and needs to reflect the improvisational spirit. The medium needs to reflect the message.

Improvisation is a particular mode of creativity, characterised by the fact that it takes place in the moment as it were. This has given rise to multiple misunderstandings about improvisation, for example, something that is made up on the spur of the moment must necessarily be an imperfect art, since as Gioia (1988, p. 66) remarks, "improvisation is doomed, it seems, to offer a pale imitation of the perfection attained by composed music". However, saxophonist Steve Lacy offers a more positive distinction between composition and improvisation. When asked to give a 15 second explanation of the difference between composition and improvisation:

> Straight away he replied: "The main difference is that in composition you have all the time you need to think about what you are going to say in fifteen seconds, whereas in improvisation you have only fifteen seconds to say what you have to say." He had taken exactly fifteen seconds to answer me. (Rzewski,1979, as cited in Lacy, 2006, p. 70)

Teaching this particular form of creativity is about enabling individuals to say what they have to say in the moment, something that requires much more than the development of musical technique. The key argument of this chapter is that the teaching of improvisation has to be undertaken improvisationally. As Holdhus et al. (2016) point out, whilst the literature on the teaching of improvisation is vast, this literature and that of the corresponding teaching practices do not necessarily address improvisational teaching skills. This is a significant omission given the emerging interest in pedagogical improvisation as a professional practice (Sawyer, 2007) and is possibly exacerbated because we do not address either music education or musical improvisation as crafts.

This chapter addresses this omission by articulating an improvisational pedagogy for teachers of musical improvisation, a pedagogy that has been described as "musical improvisation's little sister" (Holdhus, 2019). This furthers our conceptual understanding of what it means to teach musical improvisation improvisationally and to support continuing professional development of music teachers. As Holdhus (2019) observes "the literature of pedagogical improvisation in music education is sparse and I suspect this reflects a rather low level of awareness about pedagogical improvisation in the field of music education" (p. 13). This chapter offers a contribution to the literature by offering a theoretical framework that views teaching musical improvisation improvisationally as a hybrid craft derived from the craft of musical improvisation and the craft of teaching. The framework offers a third dimension of metacognitive self-reflection, characterised by the ability to transfer knowledge between these two domains and to critically reflect on this process. This approach, through raising levels of awareness of the synergies between the *what* and the how of teaching musical improvisation, enriches the discourse from being one-dimensional (based solely on music pedagogy) to a three-dimensional discourse formed from an understanding of the craft of pedagogical expertise, the craft of musical improvisation and a metacognitive/critical reflective dimension.

The theoretical framework is constructed from two sources, uniting the theory and craft of musical improvisation with the findings of research undertaken into the improvisational craft of teacher expertise (Sorensen, 2014). In the introduction to this book, Magne Espeland foregrounds the importance of experience, in particular the significance of personal experience. In doing so he makes no claims that his experiences are better or richer than the experiences of others but rather that they generate and offer new insights. I shall be following his example, given that experience is the foundation of craft knowledge. The insights that I offer in this chapter are derived from my own personal and professional experiences and include insights gained from learning (and being taught) to improvise, of leading improvisation workshops, of observing improvisation workshops, undertaking empirical research into teacher expertise and teaching drama and music.

The chapter is structured as follows. I begin by looking at the craft of improvisation, articulating the ideas and assumptions about improvisation that inform my position as a writer. I then address the issue of *what* we are teaching when we teach improvisation, identifying four dimensions that inform the craft of musical improvisation. Following this I articulate the *how* of teaching improvisationally, drawing on empirical research undertaken to explore the improvisational nature of expert teaching. The four dimensions of the craft of musical improvisation and the four processes of the craft of teaching are brought together to provide a theoretical framework to inform the craft of teaching of musical improvisation improvisationally.

The chapter concludes with some examples of how the theory is put into practice drawing on a case study of an innovative programme of improvisation workshops offered at the British and Irish Modern Music Institute (BIMM) in Bristol, UK, and offers suggestions for the further professional development of music educators.

The Craft of Improvisation: Some Key Ideas and Assumptions

Improvisation is an elusive phenomenon to pin down; it is ever present and everywhere, permeating everyday life. As Simon Rose (2017) points out, "Improvisation is a pervasive aspect of being human, in every sphere of life, enabling existence; life without the improvisational response is difficult to imagine" (p. 5). He goes on to argue that the way in which the concept of improvisation becomes constructed is of critical importance as this defines its role in practice, in education and elsewhere. It is therefore imperative to articulate the assumptions that underpin the way we understand improvisation as this informs the way it can be taught. The following assumptions are informed by my own experiences of learning the craft of becoming an improvising musician and research that I have undertaken into the phenomenon of improvisation.

Given the fact that improvisation can be found anywhere and everywhere, the first assumption that I make is that we can make a distinction between art and life, based on an understanding that the former is an expression of, and is grounded in, the latter. The phenomenon of improvisation is not exclusive to either of these contexts but is a feature; one could argue it is a defining characteristic, of both. A further distinction, one that is particularly useful within discussions such as these, is that within the field of "the arts", we find a body of conceptual and theoretical writings on the importance and nature of improvisation, an important body of knowledge that informs the craft of improvisatory practices. Until relatively recently, there have not been similar attempts to develop theories of improvisation within social (life) contexts. The long-standing tradition of describing improvisatory practices in the arts can be traced back to the Ancient Greeks and such writings, including those concerning music, are a strong cultural force.

Improvisation within artistic practice is a bounded (or boundaried) activity, and therefore it is easier to articulate intentionality and to identify the skills necessary for the craft of improvising within such contexts. This has an additional advantage in that it provides a body of knowledge that can be applied to social contexts. This knowledge can either be applied metaphorically, as in the case of using "the jazz band" as a metaphor for leadership (Sorensen, 2013) or directly by using techniques derived from drama and theatre practice to develop creativity within organisations (Dudeck & McClure, 2017). The application of our knowledge and understanding of improvisation from one context to another is at the heart of the insights offered in this chapter. In order to articulate a framework for teaching improvisation improvisationally, I shall be looking at what we know about improvisation within music (an artistic context) and combine it with what we know about improvisation in teaching (a social context).

The Craft of Musical Improvisation

As has been noted above, the way in which the concept of improvisation becomes constructed is of critical importance in defining its role in practice, in education and elsewhere. Having a clear understanding of the nature of improvisation in music is therefore important because it provides the framework for what we are trying to teach. The following definition provides the basis for understanding the craft of musical improvisation, *what* we are attempting to do when we teach musical improvisation.

Musical improvisation is a mode of intentional creative action that has unpredictable and uncertain outcomes. These outcomes are derived from *real-time* interactions, which may involve other people (musicians and/or audience) or the material environment in which the improvisation takes place. Improvisers create music within a paradoxical paradigm in that they act with the intention to be unintentional and within this context they are required to make spontaneous and intuitive decisions derived from interactions with other performers (as outlined above) and the dynamic interplay between fixed (non-negotiable) structures and the informal, dynamic and generative structures. The conditions that frame improvisational action are also dependent on the permission that the improviser gives themselves, or is given to them, to act in this way (Sorensen, 2014).

What this definition tells us is that the craft of musical improvisation involves developing a broad range of skills and dispositions that are as much social as they are strictly musical and that four dimensions inform the craft of musical improvisation:

1. The contextual dimension
2. The dialogic dimension
3. The affective dimension
4. The cultural dimension

I will provide a brief description of each of them in turn.

1. The Contextual Dimension

You can't improvise on nothing, man. Charlie Mingus – jazz bass player and composer (Santoro, 2000, p. 271)

All improvisation requires a context. This includes some form of source material, tradition or idiom that informs the basis of the improvisation, providing the material that the improviser will use and can summon up in the moment. It can also include the situation in which the improvisation takes place. Therefore, there is an obvious imperative to provide musicians with the technique, musical resources and vocabulary that will support their development as an improviser. For a jazz musician, this might mean learning to play the melody and the chord changes for a standard tune but in performance to play as if they do not know what to play, to put this knowledge to one side. Whilst this might form a substantial amount of what is, and can be, taught, it is not the whole picture.

2. The Dialogic Dimension

Improvisation is a relational activity in that it is fundamentally dialogic. The implications of this means that individual technique, whilst important, is in many ways subservient to being able to respond and react within the context of the performance: with other musicians, the audience or other material conditions of place and space. The implication of this is that improvisers need to develop the ability to listen and respond – listening is, after all, a fundamental skill for musicians. Whilst this is possibly self-evident, Lash (2003) argues that it is of primary importance for improvising musicians. For instance, the London improvising scene has been described as being one of virtuoso listening. Bass player Barry Guy describes the kind of listening that goes on as being "a decoding of the on-going musical argument" (Lash, 2003. p. 4). So a priority for improvising musicians is that they develop the ability to relate to other musicians through listening carefully to what is happening and then making decisions as to how they will respond. Consequently, there is a need for music educators to develop a pedagogy of listening (Sorensen, Gardiner, Johnson, & Jones, 2019) that addresses this relational dimension and provides them with an understanding of what to do when they are *not* playing.

3. The Affective Dimension

The affective dimension of improvisation is concerned with *feel* and goes beyond having an understanding of the context or the idiom of the musical improvisation. The importance of the affective dimension of teaching improvisation was a foundational principle of Lennie Tristano (1919–1978). Tristano was a jazz pianist who came to prominence on the New York jazz scene in the 1940s when jazz was undergoing a radical evolution due to the development of be-bop. He is considered to be one of the first teachers of jazz improvisation, and, at a time when teaching jazz revolved around technical issues, he developed a more holistic approach. His underlying belief was that the jazz musician's function is "to feel" and that this was gained through attending to listening and emulating other great jazz musicians. He stated that "you have to be influenced by all great jazz musicians, no matter what instruments they play, because the essence of jazz is feeling, it's not really the notes, it's the feeling behind" (Shim, 2007, p. 124).

I would argue that what Tristano is saying about jazz musicians could be applied to all improvising in all musical situations. It is important to be able to go beyond the notes and have an understanding of the feeling, the affective dimension of the musical situation and the social context (other musicians, audience, place and time) that define the improvisation. This is principally gained through the experience of engaging in improvisation both as a participant and as part of an audience.

4. The Cultural Dimension

A defining characteristic of improvisation is that the improviser gives her- or himself permission to improvise. This is significant as it articulates the empowering nature of improvisation. There are those who argue that creativity (and I count improvisation as a particular mode of creativity) cannot be taught but that one learns to be creative (or an improviser) by experiencing the conditions within which creative action takes place. The imperative for the teacher of musical improvisation is to create the conditions, the appropriate culture, in which permission is given to improvise.

The concept of culture (usually discussed in relation to organisations) is perhaps easier to comprehend than it is to describe. Essentially it is "the way we do things around here" and is concerned with the structures and boundaries that define the actions that are taken. Culture cannot be looked at in isolation as it is defined by its relationship to structure and power. The cultural conditions that enable improvisatory practice and learning to take place are important to understand, for, as Hopkins, Ainscow and West (1994) point out, culture (of an educational context) holds the key to improving student learning. Learning cultures provide a framework for learning, are situationally unique, have their own mind-set (in relation to what happens in the external environment) and provide a lens for the way that the world is viewed

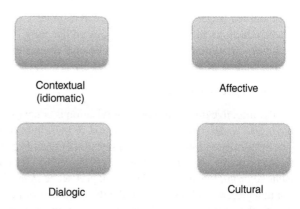

Fig. 1 The four
dimensions of the craft of
musical improvisation

Contextual
(idiomatic)

Affective

Dialogic

Cultural

(Stoll, 1998). Providing an experiential understanding of a culture that encourages improvisation is therefore an important dimension of teaching musical improvisation.

These four dimensions articulate the key characteristics of the craft of musical improvisation; they comprise the *what* we are aiming to do when teaching musical improvisation. These dimensions are shown in Fig. 1.

The Craft of Teaching Improvisationally

These four dimensions identify *what* teachers of musical improvisation need to address; they articulate the essence of the craft of musical improvisation. As we can see, this goes beyond purely musical issues and requires an awareness and sensitivity of the situated, social and affective dimensions of improvisational practice. The craft of musical improvisation includes having the ability to make judgements in the moment about when to intervene and respond within an improvisation. In the next section, I address *how* musical improvisation can be taught improvisationally. This draws on an understanding of the relationship between teacher expertise and improvisation, of how the craft of teaching, at its most developed expert level, is fundamentally improvisational.

The view of improvisational teaching that I offer is derived from the findings of empirical research undertaken to explore the craft of expert teaching by observing and interviewing seven secondary school teachers of a range of subjects in the UK (Sorensen, 2014). The findings of this research showed that the practice of "teachers with expertise" was fundamentally improvisatory and that their craft was derived from four interrelated processes: (1) utilising tacit knowledge; (2) employing a dialogic pedagogy; (3) personalisation (of learning, the teacher and the learning environment); and (4) continual adaptation through self-reflection.

These four processes are at the heart of what it means to teach improvisationally, and I shall consider them each in turn.

1. Utilising Tacit Knowledge

Teaching improvisationally demands that you are able to make decisions, professional judgements, in the moment. These decisions are not random but grounded in experience; they have become unconscious competences. Teachers with this tacit knowledge are able to draw upon a broad range of responses to situations in order to provide what may seem like automatic responses in what they do. This was clearly explained by several of the teachers who were involved in my research:

> Barbara: *I think a lot of your expertise over time becomes second nature. So whilst when I started I might plan lessons in great detail, write down every question I was going to ask, I think of these questions immediately now.*

Barbara went on to acknowledge that being able to teach improvisationally was a confidence issue, which is linked to being willing to take risks:

> Barbara: *With experience there is less fear of things going wrong and that it is OK to chuck an idea out into the open and run with it ... I think there needs to be an element of things coming on automatic pilot.*

2. Employing a Dialogic Pedagogy

Teaching improvisationally involves seeing teaching and learning as a relational and interactive process, characteristics of dialogic teaching. The dominant mode of teaching that I observed was based on skilled questioning to stimulate responses from the classes. Establishing dialogue in the classroom was one of the principle tasks that these teachers engaged in and was based on a genuine interest and engagement with their students. Dialogic teaching is by definition improvisatory, as you can never predict which ways a conversation will go. Being adept at teaching in this way meant that the teachers developed the skill of being able to take a range of different, and sometimes unexpected, contributions from the class and relate them to the lessons' main learning objective.

Eliciting responses from the class allows students to inform the direction of learning and is a way of engaging and empowering them in the learning as co-constructors of knowledge. This can be challenging for some teachers: a dialogic approach to teaching implies at least two voices, and, as Bakhtin (1993) points out, there is an underlying assumption of difference rather than identity. Accepting different views and opinions can pose problems for less experienced teachers as can being able to cope with the ambiguity of open-ended discussions.

3. Personalisation (of Learning, the Teacher and the Learning Environment)

All teaching is a relational activity, and the ability to develop positive relationships is a key skill that all teachers need to develop. One could argue that this is of particular importance when teaching musical improvisation as this, as we have seen, is very much a relational activity. One of the significant findings from the research on expert teachers was how important the process of personalisation was. The concept of personalisation is also of significance when teaching musical improvisation, as one of the major milestones for the improviser is to develop a personal sound and an approach to improvising that is identifiably theirs.

The importance of personalisation was recognised by the headteachers I inter-viewed, who had a key influence on the culture of the school. One headteacher emphasised the importance of teachers to be self-aware:

> Alan: *I think, that those teachers who struggle are often people who are not in touch with themselves … they don't come across to the children as being complete or whole.*

Alan's advice to new teachers at his school is to find an appropriate way to share something personal about themselves:

> *A picture of themselves jumping off a high diving board or rock climbing … so the children get a sense that … there is a person beyond the classroom.*

Another headteacher made the point that he wanted his pupils to experience a variety of different approaches to teaching and that pupils don't like all teachers being the same but they value the individual characteristics of their teachers. Several of the teachers that I interviewed also talked about being able to share appropriate information about themselves so that they were perceived as being a human being as opposed to just being a teacher. Being human was seen as a key characteristic of expert teachers by another headteacher (Derek) who said, "their humanity is at the forefront of all they do" and then went on to say that "the other thing that is at the heart of it is having a sense of humour".

The need for teachers to personalise their presence in the classroom, to go beyond just being seen as "a teacher", is however part of the process of personalisation. There is a reciprocal process of knowing the pupils as individuals.

> Anne: *Know the back story, that's what being an expert teacher is all about … you can read them* (the students) *like a book, that's what we are talking about when we talk about expe-rienced teachers.*

In practice "knowing the back story" means having a familiarity with the stu-dents beyond knowing their names: having and understanding of what their strengths as well as their weaknesses are and what they are interested in outside of school. This knowledge is invaluable when engaging in dialogic learning, and one of the key ways in which improvisational teaching happens is through the way that the teacher is able to respond to their pupils as individuals and adapt the course of the lesson accordingly.

4. Continual Adaptation Through Self-Reflection

The other main way in which improvisational teaching takes place is through in the moment adaptations of the lesson plan. This is easier for more experienced teachers to do as it relates to the confidence that they have in being able to respond to what happens.

The process of continual adaptation was seen in two ways, as described by Schön (1983) in his model of reflective practice. First the teachers were adept at thinking on their feet, what Schön describes as reflection-**in**-action. Given a situation in which they sense it is not working, they are able to immediately adapt and respond in an appropriate and effective way.

Fig. 2 The four processes of improvisational teaching

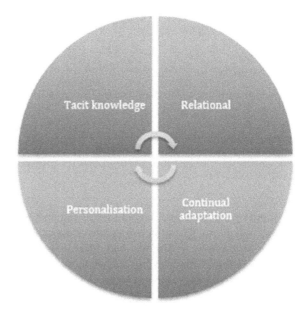

However, the expert teachers were also committed to critically appraising their work out side of the lesson, what Schon describes as reflection-**on**-action. They would think through their experiences, reflect on what did and didn't work and make changes to their practice. This might also involve informal discussions with colleagues, emphasising the importance of a non-judgemental culture within which teachers can share their failures. What was particularly important was that these teachers were willing and able to make changes to what they were teaching and to do this immediately. They were engaged in a process of wanting to continually improve what they were doing.

The four processes of teaching improvisationally are shown in Fig. 2.

A Theoretical Framework for Teaching Musical Improvisation Improvisationally

A theoretical framework for teaching musical improvisation improvisationally can be created by bringing together the four dimensions of teaching improvisation (the *what*) and the four processes of improvisational teaching (the *how*). This framework is shown in Fig. 3.

This framework clearly shows the congruencies between the *what* (of teaching musical improvisation) and the *how* (of teaching improvisationally). The context in which musical improvisation takes place needs to become tacit knowledge within the teacher and in turn informs the intuitive "in the moment' responses that they need to make as a teacher. The relational nature of musical improvisation is

Fig. 3 A theoretical framework for the craft of teaching musical improvisation improvisationally

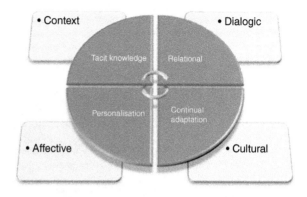

mirrored by the need for developing trusting and authentic relationships between teacher and pupils. The affective nature of musical improvisation, and the imperative for improvisers to discover and develop their own voice, is supported by the personalisation of the learning environment as the teacher gets to know the students as individuals (understanding the backstory) and allows the students to understand and relate to them as an individual. Finally, the cultural nature of musical improvisation is reflected in the continual adaptation to the teaching environment supported by reflection (both *in* action and *on* action). A third dimension, concerned with the meta-cognitive aspects, draws attention to the importance of the process of transferring knowledge from one domain to another as part of the process of critical reflective practice. This framework is dependent on a discourse that actively seeks to draw out the similarities and differences of these two crafts.

What does this theoretical framework look like in practice? I shall illustrate this with examples from an evaluative case study of an innovative course in teaching musical improvisation at the British and Irish Modern Music (BIMM) Institute in Bristol. The course, called Musical Responses and Collaborative Experiments (MRCE), comprises a series of workshops designed by three teachers (Annie Gardiner, Dan Johnson and Cliff Jones) who also lead the workshops. The classes are optional and attract between 8 and 14 students every week. Eight sessions that took place between February and March 2019 were observed as part of an evaluative case study; the findings of which, reported in Sorensen et al. (2019), provide exemplar evidence of how music improvisation can be taught improvisationally, providing insight into how the theoretical framework (outlined above) can be realised in practice. The dimensions and process of the framework are written in **bold** text.

The Framework in Practice

The MRCE sessions are designed to create a **culture** that encourages the development of improvisational skills. For each session they create a unique experience that encourage the participants encourage the exploration of new and uncharted musical topologies. They are very keen to ensure that their approach to teaching reflects a defining quality of improvisation as *a mode of intentional creative action that has unpredictable and uncertain outcomes.* This approach adopts a transformative teleology (Stacey, Griffin, & Shaw, 2000) in which outcomes and emergent forms are unpredictable and there is the movement to a future that is under permanent construction through the complex process of people relating to each other. The culture of the sessions is characterised by **relationships** that are based on trust, mutual respect and equal value in which risk-taking is encouraged.

The **context** for the workshops is open-ended; the workshop leaders are explicit in their intention that the music created in MRCE does not have to be recognisable or fit any known genre or style. They think it is important to relax the tropes or aesthetic conventions that exist around music of all kinds.

The **relational** and **affective** dimensions of teaching musical improvisation are established through the concept of the blameless space (Gardiner, Johnson & Jones, 2017) which forms an important and defining aspect of the sessions. "The blameless space isn't just a free space – it is a 'free of consequences space' – a place where, through trust and mutual abandonment of any and all judgement – students are able to focus on their own action and motivations, barriers and permissions".

Structurally the sessions are organised in two parts. The first part engages the students in musical improvisation, often without any prior knowledge or awareness of what the session will be about. This practical activity lasts between 40 and 50 min. After this there is a discussion session that typically also lasts for about the same length of time in which the leaders and participants together talk through about the improvisational activity. The discussion sessions are informed by a **dialogic pedagogy**.

The **relational** aspect of teaching improvisationally is informed by the trust that exists between the teachers and the students and the willingness for the students to risk participating in musical activities that place them in challenging situations. This is significantly developed through the ways in which they approach the assessment of the activities: "The post-improvisation discussions provide the participants with opportunities to feel, collaborate, co-create and explore, in a reflexive sense, ideas around what music, belonging and the ecologies of creativity are" (Sorensen et al., 2019, p. 10).

This approach not only builds relationships but also supports the **personalisation** of the learning experience, reflecting a core aim of MRCE to promote personal development and to refine participants understanding of the self-idiolect and creative identity.

The relationships that the teachers have with the students is a dynamic one in which they adopt a range of different roles (each of which has a differing relationship with the students). Through setting up the conditions for each session, they have the role of facilitator. When attending to the process of assessment in the post improvisation discussions, they become *witnesses of transformation*. Within this role, they mirror (or witness) key transitional moments within the improvisation process, identifying points of significance. Witnessing involves observing aural and physical responses, shifts in the affective dimension and the way the participants respond to each other. The discussion sessions are led by the student responses and initiated, if necessary, by open questions, e.g. "What did you think of that session?" "What did it feel like?" The points of witnessing are then fed into the discussion to deepen the understanding and level of reflection *on* action.

The MRCE workshop leaders recognise that they need to participate in the music making on equal terms with the students by taking on the role of co-participant. By demonstrating that they have an equal responsibility for taking risks and engaging in the improvisational activities, they are able to challenge the traditional power relationships that exist between teacher and student in order to be able to share insights and experiences in an honest way. They are also able to **continually adapt** the activities in real time (reflecting *in* action, Schön, 1983).

Conclusion

This chapter offers a theoretical framework to inform the craft of teaching musical improvisation improvisationally. This is a hybrid craft that has been created by drawing on the craft of musical improvisation (*what* is being taught) and the craft of improvisational (expert) teaching (the *how* of teaching musical improvisation). The resultant model identifies the commonalities between the two phenomena, and these have been illustrated through looking at the example of an innovative approach to teaching musical improvisation improvisationally.

This framework reinforces the importance of approaches to teaching that accept the open-ended and non-predictable outcomes of improvisation and provides opportunities for students to develop techniques appropriate to the context of the improvisational music making and then to be able to develop their improvisational skills within an environment that supports risk-taking and experimentation. Teaching needs to encourage the relational and affective dimension of improvised music making and be flexible (improvisatory) in being able to adopt a range of roles according to the demands of the situation. These roles include initiator, facilitator, participant (modelling what it is to be an improviser) and witness.

Overall these approaches accept that, given the nature of improvisation as a phenomenon, it may not be possible to teach someone to improvise. Instead teaching musical improvisation improvisationally is concerned with creating a learning experience in which students can engage with the affective nature of improvisation and through reflection (both in and on action) are able to articulate their own identity as an improvising musician. There is a unique relationship between improvisation and learning (Rose, 2017) that is derived from the "modes of creative, collaborative, embodied learning that improvisation presents" (p. 6). This is by no means a unique viewpoint: Claxton (1999) sees learning as "what you do when you don't know what to do" (p. 11) an idea that is very much aligned with Carol Dweck's concept of a growth mind-set as opposed to a fixed mind-set (Dweck, 2006). Learning, as an open-ended and on-going process, that engages in the boundaries between what we know and do not know is fundamentally improvisatory. This includes transferring knowledge, skills and understanding from one domain to another. This is the unique discourse that the craft of teaching musical improvisation improvisationally can offer to music educators. This discourse acknowledges the need to develop craft skills and knowledge in these two domains and involves the transfer of knowledge between the two. This metacognitive dialogue offers fruitful possibilities for the professional development of music educators and, with this in mind, I hope that this chapter will stimulate this discourse.

References

Bailey, D. (1980). *Improvisation: Its nature and practice in music*. Ashborune, UK: Moorland Publishing.

Bakhtin, M. M. (1993). *Towards a philosophy of the act*. Austin, Texas: University of Texas Press.

Claxton, G. (1999). *Wise up: The challenge of lifelong learning*. New York: Bloomsbury.

Dudeck, T. R., & McClure, C. (Eds.). (2017). *Applied improvisation: Leading, collaborating and creating beyond the theatre*. London: Methuen Drama.

Dweck, C. (2006). *Mindset: The new psychology of success*. Random House.

Eraut, M. (1994). *Developing professional knowledge and competence*. London: The Falmer Press.

Gardiner, A., Johnson, A., & Jones, C. (2017). Fostering creativities in higher music education Presentation at BIMM Conference: *Good practice and innovation: Addressing the challenges of 21st century modern music education*. BIMM Manchester 5 April 2017.

Gioia, E. (1988). *The imperfect art*. Oxford, UK: Oxford University Press.

Holdhus, K. (2019). Pedagogical improvisation: Musical improvisation's little sister? In G. G. Johansen, K. Holdhus, L. Larsson, & U. McGlone (Eds.), *Expanding the space for improvisation pedagogy: A transdisciplinary approach*. Abingdon, UK: Routledge.

Holdhus, K., Hoisaeter, S., Maeland, K., Vangsnes, V., Engelsen, K. S., Espeland, M., et al. (2016). Improvisation in teaching and education: Roots and applications. *Cogent Education, 3*, 1201412. https://doi.org/10.1080/2331186X.2016.1204142

Hopkins, D., Ainscow, M., & West, M. (1994). *School improvement in an era of change*. London: Cassell.

Lacy, S. (2006). *Findings: My experience with the soprano saxophone*. Paris: Outre Mensure.

Lash, D. (2003). *Improvisation: Before, during and after*. MA thesis, Oxford Brookes University.

Rose, S. (2017). *The lived experience of improvisation: In music, learning and life*. Bristol, UK: Intellect.

Santoro, G. (2000). *Myself when I am real: The life and music of Charles Mingus*. New York: Oxford University Press.

Sawyer, K. (2007). *Group genius: The creative power of collaboration*. New York: Basic Books.

Schön, D. (1983). *The reflective practitioner*. London: Basic Books.

Sennett, R. (2008). *The craftsman*. London: Penguin.

Shim, E. (2007). *Lennie Tristano: His life in music*. Ann Arbor: University of Michigan Press.

Sorensen, N. (2013). The metaphor of 'the jazz band': Ethical issues for leadership. *Critical Studies in Improvisation, 9*(1) ISSN 1712-0624.

Sorensen, N. (2014). *Improvisation and teacher expertise: A comparative case study.* PhD thesis. Bath Spa University.

Sorensen, N., Gardiner, A., Johnson, D, & Jones, C. (2019, April 23–26). *A pedagogy of listening: Supporting the facilitation of musical improvisation.* Paper presented at Research in Music Education Conference, Bath Spa University, UK.

Stacey, R. D., Griffin, D., & Shaw, P. (2000). *Complexity and management: Fad or radical challenge to systems thinking?* New York: Routledge.

Stoll, L. (1998). School culture. In *SIN research matters, 9, Autumn.* London: Institute of Education.

Phronesis in Music Education

Tiri Bergesen Schei

Abstract Phronesis and craft are complex concepts that force us to rethink what knowledge is and how little we know about how we make the decisions that underpin our actions in teaching. A question then is whether the development of phronesis is itself a kind of craft.

Introduction

It was three days before the opening night in the big public concert hall. Eighty students in music high school and their teachers were working 10 hours a day to get ready for the big event that they had been intensely preparing for months. Every student in the graduating class had arranged a piece of music for choir or band, which he or she would conduct. All song students had a solo to perform. The band players were to alternate on guitar, bass, drums, saxophone, trumpet, and piano. However, there were too many pianists. One of them, Tom, approached me during the break. He looked sullen, and said he felt redundant. Seventeen-year-old Julie, a talented singer, was hiding in the washroom. She cried, complaining that her voice did not sound as it had yesterday. In the front line of the choir, a soprano fainted and fell to the floor after half an hour's hard work with a complicated passage. Was it too complicated? Or maybe the score by young Robert just wasn't good enough? Why had we let this student come so close to the performance without helping him to produce a more suitable score? Robert was pale, his voice barely audible, as he instructed the singers in the choir.

The situation I describe is well known to music teachers. It is chaotic, unclear and uncertain. It consists of challenges that lack obvious solutions. We all work intensely; we are absorbed, constantly surveying the details and the overall progress. Will we make it on time? Will the students feel that they have succeeded as young musicians? Will they be proud? There are conflicts, small and big, between the people involved. Maybe a teacher is too domineering, or the students just tired, too hungry, too nervous?

T. B. Schei (✉)
Western Norway University of Applied Sciences, Bergen, Norway
e-mail: tbs@hvl.no

In scenarios like this, we are in the midst of music practice as it unfolds. This is where we want to be as musicians and music teachers, isn't it, in the midst of it all, where we experience with all our senses the students' individuality, their growth, their brilliance, how they manage to overcome their obstacles, how those who barely dared to enter the podium, finally do it, tremblingly, trustingly, courageously. These can be the most meaningful moments. Yet, it is also disturbing to be in the landscape of uncertainty, where I am far from assured that everything is going to be successful. I do not know which difficulties will turn up, so I cannot prepare for them in concrete detail. Whatever the problems are, there will be no ready-made solutions in textbooks or scientific papers. As one in the team of music teachers, I am put on trial. I will have to use myself as a tool, but I cannot predict whether it is my musical skills and craft, my pedagogical insight or my experience as a teacher, or even as a private person, that is needed when the students turn to me and ask for help. There are many components in my music teacher identity, many competences in my leadership craft. A competent craftsperson is more than a collection of the skills and insights that characterise that craft. Even if I am highly skilled, I do not necessarily use my expertise wisely. What is the knowledge that manifests when a music teacher uses her expertise wisely?

I am using the opening example as an entry to the thinking of Aristotle (384–322 BCE). Aristotle's ideas have survived for more than 2000 years. Some of his work, in particular on ethical behaviour in human interaction, is still considered the best guidance for understanding what it means to be a wise professional (Aristoteles, 1999; Kinsella & Pitman, 2012b). What goes on as we teach, guide and supervise? We can use Aristotle's ideas to reflect on the music teacher's mission, how we can *be* good and *do* good as music teachers and what kinds of knowledge we need to navigate in complex situations like those in the vignette. Modern language lacks words for that kind of competence. The ancient Greeks considered it a particular kind of knowledge – *phronesis*, a knowledge that is hard to learn, takes time and guidance and little by little changes us so that we tend to think and act more wisely. The simplest questions and situations can be the most vital, as well as the most complex. Sometimes we theorise too much, as if good theory could lead us all the way, give us the words, the empathy, the judgment, the patience and the actions we need to be wise practitioners. Now and then, in our theorising, we forget the individual, the student, the music, the messiness of real life and the joy of expressing music and of daring to put ourselves at stake. Aristotle writes that the ability to develop wisdom inheres in every human being; we all have the ability to grow, to learn, to develop our character in ways that will help us reach our goals and to see which goals and purposes are good and can contribute to a good life. Aristotle comes to the conclusion that it is not possible to be wise without being good—even if it is possible to be morally good without being wise (Aristoteles, 1999, p. 26). What kind of wisdom is he describing and how could such thoughts be of use to a music teacher?

What Did Aristotle Mean by *Phronesis*?

Aristotle distinguished between various kinds of knowledge or *intellectual virtues*, relevant for different tasks in human life: Three of them are *episteme*, *techne* and *phronesis*. Of these three, two have survived in modern languages, recognisable as they are: *Episteme* is the kind of knowledge that is context-independent; it is theoretical scientific knowledge. Mathematics is the classic example of exact, abstract knowledge that we can control with the help of theory (Gustavsson, 2000). Epistemic knowledge is something that is true because it can only be understood in one particular way. The physics of sound and vibration is an example from music. *Techne* is a different kind of knowledge, displayed in the skills and abilities we need to produce, to make things or carry out technical functions. In music education techne is the skills we obtain through working with scales and exercises or the outcome of work with improvisation. Aristotle deemed phronesis the highest of the three intellectual virtues. Unfortunately, it is the one concept that has been lost in modern languages, and lacking a word can sometimes make us blind.

While episteme is good *theory* and techne is concerned with good *production*, phronesis is the kind of knowledge that inheres in good *actions*—in situations where people are involved. Phronesis is usually translated as practical wisdom (Aristoteles, 1999). Phronesis is knowledge that expresses itself not in words, but through actions that are fitting, that are good and right in this particular situation. It expresses judgement and character, not only theoretical knowledge, and reveals an understanding of the complexity of a given situation, including what may be appropriate goals when things are messy and conflicted, as in the example of the music students, and also ways to approach these goals. Aristotle writes:

> Any one can get angry—that is easy … but to do this to the right person, to the right extent, at the right time, with the right motive, and in the right way, that is not for every one, nor is it easy. (Aristotle/Ross, 1999, Bk 2, Ch 9, p. 32)

Importantly the wise person's understanding is tacit, often nonconscious, and first and foremost expressed in adequate action or response. What is special about phronesis is that it implies the ethical dimension, and concepts like value, wisdom, judgement and reflection are essential. If we consider phronesis as an aspect of the crafts of leadership and guidance, it would be characterised by a practice that is not only complex and skilled, but used in a way that purposefully takes care of the persons involved in an ethical way. Phronesis is a virtue, and the person who has it, can be called a *phronimos*. When someone has a virtue, it means that he or she has developed an inclination, a tendency, to act in accordance with the moral character of the virtue (Cooke & Carr, 2014). For example, the courageous person acts courageously, the just acts with fairness, and the phronimos acts wisely. If we are lucky, virtues are learned across the entire lifespan, through experience and reflection in nourishing environments. For Aristotle, all the virtues were necessary for a person to achieve phronesis, practical wisdom. Kinsella and Pitman (2012a) write that "… all three – episteme, techne and phronesis – are required for professional practice.

The crisis, as we see it, is that episteme and techne are privileged, and the diminishing of phronesis diminishes the work that professionals aspire to do" (p. 10).

To be a good practitioner is what we strive to accomplish during our education and in our professional lives. What can be learned from Aristotle is that we tend to strive too much for theoretical knowledge and better techniques, better rules and systems, instead of asking the basic question: What kind of knowledge will help us *be* and *do* good in our actions, in situations that never repeat themselves? To master various skills in music education is craft, a competence that develops with hard work, feedback and practice. The craft is a basis for the music teacher. It would be of little help if the teacher could not demonstrate with her own voice to the student who strives to sing a complicated passage. On the other hand, if the teacher cannot connect with the girl who faints during the choir rehearsal and listen to what she has to tell about her situation and her fears, there is a lack of care and support that may, in the longer run, prevent the girl from realising her professional potential.

The type of action that according to Aristotle calls for phronesis is named praxis, with x. Praxis is wisdom displayed in social situations, it is "different kinds of actions, guided by different kinds of dispositions" in the relational field (Kemmis, 2012, p. 149). Praxis with x is ethical, as when a teacher nurtures a student to practice in a certain way. Uncertainty is an important notion of being a teacher. We do not necessarily know the right solution to the student's best approach to learning. As teachers we must acknowledge that and endure it. We sometimes even have to act as if we had the confidence. Uncertainty can be a resource for checking out what ideas others have to offer. Curiosity might also lead to improvisation and new ways of solving the problem. Our attitudes towards our own actions should be permeated with a belief that uncertainty leads to exploration, collaboration and creative thinking, and hence is good for the development of relationships and for the learning process. All relations are uncertain. This is what Gert Biesta calls "the beautiful risk of education" (Biesta, 2014). Stephen Kemmis proposes that we should ask for the capacity to deal with life in the face of uncertainty (Kemmis, 2012, p. 152).

A teacher can be a phronimos, a person who tends to know, in the face of uncertainty, what may be good for the students, if the ethics, both the moral and the intellectual virtues, are embedded in the teacher's ways of perceiving others and himself in particular contexts. This is a teacher who understands both his own vulnerability and ability and acts in accordance with the basic conditions of human existence, that we are all vulnerable and dependent, and who understands that the students' striving to establish identity and protect dignity are just as important to be aware of in the teaching situation as the concrete musical material that is to be learned – the techne and the episteme. The music teacher as phronimos—as a virtuous, ethical practitioner—will be especially thoughtful in the aspects of teaching that involve planning (Regelski, 2002, p. 23). Importantly, the good actions of phronesis are not means to an end, such as musical proficiency. Good actions should be a goal in themselves, writes Aristotle.

If I say to a weeping 17-year-old song student that she has to practice more scale exercises to be good, I am not a phronimos. A phronimos is self-reflexive; it is not enough to reflect upon the situation, it is also necessary to be aware of myself and how others see me. Who am I as a teacher in this situation? Both are necessary when I try to understand the needs of the student. Probably the student needs to practice scale exercises, as most of us need to keep up our standard of perfection as musicians, but the importance of the example is to be aware of the *person*, the living human being in front of us, weeping for some reason. If the teacher's concern is the technical perfection only, we can assume that this singer will not continue to study singing for very long.

From this, we can say that Aristotle suggests we continuously work with ourselves to consider every situation as new, with unknown facets, and hence uncertain. Uncertainty does not mean insecurity in this context. Instead, it might be considered a stimulus for prudent reflection, a precondition for mastering and solving of problems. It implies that the wise teacher must endure to fail, must understand what humility is, dare to try and dare to do wrong, have high aspirations of what may be possible to obtain and be curious.

Teacher Challenges

To contribute to students' growth, learning processes and cultural formation is every teacher's mission, but what exactly does this role imply? What is it that we want so much to offer as teachers and what pitfalls do we try to avoid? Why is it sometimes so complicated? During my years as a professional musician and music teacher, I have had many roles and struggles. What was it that I had to understand to be able to help my students when things were rough? Had I understood what I should avoid? Was it fear of shame and longing for social acceptance and self-respect that triggered me? The Danish philosopher and theologian Knud Løgstrup writes about what is at stake and hence what phronesis is about:

> One never has something to do with another person without having a part of the other person's life in one's hand. It may be a very small matter, involving only a passing mood, a dampening or quickening of spirit, a deepening or removal of some dislike. But it may also be a matter of tremendous scope, such as can determine if the life of the other flourishes or not (Løgstrup, 1997, pp. 15–16).

There was really much at stake when we worked with the students in the music high school three days before the big performance. I often experience similar situations. From voice teaching in one-to-one relations, I have learned how vulnerable most people are to being heard and seen, and to what they believe others might think of them. If we believe that "the other", be it the audience, a teacher or another musician, judges our voice or performance negatively, we tend to judge ourselves as not good enough. I have coined the concept of "voice shame" (Schei, 1998, 2011). Voice shame arises when a voice user becomes aware of the other's attention and believes the evaluation to be negative. It is as simple as that. I have met countless people, young and old, who are convinced that they cannot sing. They *know* it, because their second-year teacher, or someone in the family, told them not to sing in a performance. Once is enough to change a life, block a road to the good life, Aristotle's eudaimonia. There are other roads to the good life than singing, of course, but these are serious matters, and at the core of what we as teachers should have basic knowledge about. Shame and self-censorship can prevent the performer from seeing him or herself as good enough in the self-staging and performance.

I have worked with choirs and have had ample opportunity to practice these insights. The choir conductor is in the midst of attention, of the singers and of the audience. From this position, the conductor makes decisions and acts accordingly, continuously judging the reactions from the singers, their awareness, engagement, involvement, presence and qualities in voice production. Without the singers' support, the conductor's leadership will not be authoritative, but authoritarian. I know very well when I am not a phronimos, I can see it in my singers' faces and hear it in the music they produce. A phronimos is a person who is characterised by perceptivity, flexibility and creativity manifested in concrete action. If I am self-centred, tired or frustrated by singers who have not practiced at home, I will not be in touch with what my life experience has taught me, and I will not act in accordance with the needs of the students. I will be a conductor who is unable to realise what it takes to be a helper, so well put by Søren Kierkegaard, who says that in order to help someone, one must understand what he understands, in the way he understands it. If not, one's own understanding, however correct, scientific and wonderful, will be of no help (Kierkegaard, 1998).

What are the educational methods that might nurture phronetic ways of teaching? How can we as music teachers facilitate the development of intellectual virtues? Our most important obligation is to contribute to the students' cultural formation in every moment of our relationships with them. We influence their character development, their ability to be in good dialogue with others, their independence, curiosity, and openness—for better or for worse. This influence is mediated by *how* we think, speak and act in dialogue with our students, in the practice room when we teach one-to-one, in the classroom with 30 students or in the chaos of a big music project. The "how" of our behaviour is what Aristotle describes as acting "with the right person and to the right degree and at the right time and for the right purpose, and in the right way"—which is not within everybody's power and is not easy.

Why do we need to talk about these things? Isn't it enough that we have our tacit knowledge, our intuitive, experience-based ways of approaching the teacher's role? I will argue that it is not enough. If we cannot articulate thoughts and concepts connected to what good teaching demands of us, we will struggle with fulfilling the mission we ideally should have. If we lack clear ideas about our role, and are unable to formulate a holistic vision of what music teaching is about, it also becomes difficult to convey to non-musicians what a music teacher represents and what such a teacher can contribute with.

Thomas Regelski raises important questions about the titles "teacher", "music teacher", "musician" and "professional". The social status of a music teacher can be very ambiguous. A music teacher may have very little training in the music subjects from her teacher education and not dare to call herself a musician. Other teachers are professional musicians, but with little competence on the pedagogical level. An ambivalent professional identity arises: "Even among those who have entered music teaching as a 'calling',[28] musicianship, musicality, virtuosity, artistry, and all the other necessary criteria of being a competent musician are not sufficient criteria for being successful music teachers" (Regelski, 2009, p. 8).

So what more is needed? As I have mentioned earlier, the aim of education is *praxis. Praxis* are good actions in the field of human interacting. Kemmis writes that:

> … professional practice knowledge involves the knowledge that comes to life in the *doing* of the practice, the *craft* of the practice, and is embodied in the relationship of the practitioner to the practice and to others involved in and affected by the practice, that is, a kind of *personal* knowledge (Kemmis, 2012, p. 147).

Teaching as such is a matter of virtuosity, but not the kind of virtuosity that is self-centred or concerned with skills and competencies for its own sake. Max van Manen gives a good description of the novice teacher, who prepares every detail of the lesson and who is also very concerned about herself, how she appears in the eyes of the students. His concept of "tact" denotes a particular kind of knowledge that allows expert teachers to act confidently in the continuously changing, unpredictable and fluid situations of a classroom, where the novice, despite advanced theoretical knowledge of pedagogy, often falls short (Van Manen, 1995).

It is necessary to get experience and realise how the approach to teaching changes with experience. Kemmis argues that phronesis cannot be taught, only learned by experience and, indirectly, via praxis:

> We want something more than knowledge and technical skill in those that we aim to educate into professional practice. It is this desire for *something more*, I believe, that underpins our aspiration to develop phronesis in professional education. We not only want good professional practitioners, we want practitioners who will *do good*. (Kemmis, 2012, p. 148)

Biesta makes an interesting link to Hannah Arendt and her concept of action. What makes human beings unique is the potential we have to do something that has not been done before. We continuously bring new beginnings into the world through what we say and do; it is a miracle, something that one could not expect (Arendt, 1996; Biesta, 2005, 2014). But the newness of all situations also implies that we always have to invent new understandings and new solutions—the old rules, procedures and traditions were not developed for the situation at hand.

The concept "technology of the self", coined by Michel Foucault, denotes a practice directed by tacit knowledge and presuppositions about what are reasonable actions in a given situation. It is a disciplinary technique, a self-imposed practice that one exercises on oneself, in order to be more competent. It includes mechanisms by which we govern our social behaviour. It means that it is a craft applied on oneself (Schei, 2007, p. 34):

> Technologies of the Self permit individuals to effect by their own means or with the help of others a certain number of operations on their own bodies and souls, thoughts, conducts and ways of being, so as to transform themselves in order to attain a certain state of happiness, purity, wisdom, perfection and immortality (Foucault, 1988, p. 18).

Our praxis shows to what degree we have developed practical wisdom. We want our lifelong learning projects to take us in that direction, but how can we govern our own development, and what are the factors that decide what we learn, and how we come to experience the world and ourselves? The concept of self-technology is helpful in pointing out that we always monitor, evaluate and govern ourselves, most often without giving conscious consideration to our short- and long-term goals, our preconceptions and habits, our biases and illusions. Talking about self-technologies might help us become curious about ourselves and to explore our own praxis as teachers and as colleagues. We might decide which habits we want to continue with, which ideals we want to govern our thoughts and actions and how we can develop learning strategies that will help us become more reasonable and wise, not just in words and in our own self-image, but in the way we act with others.

Regelski points out that music teaching is not only complicated, but complex, and requires self-discipline beyond what is needed to become merely skillful:

> As concerns knowledge, music teachers as professionals need not just musical knowledge and skills, but competence relative to diagnosing and meeting both the musical and individual learning needs of students. Reason, of course, serves the ethical needs of diagnosing, planning, and evaluating instruction. And self-discipline amounts to the ethical obligation to recognise that one's teaching is never as good as it could be and that teaching, like music, needs to be "practiced"—constantly improved and updated—over the course of an entire career (Regelski, 2009, pp. 24–25).

When Biesta writes about teaching it is in a way that clearly echoes Aristotle. He says that good teaching "requires judgement about what an educationally desirable course of action is in this concrete situation with these concrete students at this particular stage in their educational trajectory" (Biesta, 2015, p. 2ff). Good judgement implies that we will know how to act as caring and trustworthy leaders when a situation arises. To find adequate words and a good way to use them when approaching a sad young pianist, a singer who hides in the restroom or a fainted soprano lying on the floor is challenging. The students should be exposed to adequate ways of dealing with crises, possibly allowing them to advance on their own path towards practical wisdom. Biesta writes that having this judgement is a virtue; it is something you *are*, more than something you *have*. He claims that teachers need to *be* competent rather than have competences and argues for a "virtue-based approach … for teachers to develop educational virtuosity".

Following Foucault, I will argue that self-technologies of many kinds can help us become competent in this deeply ethical meaning. Aristotle wrote that virtues can be learned through experience, in environments that offer critical reflection and guidance. Others have argued that all virtues start with simple politeness, where we behave in good ways for external reasons, to avoid social sanctions (Comte-Sponville, 2002). Then with time, as consequences of our good actions, we are rewarded on deep emotional levels for being trustworthy, selfless, courageous and just. Gradually we develop new patterns of intuitions, reactions and communication, and what started as fake virtuousness has become second nature; it has become us. We are no longer the same person. We have gained knowledge of the third kind, and it will manifest not as words or techniques, but as actions that are courageous, just or wise.

What, then, could be the relationship between the concepts of craft and phronesis? Embedded in the concept of craft are skills and theory, the necessary competencies for any craftsman. In addition, the craftsman may or may not display relational and contextual wisdom in his or her actions. Since "craft" may contain both professional competencies and the virtues of the phronimos, craft is a wider concept than phronesis.

The performance of a craft can be good or not so good. Phronesis, on the other hand, cannot be other than good. An unwise phronimos is a contradiction in terms.

There will be no doubt when a craftsman has phronesis. The person who has it will apply skills and perform leadership smoothly and flexibly. Complex competencies will appear to be a matter of course. A further question is whether the development of phronesis is in itself a kind of craft. It is clear that phronesis is a product of learning and that practice, experience, feedback, role models, trial and error are necessary, and also the will to work hard on one's own flaws and weaknesses. It seems reasonable to say that a phronimos is a craftsman, but a craftsman is not necessarily a phronimos.

Summing Up

Phronesis, craft and praxis are complex concepts that force us to rethink what knowledge is and how little we know about how we make the decisions that underpin our actions in teaching. We all want to be wise practitioners. The questions we need to ponder are "how do we get there" and "what are the obstacles"? A major obstacle to developing phronesis is our desire to avoid error, avoid the pain of taking risks, of making mistakes and of admitting the ones we make every day. We love the feeling of being infallible, of being right, of knowing. We do *not* like to admit ignorance, to humiliate ourselves and to ask for help and guidance. Displaying what we see as weakness evokes feelings of shame and embarrassment in us. Yet the only way towards phronesis is through acknowledgement of our shortcomings, our ignorance and our biases. Since learning this is so hard, and so fraught with emotion, there are limits to how much we can achieve on our own. We need role models; we need feedback and correction; we need support and dialogue; we need humour and forgiveness; we need a nurturing human environment. We also need theory, not because theory in itself can provide wisdom, says Aristotle, but because theory can help us realise that it is in our actions that we prove ourselves.

190   T. B. Schei

References

Arendt, H. (1996). *Vita activa: det virksomme liv*. Oslo, Norway: Pax.
Aristoteles. (1999). *Etikk: et hovedverk i Aristoteles filosofi, også kalt Den nikomakiske etikk. Oversatt og med innledning av Arnfinn Stigen* (3. utg. ed.). Gyldendal.
Aristotle. (1999). *Nicomachean ethics* (W. D. Ross, Trans.). Kitchener, ON: Batoche Books.
Biesta, G. (2005). *The role of educational ideals in teachers' professional work*. Paper presented at the C-TRIP Seminar.
Biesta, G. (2014). *Utdanningens vidunderlige risiko*. [The beautiful risk of education]. Fagbokforlaget.
Biesta, G. J. J. (2015). How does a competent teacher become a good teacher? On judgement, wisdom and virtuosity in teaching and teacher education. In R. Heilbronn & L. Foreman-Peck (Eds.), *Philosophical perspectives on the future of teacher education* (pp. 3–22). Hoboken, NJ: Wiley Blackwell.
Comte-Sponville, A. (2002). *A short treatise on the great virtues: The uses of philosophy in everyday life*. New York: Holt Paperbacks.
Cooke, S., & Carr, D. (2014). Virtue, practical wisdom and character in teaching. *British Journal of Educational Studies, 62*(2), 91–110. https://doi.org/10.1080/00071005.2014.929632
Foucault, M. (1988). The political technology of individuals. In P. H. Hutton, H. Gutman, & L. H. Martin (Eds.), *Technologies of the self: A seminar with Michel Foucault* (pp. 145–162). Amherst, MA: University of Massachusetts Press.
Gustavsson, B. (2000). *Kunskapsfilosofi: Tre kunskapsformer i historisk belysning*. Stockholm, Sweden, Wahlström & Widstrand.
Kemmis, S. (2012). Phronesis, experience, and the primacy of praxis. In *Phronesis as professional knowledge* (pp. 147–161). Rotterdam, The Netherlands: Sense Publishers.
Kierkegaard, S. (1998). *The point of view: Kierkegaard's writings* (Vol. 22) (V. Howard & Edna H. Hong, Trans.). Princeton, NJ: Princeton University Press.
Kinsella, E. A., & Pitman, A. (2012a). Engaging phronesis in professional practice and education. In *Phronesis as professional knowledge* (pp. 1–11). Rotterdam, The Netherlands: Sense Publishers.
Kinsella, E. A., & Pitman, A. (Eds.). (2012b). *Phronesis as professional knowledge. Practical wisdom in the professions*. Rotterdam, The Netherlands: Sense Publishers.
Løgstrup, K. E. (1997). *The ethical demand*. Notre Dame, IN: University of Notre Dame Press.
Regelski, T. (2002). On "methodolatry" and music teaching as critical and reflective praxis. *Philosophy of Music Education Review, 10*(2), 102–123.
Regelski, T. (2009). The ethics of music teaching as profession and praxis. *Visions of Research in Music Education, 13*, 1–34.
Schei, T. B. (1998). *Stemmeskam: Hemmede stemmeuttrykks fenomenologi, arkeologi og potensielle rekonstruksjon gjennom sangpedagogikk*. Master's thesis, Bergen University College, Bergen, Norway.
Schei, T. B. (2007). *Vokal identitet. En diskursteoretisk analyse av profesjonelle sangeres identitetsdannelse* [Vocal identity. A discourse-theoretical analysis of professional singers' identity formation]. (Dr. art.), University of Bergen, Bergen, Norway.
Schei, T. B. (2011). Kan stemmeskam overvinnes? Om helsefremmende aspekter ved profesjonelle sangeres identitetsarbeid. *Skriftserie fra Senter for musikk og helse, Antologi nr. 4, "Musikk, helse, identitet"* (Oslo: NMH-publikasjoner 2011:2), 85–105.
Van Manen, M. (1995). On the epistemology of reflective practice. *Teachers and Teaching, 1*(1), 33–50.

Approaching Vulnerability Through Contemporary Music: The Gelland Approach

Erkki Huovinen

Abstract Drawing on philosopher Richard Sennett's view of craftsmanship, this chapter argues that music education should address human incompleteness and ambiguity—as especially evident in contexts involving vulnerability. Music has often been seen as an indicator, but also as a means of overcoming unwanted psychological or social vulnerabilities. From another point of view, vulnerability may also be understood as a desired quality of openness needed for creativity and education—a quality that nevertheless requires appropriate safety mechanisms. These facets of vulnerability are illustrated through the schoolwork of the Swedish-German *Duo Gelland*, one of world's foremost classical violin duos. Using brief contemporary compositions, the Gellands elicit children's associative imagery, incorporating it in subsequent interpretations of the music in which the children may take part as conductors or musicians. Through interviews and observations from school workshops in Germany, it is shown how the Gellands create musical contexts in which children's vulnerabilities can be safely exposed and transformed. At the same time, the musicians see children's engagement as proving the social value of the music. In providing a neutralising arena for children's sometimes frightening and violent realities, the Gellands demonstrate a model for "health musicianship", challenging sharp distinctions between artistic, pedagogical and therapeutic realms.

Introduction

Philosopher Richard Sennett's definition of craftsmanship focuses on "the special human condition of being engaged"—doing good work for its own sake (Sennett, 2008, p. 20). By these lights, the claim that music education is a craft may sound like a cheap truism. However, Sennett's examples of craftsmanship in architecture, health care, and other fields also bring to the fore something much more

E. Huovinen (✉)
Royal College of Music, Stockholm, Sweden
e-mail: Erkki.s.huovinen@gmail.com

© Springer Nature Switzerland AG 2021
K. Holdhus et al. (eds.), *Music Education as Craft*, Landscapes: the Arts, Aesthetics, and Education 30, https://doi.org/10.1007/978-3-030-67704-6_15

challenging. In his view, being engaged in a craft requires embracing the difficult and the incomplete as something positive and stimulating, because it is only through hands-on work on such problems that true craftsmanship is able to develop. "To do good work means to be curious about, to investigate, and to learn from ambiguity" (Sennett, 2008, p. 48). In Sennett's examples, the incompleteness and ambiguity for an architect reside in the architectural design being crafted. If education, too, is a craft, we should probably say that what gets "crafted" there is a human being, a person. If so, Sennett's argument would seem to urge educators to focus on investigating ambiguity and incompleteness in their students.

This may sound misguided. After all, From Rousseau's focus on the child's natural goodness to models of education based on positive psychology (see Furlong, Gilman, & Huebner, 2014), we have learned not to focus on what is incomplete in children—not to see them as something imperfect to be "crafted" into a better shape. But even while embracing such ideals, I believe that Sennett's argument can be useful in another way. It can challenge us to deal with issues of *vulnerability* in contexts of education. I believe that music education, in particular, has incomparable potential for "investigating incompleteness and ambiguity" and that this requires an approach in which the educators themselves—quite like the artisan with her bare hands—also expose their own incompleteness and vulnerability.

As a case study in dealing with vulnerability in music education, I will discuss the schoolwork of the Swedish-German *Duo Gelland*. As one of the world's foremost classical violin duos, Cecilia and Martin Gelland have made a remarkable international career, having more than 200 works written specifically for them. Since 1994, they have also held children's workshops, developing what could well be described as a pedagogical method—an open set of guidelines, ideas and practices applied to engage children. In their approach, children's music-based associative images are allowed to inform musical interpretation, empowering children as co-creators of the music. In using repeated hearings of composed music, in helping children to explore the music through their own activities, and in connecting associative listening to musical structure, their approach has a lot in common with Magne Espeland's (1987) pioneering classroom experiments in the project *Music in Use*. The difference is that Gellands perform the music themselves on their instruments and that they seem to heighten the level of interaction by having the children participate in and guide their own music-making. Such mutuality suggests a craftsmanship-like character to Gellands' work: what is achieved is achieved right there in a tight hands-on coupling between them and the children. Interestingly, all of this takes place through what many might consider an unlikely choice of music to be played with children—highly complex contemporary music.

The chapter is based on observing eight of Gellands' workshops (with groups of 9–13 fifth graders) in a German *Gemeinschaftsschule* in 2017 and on a series of interviews with the musicians before, during (stimulated recall), and after the project (conducted in German and Swedish). We had agreed that each workshop would involve the first two brief duo pieces from the Scottish contemporary composer James Dillon's *Traumwerk, Book 1* (1995), both of them in three consecutive performances. After the first performance of one of these pieces, the musicians' question of "What did you hear?" always led to incorporating the children's imagery in the subsequent performances in whatever ways deemed appropriate. To highlight some of the typical outcomes, the participants might be given drums to articulate their images in the music as co-musicians, or a participant might be chosen as a conductor to guide the musicians or the other children in shaping the next performance dynamically in accordance with the imagery. Gellands' workshops suggest an improvisatory attitude to contemporary concert music hardly intended or foreseen by many of the composers themselves. Instead of a systematic account of the pedagogical approach as a whole, I will here adopt a narrative approach to focus on what I interpret as central to Gellands' work—dealing with points of vulnerability in the children.

According to information provided by the coordinator of the school we visited, around 50% of the children were "financially supported through so-called educational funds, that is, many of our pupils come from families with unemployment or low incomes, a part of them with a long-term dependence of social welfare provision". The other half was more heterogenous, but notably included many "children from families that have been with us only for a short while after fleeing from a war zone in the Middle East". In such contexts, visiting musicians have the drawback that they cannot be informed of the children's individual backgrounds to engage with their individual needs, nor can they extend their work with the children beyond one workshop. Still, I argue that Gellands' work provides a model case of how an aspect such as human vulnerability might be empathetically addressed in musical engagements with children. Let us begin, however, by examining the notion of vulnerability in the context of music.

Vulnerability to Be Overcome and Vulnerability as Openness

Vulnerability is a broad notion that can be seen as connected to music in two very different ways. Firstly, music may be seen as an indicator or even a cause, but also as a means of overcoming unwanted psychological or social vulnerabilities. On the social plane, consider how music-educational programmes may involve "marginalisation and exploitation of vulnerable populations", but also "potential as [sites] of resistance and social transformation" for overcoming such problems (Matthews, 2015, pp. 238–239). In individual psychology, music may similarly be seen as double-edged. For instance, research on music and mental health has shown that preference for certain musical genres might be indicative of underlying emotional disturbance or vulnerability (see Baker & Bor, 2008). A typical research topic has been the potential association between adolescents' preference for heavy metal music and suicidal thoughts (e.g. Martin, Clarke, & Pearce, 1993; Scheel & Westefeld, 1999). Research may also encourage a more positive perspective in terms of striving for broad musical exposure. For example, the finding that youth with eclectic musical tastes have less problems in negotiating their adolescence than ones with "heavy" or "light" tastes suggests that "exposing such adolescents to a greater variety of music may promote greater self-exploration, validation, and normalisation of their issues, thus enhancing their development" (Schwartz & Fouts, 2003, p. 212). As in the social argumentation mentioned above, what is of importance, then, is not simply that any old music (or music education) is present in an adolescent's life, but exactly what is done and how. In these discussions, vulnerability appears as something unwanted that is either aggravated by or overcome through music.

Secondly, vulnerability can also in itself be seen as something of value. A bestselling author on the topic defines vulnerability as uncertainty, risk and emotional exposure, but, as such, sees it as the heart of meaningful human experiences (Brown, 2012). In similar terms, educators have seen vulnerability as a necessary prerequisite for true learning. "Learning—fully engaged learning—requires vulnerability. It requires the capacity to leave oneself open to criticism and willingly seek and provide support" (Nakkula & Toshalis, 2010, p. 113). Such vulnerability explains why safe and supportive learning environments are so important. Understood as openness or exposure, vulnerability also becomes a desirable precondition for creativity, and here, too, it has to occur within protective constraints. Consider the connections between creativity and psychopathology—for instance, the relative tendency of professional musicians toward positive schizotypy (Rawlings & Locarnini, 2007). According to the *shared vulnerability model*, creative achievement and psychopathology share some cognitive features that increase access and attention to material that would usually be processed below the level of conscious awareness. Unregulated attention to such material would overwhelm the person as chaotic, and thus the model also attributes creativity with certain protective factors (such as high IQ, working memory skills, and cognitive flexibility) that allow a person to process and manipulate the increased range of stimuli without "going mad" (Carson, 2011). Both in education and creativity, then, individual vulnerability may be understood as a desired quality of openness, but it also optimally requires appropriate safety mechanisms.

In an interview study on musicians' learning, Wiggins (2011) found vulnerability to emerge in both positive and negative guises. A music student might not feel ready to share his or her music with others, feeling vulnerable to others' judgement because the sonic nature of music makes all necessary doodling instantly public. While vulnerability may thus inhibit musical agency, Wiggins also found that understood as openness and sensitivity to the music, it may itself be a component of musical agency. The statement made by one of her interviewees, "The more open and vulnerable I am, the better the eventual product" (Wiggins, 2011, p. 359), may indeed represent a rather common attitude among musicians.

Painting the Music: Neutralising Vulnerability

Before discussing the observed workshops which were distinctly interactive in nature, we may take a look at a somewhat simpler approach that the Gellands have used with children—one in which children "paint a portrait of the music" they hear and then discuss the paintings. In talking about this exercise in the interviews, the Gellands often returned to formative experiences they had had with children in vulnerable positions. For instance, Cecilia remembered "a child recounting how one almost drowns—this child had been along in the [refugee] escape over the Mediterranean". As Martin explained, such personal content cannot be forced into the workshops:

> MG: One girl [in a Swedish school] had painted herself in a cage, and afterwards we found out that it suited her biography well. She had had problems in her family, and had painted herself accordingly without saying anything about it. Had we said, "Please, paint now your own biography or how you feel," she would certainly not have painted herself, but through the music it broke free, and she painted something that was significant for her. Another time a teacher told us afterwards, "This boy had never before painted in colour, but only in black and white. This was the first time that he used colours".

According to Cecilia, describing music in painting works in this way because it allows any difficult experiences to be *neutralised*. Hence the activity may assume therapeutic significance:

> CG: I remember one girl in Lapland [...] who narrated about the music that there had been an assault—she described this in the music. And afterwards the teacher came to us and told that what the girl had described was personal. She had never been able to talk about it, but [...] it was something about his father abusing her. This way, it was neutralised: She did not tell about herself, but she described the music. I remember another time when the children had painted pictures to [the music of the Swedish composer] Allan Pettersson. [...] There was a girl who described her picture as being about a girl who is raped by her boyfriend, and, on such occasions, it is really hard to know how to react. But I listened to what she said—this was when we went around looking at the pictures, while they were still painting, and she whispered... I didn't make more of it, but later, I have thought that it may well have been something personally experienced. It need not have been that, but it may have been. [...] I hope that it was okay to have been able to express it in a neutral way.
>
> EH: It is interesting that many of the stories and experiences emerging in these situations would undoubtedly be understood as therapeutic in other contexts.
>
> CG: And they are therapeutic. I mean, to interpret music is also therapeutic. I don't know if I would listen to somebody who did not offer much of him- or herself—so as to also be therapeutic—and it is the same thing when you listen.

In this perspective, music is therapeutic by way of allowing the children a neutralised view of their inner experiences, but this also requires that the musicians live up to the challenge by offering enough of themselves. Cecilia's comments thus strongly suggest a mutuality or dialogism as an ideal for the meetings with children. Indeed, a genuine attentiveness to what children have to say quite naturally leads to welcoming mutual improvisatory processes—and Gellands, as we will see, incorporate improvisation in their workshops to a far greater degree than is usual for contemporary concert music. Their notion of improvisation seems very much in accordance with the above-mentioned idea of vulnerability as openness: It is an attitude that requires exposing one's own shortcomings to the audience:

CG: From children, we have also learned to test new things which we wouldn't have come upon by ourselves. Among other things, to improvise in the way we do: This is something we have, in fact, learned from children. [...] We are chamber musicians, classically schooled, with good ears, but we did not come to where we are through being taught to improvise anywhere. It was rather through our experiments in the classroom that it has become like this. I feel it as a responsibility that in all encounters with an audience, I am to some degree willing to fall out of my frame, so to speak—which also implies that I offer my own shortcomings. You cannot be perfect—whatever that might mean—and it shouldn't be so important that I myself stand in the way of the idea or vision or inspiration, or whatever it is that one mediates through music.

The above interview extract well exemplifies how the Gellands' accounts of musical processes often were couched in ethical notions. The notion of responsibility, mentioned by Cecilia above, seems to be informed by the recognition that any brief school visit might be of pivotal importance to someone in the class. When describing their motivation to work with children, both of the musicians narrated a personally significant event that had taken place in Sweden 16 years before our interviews:

MG: There was a boy in this class, perhaps on the fifth or sixth grade. We did not know that he was bullied in the class. The parents being in free church, he was a bit separated from the others. [We did not know] that when he had come home, it had been the first time that there had been something fantastic in school, and his greatest wish was that we would always come again. And he had had a violin—he was allowed to play the violin—but we did not come again at that time, only later. Half a year later, he had committed suicide. And he just wanted really to play the violin, and was made fun of by the other kids.

Violent Realities

It appears that experiences such as described above have made the Gellands listen very carefully and respectfully to what the children have to say, even when the latter might be lacking in words to express themselves. In the workshops I observed, the musicians' genuine interest in responses to the question "What did you hear?" was tangible. Even simple and stereotypical responses such as "high notes" or "It was loud" were treated as if they contained new insights about the music. Cecilia later explained that when she notices a child feeling insecure, she may choose to "ask a question that is so simple that it would almost be impossible not to answer something". In working with children, she continued, there is often a sense that "they experience, they listen carefully, it seems that they hear everything—but that one cannot talk about everything that one experiences". Hence, even associations that might superficially seem far off from the heard music were always treated with respect for the underlying experience and with an understanding that the children are simply making use of the means available to them. As Martin pointed out, it would be inappropriate to condemn images related to films and computer games as bad descriptions of heard music: "These are the images that children have at their disposal".

The children's realities that provide them the images and concepts to work with might thus also include aggression and violence. In the school where we carried out the project, a teacher told us that the children saw a lot of violent movies, and Cecilia later informed me that the suburb was also known for having more violence than other parts of the city. Not surprisingly, then, images of violence emerged in the workshops. Let us consider the reactions of Group 3, consisting of 11 boys, to the hyper-energetic *Traumwerk*, Movement 1. The most immediate listener reaction involved a personifying interpretation: "I heard it as if... in the freaky playing [imitates the musicians' fast right-hand movements]... as if he escapes, and then looks back or [sees if someone] is chasing him". The other boys in the group continued developing the image by describing the "panic" of the protagonist, his "gasping for air" while occasionally "hiding" before running again and how he either "was saved" in the end or how he was "shot" and was "dying" with the "sorrow music" at the end of the piece. These themes were enthusiastically developed with fleeting references to the horror film *It*, to a hunter chasing Bugs Bunny and to "being with a woman" in the end. Finally, the image that the protagonist "is in a hospital just before dying, so that his heart is beating hard" led Cecilia to suggest "an experiment" in which conga drums would be added as heartbeats to the next performance of the piece. The musicians also suggested that changes between escaping and stopping to take a breath would be indicated by loud breathing and by the rapidity of the drums' heartbeats—an example of how children's imagery might be constructively used for open creative tasks that require attention to the music.

When I later asked the musicians about such associations to violence, Cecilia replied, "We feel we must respect what they place in the space". This, of course, is not a self-evident reaction in the face of violent imagery. The musicians recalled an earlier workshop in which a boy had painted a war scene to the music, but the regular teacher had disallowed this, insisting the boy to paint another picture. Cecilia remembered that "it was totally absurd, but at the same time I didn't want to interfere, for it might have gotten even worse for the children afterwards, had we argued with the teacher". In Cecilia's own view, music may sometimes help to "channel emotions, and perhaps especially emotions that can be difficult to channel in an accepted manner—like aggressivity, for instance". Instead of forbidding aggressive images, the musicians may thus let them enter the musical context when they emerge from the group. Again, the idea is that by placing them into the musical context, such images may be observed in a neutralised setting:

CG: If we create a secure situation, and if a [violent] memory like this is placed into the secure space where we show that we are reliable and respectful, and where the children themselves can feel safe, then it should neutralise the experience. [The experience] has been put in a place where it is possible to examine it.

Treating violent images with respect may leave room for the music to suggest new perspectives to the imagery. Cecilia recounted a previous workshop in which the children's task had been to "compose" their own music by telling the musicians what to play:

CG: On one occasion it felt as if it [i.e., violent imagery] had a cathartic function. [This was] grade four, I think, in Jämtland [county in Sweden]—a class that we had met before. And it was exactly when the Iraq war had been in the news—that it would break out. And so they came up with their music: There were kids heard playing, rain would be there, there was a brook, and I'm not sure, but maybe there were birds, too—and then suddenly there is this little boy who says: "And now comes the bomb!" I saw that the teacher jumped a bit…

MG: Atomic bomb.

CG: Oh, he said "atomic bomb," okay. I myself also felt stiff for a moment, but we played the atomic bomb that shred everything to pieces, and then it continued. […] And afterwards: "Now comes the rain, and now comes the brook, and now come the children"—and so it was finished. It was almost hard to hold the tears—it was so strong. And there was no question that there would have been something wrong with it, as it became so clear what function it had served.

Such transformative experiences may be most meaningful for individuals who have themselves experienced violence in their lives. This became most tangible in the Gellands' account of their recent visit to a correctional youth facility in Nebraska to meet adolescents waiting for their criminal sentences. Together with members of the 113 Composers Collective from Minneapolis, the Gellands had again asked the adolescents to paint the music. Note how the situation involves a continuing feedback loop between an initial musical performance [not described here], an associative picture, its further transformation to some new music, and, again, the painter's account of his life conditions:

CG: Among them there was one boy […] who painted […] "a knife, a dagger, a pistol, and handcuffs." This was his picture. And we asked—it is very important not just to talk about the picture—if they would wish that sound would come out of their pictures. […] So, they told us what we should do to deepen them [i.e., how to transform the pictures to sound]. When it came to these handcuffs, the boy said: "Now, it will be glad music!" I thought for a moment that he was just fooling me—that he didn't take it seriously. But we did as he had asked, and he became so moved. […] Tears glimmered in his eyes. And it turned out that his environment was so frightening that when the police finally comes, he is glad, because then he will get away to a place that is safe. With many others, too, when they described how the music should be that would come out of their pictures, there was a very strong emotional presence, a depth that was extremely touching.

In working with children's or adolescents' associations to live contemporary music, it seems that a respectful embracement of their responses invites their life realities—even violent ones—to be revealed. In fact, avoiding this altogether might require a distancing and less empathetic attitude towards the children or—as in the above-mentioned teacher's case—explicitly forbidding certain kinds of imagery. It is no wonder, then, that questions of responsibility were often mentioned by the musicians in connection with strong imagery. Cecilia noted that sometimes she has thought to herself "whether it is right to let these things be evoked, when we have to go from there and cannot help them to handle it—for there is no-one else that could take care of it". While the Gellands do not pretend to be professional therapists, Cecilia seems to suggest that the musicians themselves may have a key role when it comes to helping individuals to cope with experiences awakened by the music. In the workshops that I followed, violent images were not just allowed to emerge, but when they did, they were consistently worked into musical interactions in which they could be collectively observed and even transformed to something else. The chasing scenario described above, for instance, could be seen to involve "externalisation and re-enacting scenarios in which violence can occur" (McFerran & Wölfl, 2015) exactly as recommended by music therapists for working on violence with young people in schools.

Confidence in the Music and the Incomprehensible

A recurrent theme in the Gellands' talk about their work was the way in which children's imagery may feed into the interpretative process of the musicians. Cecilia noted that if the interpreter's role were just to "count correctly", working with children would not be of much use. In fact, however, the interpreter's work involves being "in a process together with the work—one that perhaps even involves a certain friction". It is "research work" akin to how an actor works to get inside of a role: "This is not just something done consciously with the fingers, but something in which you apply your whole unconscious. You thus have to feed it to be ready inside".

When commenting on the school workshops in stimulated-recall interviews, the Gellands often mentioned their increased "confidence with the [musical] work" in question. Sometimes, this had to do with new perspectives opened into the particular composition through the children's imagery and through the ensuing collective interpretations carried out in class. For example, the above-mentioned boy group's imagery of escaping and stopping to take a breath in *Traumwerk* Movement 1 resulted in a narratively structured performance of the piece that was fun for the children, but also recalled with enthusiasm by Cecilia later in the interview:

CG: There is something about energy or fluctuation in the first movement that I now see
      that I had not grasped before. Something about how one runs and stops, and runs again
      […]: I had seen it more just as having one motion from the beginning to the end […]
      but now it became a transformation, became clearer.

Martin, in another interview, described his change of perspective regarding *Traumwerk* Movement 1 in similar terms. In its duration of less than 1 min, the piece had previously felt simply like one "brief, fierce motion", but the children had made him realise that the piece "had a bunch of stages, moods were built up—there were so many things to be found within the brief movement: just to listen once and then already be able to apprehend so much!"

Quite often, an increased "confidence in the work" seemed less related to new music-structural insights and more to the very possibility of creating a genuine dialogue through the music. With Group 5, the final performance of *Traumwerk* Movement 2 involved the children closing their eyes, listening to features (e.g. brightness or darkness) that they had heard in the music on the two previous performances and "painting them with sound" on their drums. Cecilia later commented: "It feels in such a situation that there is a great confidence between us and the children, but also between the music and the children, as they are willing to open themselves like that, close their eyes, and play their emotions to us".

In their subsequent treatment of *Traumwerk* Movement 1, the group ended up in a performance in which one pupil was chosen to conduct the dynamic levels of the music by raising and lowering his hands. With his right hand, the conductor first led the other children into a prelude on their conga drums. Then, using his left hand, he conducted "Tom and Jerry"—as the two violins had been identified in the previous group discussion—thus affecting the moment-to-moment intensity of the composition and calling forth improvisatory insertions to the piece by the violinists. These two movements had been agreed upon, but the conductor also chose to invite a conga postlude to the piece. In her comments on this performance, Cecilia noted the "enormous fragility called forth by the music", continuing: "It gives us an enormous confidence in the music that such dialogues can emerge [...]—that the music can play a part in this". Even if the children's responses centred on rather simple sensory qualities (brightness/darkness) or filmic associations (Tom and Jerry), their contribution did not stop here. Rather, such responses only served to offer perspectival orientation to collaborative musical activities in which Dillon's music was imbued with freshly identified meanings and thus validated as a potent springboard for musical interaction. It may well have been the children's openness toward musically exploring their own images—rather than their spoken responses as such—that carried the most weight for the musicians, both in suggesting the depth of experience behind the expressed images and in proving the social value of the music.

At times, however, the children's images were more complex. In Group 6, such a response emerged after the first performance of *Traumwerk* Movement 2. After a series of other responses such as "sad and good", a girl with a refugee background suddenly came up with an image of the *Incomprehensible*:

Girl:	Frightening [*Erschreckend*].
CG:	Something where one also gets frightened?
Girl:	Yes.
Children:	Yes! Yes!
CG:	Yes.
Girl:	So, you cannot grasp it that... you cannot grasp what is being done—the Incomprehensible [*das Unfassbare*].
Boy:	[You cannot grasp it] through language?
Girl:	Yes. Through language.
CG:	So, you mean that something happens, and you cannot grasp...
Girl:	Yes.
CG:	...that it has really happened? All right.
MG:	Would you like to try it on the drum?

Girl: Yes.
MG: How could it sound?
Girl: [Plays quiet, quick rhythms on the conga for 25 s.]
CG: It is beautiful. It creates a special mood, almost a kind of tension.

Cecilia later approvingly commented on Martin's quick decision to ask the girl to try and *play* the Incomprehensible: "I wouldn't have dared to do it. [...] It was a really difficult task to show the Incomprehensible on a drum like that, but she did it, and there was such a tension in what she did—it was fascinating. And it became something to build upon". Along with other qualities heard in the music by the children, the Incomprehensible finally received a role in a prelude that was negotiated to precede the final performance of *Traumwerk* Movement 2. After some other structural suggestions had been tossed around, the above girl came up with the final version: "An idea: First, there is the Frightening, and then the Fast, and then the Slow, and after that comes the Incomprehensible [Cecilia: Yes!], and then I can do the Incomprehensible like this [scrapes the drum head]". In the final performance, a prelude with this structure preceded the violin piece, and in the end Cecilia signalled the drums to "come back" one by one.

In being shown the video recording of the performance in their respective interviews, Cecilia and Martin both extensively pondered upon the image of the Incomprehensible. Cecilia's understanding of this "fabulous image" seemed related to the fact that before the above-quoted discussion, she had asked the children if the music could be heard as a question. Thus, the girl's talk about something frightening provided a key to the incomprehensibility:

CG: She explained it as if something had happened, and I understood that she meant that
       something of a traumatic character had taken place that one cannot grasp—as when
       someone has died or something. It is beyond what one can take in. And there, this
       music was it [i.e., the Incomprehensible]. That is, what had happened had happened
       before the music—so it provided a sort of answer to the [question in the] music.

Half a year later, in a seminar with composition students at the Royal College of Music in Stockholm, Cecilia's recollection had been simplified a bit: "One child was explaining that this music was happening after [...] something really terrible [had] occurred—*this* is *afterwards*. So, we had her play on the drums the Before, and then we played the Afterwards". In this interpretation, the Incomprehensible was located in the violin piece where the girl first had heard it, and the collaborative drum prelude represents something frightening or terrible that may have preceded the Incomprehensible, thus providing an "answer" to it or rendering it understandable.

In a separate interview after the workshops, Martin proposed an even more detailed psychological explanation to the Incomprehensible—one that was interestingly congenial to one of his own writings. The main idea in his philosophical article is that for a human being, a total catastrophe (such as the Holocaust) is un-experienceable, while it erases all points of orientation due to its immense dimensions and thus cannot be comprehended at all. In this view, a catastrophe can better be represented in artistic ways, by creating a parallel world, a personalised response (Gelland, 2014). In his explanation of the workshop, Martin saw the girl provide this sort of response to the state of incomprehensibility that follows a catastrophe:

MG: I assume that when she said the word "Incomprehensible"—a really advanced concept for her age—that she meant... It was interesting: She said "terror" [*das Erschrecken*], and [with the Incomprehensible] she meant *after* being frightened [*nach dem Erschrecken*]. [...] This girl was certainly from Syria or thereabout: She may have such a background. [...] She may have herself experienced a catastrophe, or had a connection with it—with such experiences. [...] This is an example of how something that has autobiographical import for a child may get a musical representation without her saying it. [...] There is no need to explain in words what she or her family may perhaps have experienced.

EH: But how is that mediated in the group situation? How does it work with the other children being there?

MG: Well, everyone took her seriously. The others do not need to know the [exact] context. What is important is just that they take it seriously—this pattern of being terrified and what comes after it—that it is given a concrete representation. This image will also stick with the others. [...] They can respect it, as they may themselves have experienced something serious.

From this perspective, the collaborative prelude in which the Incomprehensible followed after the Frightening was not just any concatenation of ideas suggested by the children, nor was it just a representation of the Frightening (as in Cecilia's later recollection). Rather, the prelude provided a complex emotional structure through which to address an unspeakable experience and its aftermath. In this interpretation, the Incomprehensible was centrally represented by the girl's own drum part in the prelude:

MG: [The resulting musical situation] is meaningful, even though it might not sound so very interesting in acoustic terms, but...

EH: It was more about the semantic interpretation.

MG: Yes. It is the concept. [...] She did only that one thing [i.e., played the Incomprehensible], and the Frightening was done by the others [before her]. In other words, the situation was described collectively, in the group, through group work. [...] It is all about structure: You process the structure of a situation. Not just one emotional state, but a structure...

EH: It was not just a musical structure, but rather...

MG: No. A human structure.

EH: An experiential structure, or...?

MG: Yes.

It is notable that the original workshop discussion in which the image of the Incomprehensible emerged was rather sparse, and it takes a few leaps of imagination to interpret the image as Martin does here. The factual accuracy of the musicians' various interpretations may nevertheless be of lesser importance than the way in which the strong image sparked the imagination of everyone involved, leading to a creative, collaborative staging. Even if Martin would not have been "correct" in hearing the notion of the Incomprehensible in relation to a catastrophe, the situation undoubtedly did involve working on a structure of rather complex emotional qualities that had emerged from the children's own sphere of experience. For the musicians, the level of children's involvement confirmed the value of the music they provided and inspired them to meet the children with a thoroughgoing openness:

> CG: The meetings with the children proved that coming into contact with these two pieces can lead to a kind of spiritual experience, and that it touched their own spirituality, as exemplified by the girl who talked about the Incomprehensible [...]. In many of the things they did, it felt that they were so generous to share their innermost. It gives me a sort of confidence, and also a mandate to apply my own spirituality and my own depth when I interpret the music.

Discussion

Noting how professional musicians' school visits often suffer from a one-directional sender-receiver relationship between the musicians and the audience, Kari Holdhus has argued for tighter musician-teacher collaborations, suggesting that "visiting artists' practices must be school led and school based" (Holdhus, 2018, p. 27). The work of Duo Gelland illustrates an alternative approach in which the musicians are holding the strings—in the workshops I observed, the teacher either sat in the background or was absent from class—but in which the sender-receiver relationship is broken down. The Gellands clearly exceed the minimum expectation for school music projects to provide interesting cultural experiences. Indeed, they exemplify what Even Ruud has called "health musicians"—individuals who possess "the necessary musical and performative skills, the methodological equipment, and theoretical familiarity, and not least, the personal, ethical, and political values to best carry out [...] health-musicking projects" (Ruud, 2012, p. 95). While neither of the Gellands has an education as a teacher or therapist, their ethical thinking draws heavily on their readings in anthropology (Cecilia) and philosophy (Martin), and my impression was that their classroom presence was not merely imbued by musical excellence, but even more importantly by an ethics of parental care and steady democratic ideals.

It is notable that much of what the Gellands do in class has parallels in expressive arts therapies. For instance, Martin's understanding of the image of the Incomprehensible discussed above is reminiscent of views in the arts therapies according to which a trauma should not be provided a rational "meaning", but it rather needs to be re-imagined in artistic "ways of representation that are true to its chaotic and meaningless character" (Levine, 2009, p. 18). Similarly, Cecilia's suggestion that the arts provide a neutralising arena for safely negotiating difficult inner experiences and violent impulses is, in effect, an art-therapeutic maxim. Earlier, I mentioned how creativity has been distinguished from psychopathology by the presence of protective factors; similarly, music provides here a structured, protective framework in which human vulnerability can be channelled in a controlled way instead of leading to inner chaos.

The Gelland approach to health musicianship thus directly challenges sharp distinctions between "artistic", "pedagogical", and "therapeutic" realms. In particular, it challenges the idea that there should be an essential distinction between "human communicating in sound" or "playing oneself" that can take place in music therapy improvisation in the presence of an educated therapist and "artistic" musical improvisation that is simply "about making music" (Pavlicevic, 2000). Indeed, such distinctions might be questioned by many improvising musicians, too—witness the German clarinettist Theo Jörgensmann's (b. 1948) notion of improvisation as "coming-to-oneself" and "becoming-aware-of-oneself" (Wilson, 1999, p. 12). For the Gellands, the interpretation of contemporary music in children's workshops is likewise informed by an improvisatory stance which not only allows but indeed requires that the musicians are constantly "playing themselves"—exposing their own human selves. The musicians' openness to expose their own vulnerability becomes the key in reaching out to any such vulnerabilities in children that the music might help to overcome.

The most obvious challenge to music educators and music therapists that is implicit in the Gelland approach might be the level of musical craftsmanship with which they operate. Although not explicitly discussed above, the immediacy of musical interchange in the workshops was palpably rooted in musical excellence, reminding an observer of the importance of musical quality when working with children. For musicians, in turn, the most obvious challenge might be to break down patterns of one-directional performativity in school concert visits and community projects: In music, interactivity implies education, and succeeding in this should not be seen as an exclusive domain of professional teachers. The deeper challenge to musicians, teachers, and therapists alike, however, lies in dropping such professional titles and opening oneself as a vulnerable human being in front of the children. According to the view unfolded above, it is only by offering to expose one's humanity and one's shortcomings in true dialogue that the musician may reach out to offer relief to vulnerable others—be they adults or be they children. This, to me, seems very close to Sennett's definition of craftsmanship—"the special human condition of being engaged".

References

Baker, F., & Bor, W. (2008). Can music preference indicate mental health status in young people? *Australasian Psychiatry, 16*(4), 284–288.

Brown, B. (2012). *Daring greatly: How the courage to be vulnerable transforms the way we live, love, parent, and lead*. New York: Avery.

Carson, S. (2011). Creativity and psychopathology: A shared vulnerability model. *The Canadian Journal of Psychiatry, 56*(3), 144–153.

Espeland, M. (1987). Music in use: Responsive music listening in the primary school. *British Journal of Music Education, 4*(3), 283–297.

Furlong, M. J., Gilman, R., & Huebner, E. S. (Eds.). (2014). *Handbook of positive psychology in schools* (2nd ed.). New York: Routledge.

Gelland, M. (2014). "…um etwas davon plötzlich aufleuchten zu lassen": Darstellungsprobleme individuellen Erlebens. *Zeitschrift ästhetische Bildung, 6*(2), 2–7.

Holdhus, K. (2018). Teacher-musician collaborations on the move: From performance appreciation to dialogue. In C. Christophersen & A. Kenny (Eds.), *Musician-teacher collaborations: Altering the chord* (pp. 27–38). New York: Routledge.

Levine, S. K. (2009). *Trauma, tragedy, therapy: The arts and human suffering*. Philadelphia, PA: Jessica Kingsley Publishers.

Martin, G., Clarke, M., & Pearce, C. (1993). Adolescent suicide: Music preference as an indicator of vulnerability. *Journal of the American Academy of Child and Adolescent Psychiatry, 32*(3), 530–535.

Matthews, R. (2015). Beyond toleration—Facing the other. In C. Benedict, P. Schmidt, G. Spruce, & P. Woodford (Eds.), *Social justice in music education* (pp. 238–249). Oxford, UK: Oxford University Press.

McFerran, K. S. & Wölfl, A. (2015). Music, violence and music therapy with young people in schools: A position paper. *Voices, 15*(2). Available at: https://voices.no/index.php/voices/article/view/2280/2035. Viewed 9/19/2018.

Nakkula, M. J., & Toshalis, E. (2010). *Understanding youth: Adolescent development for educators*. Cambridge, MA: Harvard Education Press.

Pavlicevic, M. (2000). Improvisation in music therapy: Human communication in sound. *Journal of Music Therapy, 37*(4), 269–285.

Rawlings, D., & Locarnini, A. (2007). Dimensional schizotypy, autism, and unusual word associations in artists and scientists. *Journal of Research in Personality, 42*(2), 465–471.

Ruud, E. (2012). The new health musicians. In R. A. R. MacDonald, G. Kreutz, & L. Mitchell (Eds.), *Music, health, and wellbeing* (pp. 87–96). Oxford, UK: Oxford University Press.

Scheel, K. R., & Westefeld, J. S. (1999). Heavy metal music and adolescent suicidality: An empirical investigation. *Adolescence, 34*(134), 253–273.

Schwartz, K. D., & Fouts, G. T. (2003). Music preferences, personality style, and developmental issues of adolescents. *Journal of Youth and Adolescence, 32*(3), 205–213.

Sennett, R. (2008). *The craftsman*. London: Allen Lane.

Wiggins, J. (2011). Vulnerability and agency in being and becoming a musician. *Music Education Research, 13*(4), 355–367.

Wilson, P. N. (1999). *Hear and now: Gedanken zur improvisierten Musik*. Hofheim, Germany: Wolke Verlag.

The *Kraptr* of Aging Folk Musicians: Mental Practice for the Future

Eva Sæther

Abstract This chapter rests on participant observation and interviews from Malungs folkhögskola, the distance education "Folkmusik fiol", led by the doyen of Swedish folk music pedagogy, Jonny Soling. With his life-long experience of fiddle education for grown-ups, Soling has unique knowledge of holistic fiddle didactics. At the age of 73, he still attracts course participants from all ages and all parts of Sweden, and many of these students are aged 60 plus. What is it that inspires these aging folk musicians to invest time and energy in challenging further training? What are the characteristics of the *kraptr* in folk music and of Jonny Soling? In the invitation to contribute to this book, Magne Espeland introduces an expanded notion of craft, giving space to a multiplicity of interpretations. The shared continental and old English use is associated with power, physical strength and skill. With the old Norse *kraptr*, virtue is added to the list. In this chapter, another dimension is suggested, opening up for ethical dimensions of sharing knowledge, including the experience that comes with age.

It didn't take long after the invitation to this book on kraptr jingled into the mailbox, before I, with an introverted smile recaptured a scene from a PhD defense party. The opponent, Magne Espeland, pulled up a recorder from the inside pocket of his jacket. With this instrument, maybe the most bullied in the history of music education, he delivered an elegant and appreciative comment to the new doctor in music education.

On stage, close to the opponent, was the happy respondent and fiddler, ready to through and with his fiddle give his thanks to the opponent, the committee, fellow folk musicians, colleagues and family. Through the presented thesis we had all delved into the craft of folk music, and now we were reminded of the sounding dimension, improvisation in the playing and the performing of folk music – and the ability of music to reach beyond words.

My introverted smile from this memory was reinforced by the tone of the invitation. Of course, the retiring (?) master of recorder can't resist being part of this collaborative book project, and of course the theme is addressing the future. Where are we heading with our shared understanding of the craft of music education? How can we include groups, genres and instruments from the margins, how can tradition and innovation co-exist, how do we combine theory with practice? How do we apply post-colonial approaches in our ambitions to develop culturally sensitive music education? All these challenges are waiting for attention and care, but in this context, they are drowned out by other, more instantly burning questions:

E. Sæther (✉)
Lund University, Lund, Sweden
e-mail: eva.saether@mhm.lu.se

© Springer Nature Switzerland AG 2021   207
K. Holdhus et al. (eds.), *Music Education as Craft*, Landscapes: the Arts,
Aesthetics, and Education 30, https://doi.org/10.1007/978-3-030-67704-6_16

- *How is meaningful aging connected to musical learning?*
- *How can aging inform the kraptr of music education?*

This chapter rests on participant observation and interviews from Malungs Folk High School, and more particular in regard to the distance education of "Folk music fiddle", led by Jonny Soling, the doyen of Swedish folk music pedagogy. With his life-long experience of fiddle education for grown-ups, Soling has a unique knowledge on holistic fiddle didactics. Since 1978, when the regular courses started at Malung Folk High School, approximately 15.000 musicians have been fostered by him. At the age of 73, he still attracts course participants from all ages and all parts of Sweden, many of these students being 60 plus. What is it that inspire these aging folk musicians to invest time and energy in engaging in challenging further training? What are the characteristics of the craft in folk music and of Jonny Soling?

A body of research exists on the effect of older musicians' participation in musical ensembles. The benefits thereof have been found to include enhanced social cohesion, personal development and empowerment, as well as contributions to recovery from depression and maintenance of personal well-being throughout the later stages of life (Balbag, Pedersen, & Gatz, 2014; Creech, Hallam, McQueen, & Varvargou, 2013).

Musicians require many years of practice in order to gain proficiency in their chosen instrument. Ericsson, Krampe, and Tesch-Romer (1993), in exploring what separates those who achieve true excellence on their instrument from those of lesser ability, conducted a landmark study of young violinists at the Music Academy of West Berlin, Germany. They discovered, after testing and surveying students across multiple categories, that one category alone distinguished the best students from others, namely, the amount of time spent on practice. The determining factor, however, was not just the quantity, i.e. conducted over many years, but also the quality of practice, which is goal-oriented, highly focused, including plentiful feedback, and being mentally challenging and tiring.

The aim of this chapter is to investigate and analyse practice habits and methodologies among older folk musicians, their reasons for engaging in physically and mentally demanding practice, the motivation that drives them to continue over time and, most importantly, the implications for our understanding of future-oriented *kraptr* that can be found from a study on and with aging fiddlers.

People get older. During the next coming decades, the demographic old-age dependency ratio within the EU will radically change. In 2010, the ratio was 25%, which means that the working-age population (15–64 years) balanced the smaller group of old-agers (64 +), although with concerns about shrinking funds for retirement pension. With changing life habits, it is expected that in 2070 the ratio will be 51.2%. With increasing life expectancy, there will be only two working-age persons for each 64+ person (Kristoffersson & Nilsson, 2018). This group of elders is to this date scarcely discussed within music education research. Furthermore, this group in Western societies tend to be regarded as a problem rather than an asset.

In her study on music as a promoter of well-being for older men, Lindblad (2018) refers to research that shows that young and old people are more content with their lives than other age groups. Older people tend to spend their time with whatever puts them in a positive state of mind, for example, music.

> Music has been shown to give substantial health benefits, at mental, social, existential as well as physical levels. To engage in music can create a sense of meaning and purpose in life, strengthen self-esteem or support social engagement and a sense of belonging. (Lindblad, 2018, p. 102).

In general, education is planned for young people. However, life-long learning is in the forefront of research on "successful ageing". Schoultz (2018) refers to a study showing that music, arts and informal evening courses have significant importance for the well-being of elder people, while sports and more formal courses did not show any significant effect. The definition of successful ageing entails (i) avoiding illness, (ii) retaining a high level of physical and cognitive ability and (iii) participating in social and stimulating activities (Schoultz, 2018, p. 123). There is a need for more studies on the relation between elder peoples' learning and health benefits. We need to know more about content and methods, and we need to know more about learning processes in diverse contexts. The question for a sustainable future is if and how education can enhance a sense of coherence and strengthen general resistance resources (Schoultz, 2018). In this chapter, the life-long learning processes that flourish at Malung Folk High School are reviewed in the light of a conceptual framework that highlights sustainability potentials for societies with ageing populations.

Methodology

The methodological inspiration for this study stems from interviews performed in Gambia (Sæther, 2003) where the questions, in a sense, were asked by the kora,[1] played by my co-researcher jali Alagi Mbye. In the interview with the ageing Kanuteh brothers, the ostinatos played on the kora, accompanying the conversation, skilfully guided the expert musicians to discuss and reflect on pedagogical and societal aspects within their own tradition. The old master musicians were concerned about problems with recruiting new students and a decline in the quality of young performers. Times were better before, they argued, when boys born in a jali family stayed within the regimen of the tradition and learned how to play the kora by "obeying" the old masters. On the other hand, the younger master Alagi Mbye was concerned with widened participation, a music education for all, including children from non-jali families, regardless gender. He had at that time already violated the "traditional curriculum" by opening a school for all – much in line with Jonny Soling's distance education "Folk music fiddle", open for all.

In research projects following the study in Gambia on what we can learn from studies in orally transmitted musical cultures, the experience from the

---

[1] 21-stringed harp lute, played in Gambia, Senegal and surrounding Mande areas.

ostinato-guided interview has been used in projects at home, exploring intercultural learning contexts such as the Persian music school in Malmö (Sæther, 2010), and the implementation of El Sistema in socio-economical vulnerable parts of Malmö (Sæther, Bergman, & Lindgren, 2017). *Sensuous scholarship*, as suggested by Stoller (1997), and methodological openings from the arts as presented in Bresler (2015) inform the design of this ongoing study on ageing Swedish folk fiddlers. As sensuous scholarship asks us to include more senses than the dominant visual sense in our efforts to expand knowledge, my own fiddle is part of the field study, performed together with the 24 other students at the "Folk music fiddle" course of 2018–2019. During 4 weeks spread over the academic year, me and my fiddle travel to the little village Malung in the region of Dalarna, to learn from the master. Being one of the students, and myself 60 plus, a participant observation study including questionnaires on participant aspirations and experiences and interviews with Jonny Soling and selected participants is presently in process. The data generation will in later stages be informed by theoretical concepts from the field of social sustainability in music education. For this chapter, the data presented rests on field notes from the first week of lessons in Malung, September 17–20, an interview with Jonny Soling and results from the questionnaire on student expectations, background and aspirations. The participants have been given names to protect their anonymity. Ethical rules and procedures as prescribed by Lund University and the National Agency for Research have been applied.

Tuning in to the Results

> *I wake up early. Someone is playing the fiddle. I have been given a temporary home in one of the small school houses and notice that the furnishing in my room hasn't changed since the 1980's. Shower and bathroom are shared with the other course participants, in my room there is a basin for tooth brushing, an empty stock shelf from IKEA that I remember from my student period, two narrow beds and a writing desk. It is perfectly ascetic. Here we are with our fiddles, soon we will meet Jonny. The first lesson starts 08.30.*

> *During the long car ride to Malung with two fellow participants, there was plenty of time to talk about our personal projects. Olof hesitates: "Is it ok to say that I want to learn all Jonny's tips and tricks before it is too late?" We agree that this is a relevant project, as is of course Olof's ambition to dig deeper into, transcribe and organise his knowledge on tunes from his own geographical roots. Stina simply wants to improve her fiddle playing. I claim that I want to learn how to hold the fiddle. "What?" Yes, hold it, in balance, without muscle efforts. And I aim to learn how to love etudes and scales. At the end of the period I hope to have acquired a repertoire of tunes from the late fiddler Hans Lisper (1946–2007).* (Field notes from the first morning, 180917)

Later that same first day I hear Jonny Soling touching all of my focus areas: "I adjust the resonances in my body according to my inner singing" he says on finding a rich tone quality. "It's not about how you hold the bow, it's on how you move it", he continues. I realise I have to shift my attention from the fiddle to the bow, in order to learn how to hold my instrument in a balanced manner. I also have a feeling that there is more to it: "Music is a good way to coordinate the body, it's a good way to keep alive until it is over". This day, as all other days of the week, Jonny starts teaching at 08.30 and stops at 15.00, in one continuous flow of storytelling, etudes, laughter, tunes, moving around in the room, more scales and etudes, only interrupted by breaks for coffee or food.

We are 25 students in the room, most of us with white hairs – the first preliminary results from the questionnaire show that the majority have passed 60 years, a few have passed 70. In order to avoid wasting any time on superfluous introductions of our names or the course structure, Jonny starts with the essentials. Sitting in front of us, he gives us the narrative on how he started to play the fiddle as a grown-up, 25 years old, against all advice – to show the importance of motivation and pulverisation of prejudices. Directly after the storytelling, we move our chairs into a circle and are served with the first scale, G-major, semiquavers in a variation of bow patterns.

As the week proceeds, we are presented with a rich flora of histories about traditional masters that have informed Jonny Soling's craftsmanship, musicians that in this context serve as motivators and inspiring models for our own practice. We are also playfully guided into the scales and etudes that we are now supposed to engage with an hour a day. There are no shortcuts to mastery. And you never get done. Jonny Soling talks about musical exercise as skills training ("färdighetsträning" in Swedish) as a never-ending polishing and development of skills, where you are never "färdig", done.

In the field notes from the first day, I find a collection of one-liners from Jonny Soling's pedagogical tool box, a box that has been equipped during more than 40 years of teaching. As a teacher he never makes any lesson plans; however he prepares himself to have full access to the imaginary tool box, mentally and physically: "It's fair to guess that with age follows experience. The body needs maintenance, if you don't act your physical and psychological skills deteriorate" (field notes, 180,917).

> Bowing happens in both arms. Then you pump blood, and blood is life. The fiddle is a vibrator, so is the bow, I allow the string to meet the flesh of my fingers, I don't press, I have a love relation to my instrument. (From the collection of Jonny Soling's one-liners, 180917).

Three days later, we eventually present ourselves to one another; now we have played with Jonny Soling at daytime, and at nights gathered in smaller informal groups to get to know each other through jamming and sharing tunes. This is also the day I choose for an interview with Jonny Soling. In the following section, our conversation is structured according to the emerging themes, five dimensions of craft in the pedagogy of Jonny Soling: the child's attitude, breaking prejudices on age, storytelling, mental practice and inclusion of all.

The Craft of the Child

As we struggle with our bowing patterns and triplets, Jonny Soling dances around in the circle, curiously capturing how every individual is doing, from the beginners to the veterans who have already spent a long life developing their fiddling skills. There is something in his body language that reminds me of the playfulness of a child, and this is no coincidence. His movement in the room is part of a strategy to refuel us, the (ageing) course participants, with the energy and engagement of a child: "It's about conquering new fields or discovering new ideas and skills", he says. In his view most of us turn "into adults" already as teenagers, wiping away the child's capacity to nurture an interest towards almost anything. "There is a tremendously powerful pedagogy in the approach towards learning of a child, that I now strive to recapture…I am not saying this is the alone salvation, but I think it is an attitude, and if you combine that with the brain of an adult, the experiences of an adult, that combination is very strong". When talking about why he has focused so much on the bowing during the first week the course, Jonny Soling relates to the rediscovery of the approach towards the learning of a child. He is convinced that people and musicians that reach their goals do not find any obstacles that they avoid. Instead they find things that are "interesting". He underlines:

> … because those who have that [the approach of a child] grow naturally, they need very little, actually they don't need one single course. Actually they can take courses, it doesn't need to stand in the way for their learning, since they have a creative attunement towards whatever they are doing to constantly be in a learning mode".

This approach concerns not only the participants in the course, the learners, but very much the teacher. It is obvious to us, the participants, that Jonny Soling enjoys teaching; being in the classroom in many ways resembles being at an interactive theatre play, where we move in and out of different roles. He never writes down what to do during a full day of teaching, but intuitively takes in what the room needs, a habit that makes and keeps him alert. There is, he says, nothing that can stop him from teaching: "I love to analyse, to strip down, to rebuild, and I am very fond of mediation and communication. And this concerns all aspects of life. The classroom is just one channel".

Ultimately, the craft of the child approach lends Jonny Soling to choose the difficult and avoid the easy. For example he chooses to teach 25 persons in a group, covering almost complete beginners to advanced players. It is, when performed in action, in the bowing patterns, he gives us as learners the impression that the difficult is easy, if performed with a playful mindset.

The Craft of Breaking Prejudices on Age

The experiences from teaching students of all ages, including the ageing population that dominate the distance courses, have not changed Jonny Soling's teaching methods. On the contrary, the elder students have confirmed his belief that learning is not about age, it is about engagement. "There are so many prejudices in society on music, and the music institutions seem to take these for granted", he says. His own life story serves as an illustration that very few of the common ideas on music and musicality need to be true. "You have to be young, you have to be musical, there is a whole menagerie of prejudices connected to the music I am playing...nowadays it is too late to start when you are 7. You have to start at 3" (laughing). Here Jonny is referring to the influential Suzuki method, that when spreading from Japan to other parts of the world has led to a focus on a very early start for violin students. Many years ago, Shinuzi Suzuki himself visited Jonny Soling's home in Dalarna. At this occasion, Jonny seized the opportunity to question the age discourse. After telling his story, which entails fighting for a teacher since no one wanted to teach a 25-year-old, he played some tunes and then asked about the importance of starting young. In the educational system of Japan, the mothers are involved a lot, playing and learning together with very young children. "It is a pedagogical system – not a biological", Jonny Soling argues. And the story goes that Suzuki himself, visiting Jonny Soling in a little village in the most famous folk music district in Sweden, concluded after being asked at what age you should start playing the violin: "Well, you start when you start".

It has become one of Jonny Soling's missions to tear down all kinds of hindrances that can be used for not believing that musical learning is possible at all stages of life: "You can say you are too old, or you don't have the right parents, or you name it, this is what I want to pulverize". One way of doing this is to reduce fears and installing an appetite for etudes among us, the adult learners: "There is a strange conception of practise as duty. If I wake up early, I can play all the boring scales for the prescribed number of hours, and then, when I am free, at last I can play the music. To me this is pure madness. All the musicians I know, most of them are self-taught, they say yes to everything". By playing around with us in the semiquavers and triplets, Jonny Soling strives at installing a kind of investigative mentality, for us to continue to play with the exercises, beyond concepts of duty and age.

The Craft of Storytelling

Every morning, as we enter the classroom that is already furnished with chairs in lines, we learn that now it is story time. We take our seats, fiddles still in their boxes, and listen to an endless stream of stories on old fiddlers or key moments of Jonny Soling's musical live story. These stories alert us on possibilities, hindrances, motivation, desire, devotion, stubbornness and historical use and misuse of folk music as a genre. During the morning hours, the stories guide us to reflect on issues in our own active music making, issues that Jonny Soling has observed need our attention:

> I nourish the art of story telling a lot, like I still practice my solo playing. You know, when friends pass away (laughter) I tell myself that I enjoy playing solo. This does not mean that I don't like playing with other, but I like giving talks, and I like to have a voice, to influence. But this has to do with confidence and avoiding fears. When I see that students are tired I break in with a story, or something else that brings new air to the room.

In his teaching, Jonny Soling uses the stories both to interrupt fatiguing efforts and to convey knowledge that he considers important to transmit. Some of this knowledge is related to specific master musicians, especially what their characteristics are, and why they have managed to develop certain specific skills. Additionally, there is an aspect of well-being in the storytelling situation and a pedagogic quality. When narrating the life story of the famous fiddlers Påhl-Olle and Nils Agenmark, he focuses on the key qualities of their learning capacities and their driving motivation to continue to develop as musicians until the very end: "If I, as a pedagogue, am able to contribute to winkle out this driving force within a few more, then I have been very successful". The storytelling includes playing tunes, asking us to listen with closed eyes or to imagine the vibrations and tone qualities that a good fiddler is searching for in the bowing movements, the body balance, the relaxed fingering and the musical curiosity, the approach of a child, both telling and learning from stories.

The Craft of Mental Practice

In Eriksson's (2016) thesis on Jonny Soling's pedagogy, she emphasises his focus on mental training, practicing without the instrument. Surprisingly, during the first week of the distance course, we were immersed in very practical exercises. However, later on we will learn how to play mentally: "When you have learned how to do that, when you have practiced how to practice without your instrument, there is no difference between practicing with or without your fiddle. You are playing…which means that if you are bored at a party you can always play". Jonny laughs again and talks about how one of his former students has learnt how to practise during long car transports between gigs. I wonder whether this might be potentially dangerous: "Well, that depends. If the playing is in the foreground and the driving in the background. You have to learn how to handle that, but the brain can work on different levels, simultaneously".

The capacity to work with mental preparations is often used by Jonny Soling to put himself in a state of mind where a concert is possible. "You can't always pick your best performance from your arms sleeve, it is not always there, but there is a state of mind where it is possible". As in almost all lessons, even in the interview, Jonny Soling relates music making to wider issues on general levels. The craft of mental practice, for example, is related to the necessity to apply a specific mental platform to any situation in life. Being with a child demands a certain mentality that needs to be activated, helping an old person over the street needs a relation: "…you cannot just drag him. I think a lot like that, now it gets deep (laughs), I think of life as a theatre. That means that I want to be able to take different roles". This is an idea that has grown from observations of the late fiddler Påhl-Olle, who had the skill to walk into any room, read the room and sense what positions that were available and free: "He never took over, he never just grabbed a chair, he contributed to the room".

In many respects, this skill is crucial for a pedagogue who needs to both give and take space in order to build relationships that enhance learning.

The Craft of Inclusion

Quality is in focus during all our learning sessions at the first gathering of the distance course, quality of tone, of intention, of balance, of bowing, of presence, of every detail. As students we sense that our playing skills are scrutinised; still we have not been asked to perform an entrance test or to even give any information on our imagined level. Jonny Soling, with all his experience from serving as a judge at numerous prestigious events knows how little he knows: "Who am I to say that you are not accepted? Everyone who thinks that he or she wants to take this course should have the possibility to do so. There are no good incentives for exclusion, and only if we have more applicants than the room can take, I have had to say no. In those cases I have used lottery to decide."

In the interview we talk about the societal benefits of people being fully occupied with meaningful activities. "I believe that in order to stay alive until you die, which I have taken as my project, then you have to make sure that you are busy with interesting tasks every day, all the time. Interesting things. And by all means, it might as well be difficult". I think that other teachers would have hesitated or refused to teach such a diverse group as ours, but to Jonny Soling the most important limit is the physical room, when it comes to pedagogy it is the teacher's competence that determines the possible size and nature of the group. When beginners get worried about not coping with a bowing pattern, he is there persuading them to take it easy and just listen, and stay assured that with time the knowledge will be there, in the arms. As a pedagogue, he is convinced that when fear is substituted with longing, you have reached halfway. A couple of participants at this distance course are returnees; taking part of Jonny Soling's courses has to them become a lifestyle.

Fading out Towards the Discussion

In the sections above, the craft of ageing folk musicians is discussed through the experience of Jonny Soling, aged 73. With his inclusive approach, he attracts students from all over Sweden, most of them belonging to the growing group of people in Europe aged 64+ years. In order to capture the expectations and driving forces of this group, a questionnaire was sent to the 25 participants in the distance course of 2018–2019. Based on the preliminary result of the answers, some of the students are very well aware of what they are looking for.

The answers to the question on the most important reason for choosing to participate in the course include Jonny Soling's pedagogy: "Specifically Jonny's holistic perspective on teaching. Folk music isn't only about the tunes, there is much more to it. Peoples' approach towards life, tradition, development and present times. Jonny is inspiring with his lust for life and his way of "living" pedagogy". When specifying expectations, the participants mention playing technique and acquiring tools for continued development of skills. For those who have already retired, the distance course offers possibilities to learn from the best, and for those that are still busy with a full-time profession, the format with four intensive "boarding school" weeks opens up for "a possibility to break the hectic everyday life and provide a chance to lay hold of music making". The answers also testify to the elder students living an active life between the course weeks. Among the ageing folk music students, we find a yoga teacher, a manager of a ceramics company, a supply teacher, a carpenter with special skills in house renovation and a student – together the student group challenge notions on age as a hindrance for living a meaningful life.

Turning Back to Kraptr for the Future

In the invitation to contribute to this book, Magne Espeland introduces what I understand as an expanded notion of craft, giving space to a multiplicity of interpretations. The shared continental and old English use is associated with power, physical strength and skill. With the old Norse "kraptr", virtue is added to the list. In this chapter, another dimension is suggested, opening up for ethical dimensions of sharing knowledge, including the experience that comes with age. The two questions that were posed in the opening: "How is meaningful ageing connected to musical learning?" and "How can aging inform the kraptr of music education?" have not yet been fully answered. This is a good sign, because with all questions answered there would be very little room for curiosity and directions for future directions within music education. As the kraptr practiced at Malungs folkhögskola points at, there are many good reasons for higher music education to rethink how life-long learning might influence both content, methods and widened participation.

References

Balbag, M. A., Pedersen, N. L., & Gatz, M. (2014). Playing a musical instrument as a protective factor against dementia and cognitive impairment: A population-based twin study. *International Journal of Alzheimer's Disease, 2014*, 1–6. https://doi.org/10.1155/2014/836748

Bresler, L. (Ed.). (2015). *Beyond methods. Lessons from the arts to research methodology* (Vol. 10). Lund, Sweden: Malmö Academy of Music, Lund University.

Creech, A., Hallam, S., McQueen, H., & Varvargou, M. (2013). The power of music in the lives of older adults. *Research Studies in Music Education, 35*(1), 87–102.

Ericsson, K. A., Krampe, R. T., & Tesch-Romer, C. (1993). The role of deliberate practice in the acquisition of expert performance. *Psychological Review, 100*(3), 363–406.

Eriksson, C. (2016). *Att spela fiol med hela kroppen: En studie i Jonny Solings pedagogik*. Examensarbete (10hp). Kungliga Musikhögskolan.

Kristoffersson, E., & Nilsson, K. (Eds.). (2018). *Successful ageing in an interdisciplinary context: Popular science presentations*. Örebro, Sweden: Örebro University.

Lindblad, K. (2018). Music as a promoter of well-being for older men. In E. Kristoffersson & K. Nilsson (Eds.), *Successful ageing in an interdisciplinary context: Popular science presentations* (pp. 98–106). Örebro, Sweden: Örebro University.

Sæther, E. (2003). *The oral university. Attitudes to music teaching and learning in the Gambia*. Malmö, Sweden: Malmö Academy of Music.

Sæther, E. (2010). Music education and the other. *Finnish Journal of Music Education, 13*(1), 45–60.

Sæther, E., Bergman, Å., & Lindgren, M. (2017). El Sistema: Musiklärare i en spänningsfylld modell för inkluderande pedagogik. *Pedagogisk forskning i Sverige, 22*(1–2), 9–27.

Schoultz, M. (2018). The learning activities and health of older adults: A salutogenic perspective on successful ageing. In E. Kristoffersson & K. Nilsson (Eds.), *Successful ageing in an interdisciplinary context: Popular science presentations* (pp. 121–127). Örebro, Sweden: Örebro University.

Stoller, P. (1997). *Sensuous scholarship*. Philadelphia, PA: University of Pennsylvania Press.

Music Education as Craft: Reframing a Rationale

Magne I. Espeland ⓘ

Abstract This chapter is an attempt to discuss the question of rationale(s) for music education. I shall argue that in light of considering and exploring "music education as craft", it is meaningful to reframe our rationale for this profession and ground our music education practices better in experience-based as well as philosophically and research-based knowledge and skills. I focus on what I have called a "common topos of significance" when considering music education as craft. I bring to the rationale table the following aspects of music education: (i) the significance of a dynamic interplay between the traditional and the innovative in our approach to music education practices; (ii) the significance of the creative and the improvisational in teaching as well as in learning processes; (iii) the significance of the material, and embodied practices in teaching as well as in learning environments; and finally, (iv) the significance of the relational and the democratic in our dealings with learners and colleagues. I have argued that it is of the utmost significance to foster, develop, discuss, and critique these aspects of music education in order to maintain, develop, and perhaps even to reframe a sustainable rationale for music education in a changing world.

Introduction

Twenty years ago, as we were celebrating a new millennium, I had the privilege of being invited to American professor, Bennett Reimer's, Northwestern University Music Education Leadership Seminar (NUMEL) that took place at the university campus in Chicago, United States. During a hectic and very interesting week, invited music educators assembled—not to present as we usually do at conferences—but to *discuss* topics particularly relevant for the rationale and practices of international music education.[1]

---

[1] In the foreword to the accompanying published book, editor and participant, Dr. Maud Hickey (2003) writes: "Imagine having the opportunity to spend five uninterrupted days with a small core

---

M. I. Espeland (✉)
Western Norway University of Applied Sciences, Stord, Norway
e-mail: magne.espeland@hvl.no

219

One of the guests at the Reimer seminar was Canadian composer, Raymond Murray Schafer, a well-known Canadian music educator and a pioneer of what often is referred to as the composition movement in music education (cf. Barrett, 1998). Schafer introduced his talk by recollecting a personal story from his music conservatoire student days where he was *expelled* from his institution because of his musical and educational viewpoints and how this dramatic event in his life became the start of his ground-breaking educational work in music composition. His story is one of the many in music education where opposition to established rationales and practices, and individuals' experience and thinking connected to a music educa-tion practice, sometimes lay the ground for hugely influential movements in music education.[2] Schafer's 40-year-old story was narrated at the Reimer seminar with humour in hindsight, but it can be understood as an example of how old rationales for practices in professional fields such as music education eventually cede to new ones in a seemingly endless trajectory of renewal and development.

This chapter is an attempt to focus on the question of rationale(s) for music edu-cation, that is, the underlying principles or fundamental reasons and justification for the future of music educations and its development in a changing world. I shall argue that in light of considering and exploring "music education as craft", it is meaningful to reframe our rationale for this profession, not only by trying to build new and innovative practices in our field but also to ground our music education practices better in experience-based *as well as* philosophically and research-based knowledge and skills.

A Common Topos of Significance for Music Education Practices in Our Age

Attempting such a bold endeavour, it is inspiring to know that I build on a long tradi-tion. For example, 105 years ago, a composer at the Royal Academy of Music in London, recognised as the institutor of the Music Appreciation Movement, Stewart Macpherson, wrote in his book *The Musical Education of the Child* (1915)[3]:

---

of colleagues who have the same research interest as you and have devoted a considerable amount of time and energy to this research. While in the past you've not had more than a passing 10-min conversation (if any) with some of these scholars, these 5 days offer time that is completely dedi-cated to brainstorming, discussing, questioning, and challenging ideas in the field" (Hickey, 2003, p. vii).

[2] In the case of Raymond Murray Schafer, the clash with the music conservatory he attended, a prominent music institution in urban Canada in the 1950s—with its many rules and conventions— became the very reason for a young composer's radical entrance into the field of international music education where he met other pioneers with similar ideas and rationales for music education (Schafer, 1965, 1969).

[3] Stewart Macpherson was professor of Music at the Royal Conservatory of Music in London. Between 1910 and 1916 he published a number of theory books for higher music education, but he

If we apply this thought to the teaching and learning of music, how does it all work out? What is the net result of all the vast amount of effort—honest, dogged, painstaking effort—that has been and is being expended throughout the land in connection with the child's lessons in music? For that the majority of music-teachers are some of the most hard-worked and hard-working members of the community—men and woman who bring to bear upon their work a degree of zeal, energy and patience which those in many another and better-paid walk of life might envy—is in reality a commonplace of experience, a truism which few will care to deny. (Macpherson, 1915, p. 2)

To me, it is both moving and thought-provoking to encounter a text written in the beginning of the horrors of the First World War, expressing such a strong belief in what he describes as "a commonplace of experience" and belief-based practices of hardworking music teachers. I share Macpherson's deep respect for the practitioners of music education and practices based on truism and experience rather than on a form of knowledge we often refer to as research-based. One of the questions I have asked myself lately however, when thinking about craft and craftsmanship, is the extent to which there might be a *common* place, a common topos, where it would be possible to describe and discuss a number of contemporary aspects of music education as particularly *significant,* that is, if and when we think about these practices as representing a craft and craftsmanship.

Even if I have a deep respect for the pioneering, experience-based practices in our long music education tradition, I shall argue that the list of pioneering practices and their adherents in music education, i.e. those connected to international pioneers such as Émile Jacques-Dalcroze, Stewart Macpherson, Carl Orff and Gunild Keetmann, Zoltán Kodály, Dmitry Kabalevsky, Eunice Boardman, John Paynter, Violeta Hemsy de Gainza, Meki Nzewi, José Antonio Abreu, Lucy Green and others, also need to be grounded in research and in a solid theoretical framework.[4] Indeed, this was the very intention of Bennett Reimer's NUMEL seminars. However, neither Reimer nor Macpherson seemed to take much notice of the wider context that they, or other humans, were and are a part of. Macpherson, when discussing music education without mentioning the wider and horrifying background of a World War, and the Reimer seminar participants paying very little attention during the seminar to the fact that we are all ecologically responsible individuals seemingly living in the age of the Anthropocene.[5]

Although I have been a researcher in music education for decades, I still believe that we can never reach a point where we can base a rationale for music education on research-based knowledge alone, simply because quality empirical research recognises its own limits as well as the complexities of music education practices. To

---

also was very much involved in supporting and advocating music in schools nationally and internationally (cf. MacPherson, 1910, 1912; Macpherson 1915).

[4] The list of names given here is just examples. I am fully aware that the production of a complete list giving credits to individual pioneers of music education practices is far beyond my limited knowledge of the field (See: Cox and Stevens 2017).

[5] According to Wikipedia, "The Age of the Anthropocene" is "a proposed geological epoch dating from the commencement of significant human impact on Earth's geology and ecosystems". (Wikipedia, 2020)

me, a reframed rationale for music education as craft can neither escape a reliance on truisms based on experience, nor can such a rationale avoid philosophical reasoning and argumentation. This does not mean, however, that anything goes, or that all knowledge is equally important, be it research-based, experience-based or based on philosophical and ontological theories. A common topos of significance for music education as craft needs to rest on our *knowledge* stemming from all of three sources of experience and sharing I have referred to above: (i) experience-based knowledge acquired through a myriad of excellent music education practices over a long time; (ii) knowledge, based on ontological and philosophical arguments dealing with the basic and big questions of our time and existence and, finally, (iii) our ever-expanding research-based knowledge in a number of science disciplines as well in music education and other relevant educational practices.

By applying such a tripartite framework for a knowledge-based approach in a discussion of a reframed rationale for music education as craft, my intention is not to reach a conclusion aspiring to be "the truth", but rather to inspire a *discussion* about what I have referred to as a common topos of significance, a commonplace of experience together with the research-based and philosophical knowledge that comes to mind when we think about music education as craft. In such an approach, I find support in the Indian philosopher, Joseph Kaipayil's fairly recent theory of *Relationalism: A Theory of Being* (2009), where he links knowledge, truth and beliefs. He writes:

> Finally, knowledge is relational in its truth dimension. Truth belongs to belief, for truth is acceptance of a belief to be the case about the object....
>
> It is possible to have multiple beliefs about one and same object; each of these beliefs can be true provided its claim has justification for the facts about the object. But the problem is how we can know the facts about an object in order to determine whether a belief relates to a fact it refers to. First of all, we should admit that reality is complex and that there is more to it than our description of it. Secondly, we need to accept that each of our description or beliefs is indeed an interpretation of the object under consideration and hence limited representation of that object. Thirdly, it is important to recognise poly-alethism that the truth about an object can be manifold. (p. 45)

Our object is music education. A strange thing to say maybe, but even so Kaipayil's ontological claim seems very relevant to me, especially since my intention for the following sections of this chapter is to fill my topos of significance with *my* choices, *my* interpretations, *my* suggestions and *my* invitation to a deeper and prolonged discussion far beyond this chapter and this book. Such a discussion may well be the beginning of an attempt to answer, at least to some extent, the questions I posed as an invitation to this volume:

> How should the diverse and long traditions of music education crafts respond to a rapidly changing environment in society and education? How could music education conceived of as craft contribute to creative and sustainable solutions to societal and educational challenges created by multiculturalism, globalisation, technology and accountability? And what kind of music education skills, virtues, and rationale (*kraptrs*) need to be changed, modified, developed, invented, dismissed or kept? How, and for what reasons and to what ends?" (Editorial group, letter of invitation to authors)

Each of the questions above is an invitation to explore as well as express our knowledge (based on experience and truism as well as research and philosophy) about what a topos of significance for music education as craft might consist of and how such a topos can be argued for as well as critiqued. In my case, I do not consider what follows as a well-defined and definitive collection of important characteristics and aspects of quality and sustainable music education, but as a commonplace for discussion about significant theories and practices.[6] In the next section therefore, it is my privilege to argue that such a commonplace of significance with regard to music education as craft needs to address: (i) the significance of a dynamic interplay between the traditional and the innovative in our approach to music education practices; (ii) the significance of the creative and the improvisational in teaching as well as in learning processes; (iii) the significance of the material and embodied practices in teaching as well as in learning environments; and finally (iv) the significance of the relational and the democratic in our dealings with learners and colleagues.

Music Education as Craft: What Is Significant and Why?

The Significance of a Dynamic Interplay Between the Traditional and the Innovative

Music education and music teaching and learning have a long formal as well as informal history. We know quite a bit about this tradition from research as well as from experience, be it about formal education in institutions or informal music teaching or learning in families or in garages. For example, the history of informal musical transmission from parent to child builds on a principle of apprenticeship which resembles similar trajectories of learning and professionalisation in craft guilds. Other parts of the history of music teaching and learning in schools, institutions or organisations are often described as specific and sometimes radically new methods or systems emerge, seemingly created by innovative and visionary music education pioneers and often connected to specific theories of learning and teaching. Not all education subjects or disciplines have such histories. To discard some of these achievements of music education history seems inevitable: some die away naturally; some persist only as a result of a few committed individuals who feel very strongly about something they believe has value; but others thrive and blossom. I have often wondered why. Is it because of the musical or pedagogical quality of the system in question—or lack thereof—or is it for other reasons?

---

[6] In many ways, music education can claim to have many "commonplaces" of this kind thanks to a multitude of writers and thinkers who have followed in Stuart McPherson's footsteps. Especially since the beginning of the 1990s, the international literature production with regard to research in music education has been impressive, e.g. in the form of comprehensive handbooks such as Richard Colwell's (1992) *Handbook of Research on Music Teaching and Learning* and its followers.

Some 20 years ago, I observed a student activity which can serve as a good example of what I would like to call a dynamic interplay between the traditional and the innovative in a music education practice. Bachelor students studying folk music from four countries and many institutions gathered for a week-long conference.[7] New to each other, they started off by teaching each other by ear—in instrumental or vocal groups of four—a simple chosen tune. This was in a tradition they were familiar with: the master-apprentice model of indigenous music teaching and learning very common in western as well as other music transmission traditions. Over the following couple of days, they elaborated on these simple melodies to create new pieces of music to be performed in an evening concert, more or less within a chamber music context and tradition. To observe these students when developing their work through negotiations and ear-based as well as notation-based trialling was an illuminating experience for me. It demonstrated how the students used their traditional master-apprenticeship model when appropriate. They moved towards models involving musical thematic invention and elaboration, discussions about harmony, counterpoint and form, numerous musical try-outs and verbal as well as musical negotiations when needed, going back and forth, driven by the desire to progress towards a common and accepted goal. The concert was awesome, and I still remember some of the music and the atmosphere. As such, the whole process can be described and characterised as a process of ongoing change and dynamic interplay from one mode of learning and teaching philosophy to another.

Few have written more convincingly about the need for *change* for music education than American philosopher, Estelle Jorgensen. In her book, *Transforming Music Education* (2003), she argues that what music education as a profession needs, is "transformation" justified for two main reasons:

> First, the mortality of human beings and the fact that education is carried on by one generation after another necessitates transformation if it is to succeed in the long run. Second, because it is undertaken by human beings, music education is beset by systematic problems that afflict the wider society. (p. 19)

Her first reason is simply rooted in the fact that generations have to adapt to a changing world and changing circumstances and that they should be developing practices of their own while still keeping some of the tradition. Her second reason is more complex and connected to values and what she calls a "humane" education, which she describes as a "radical and critical pedagogy" (p. x). While I am very sympathetic to the idea of "transformation" with regard to some very important aspects of music education, for example, its overall justification in humane values and systemic flaws in institutions and frameworks, I remain sceptical of an analysis which seems to rely on the passing of time and generations as a major and dominant element in educational renewal and, and I assume, quality signatures of music education. True, music education achievements of the past may well be flawed, and

---

[7] The *NorTrad* annual conference is arranged by the NordTrad Folkmusic Network consisting of 16 higher education institutions in Finland, Estonia, Sweden, Denmark and Norway and the Baltic countries.

some might appear to exist more or less as music education museums, but this does not mean that the age of a method or system in itself should be disqualifying. The most important criteria, as I see it, should be educational and pedagogical quality within a framework of societal sustainability and social, educational and individual relevance for the practice and purpose in question. Applying the lens of "music education as craft" means, first and foremost, a critical recognition and appraisal of the pedagogical repertoires and reservoirs—to use Basil Bernstein's (2000) concepts—developed over time as vertical knowledge and discourse structures by the music education profession in a broad sense—often including musicians and parents—and by other relevant disciplines, professions and, not to forget, political initiatives.[8]

Let us for a moment consider the question of tradition and innovation from an example of a well-established music education system that emerged a little less than one hundred years ago: Orff Schulwerk. Developed as a pedagogical practice in the Günther Schule of the interwar period in Germany, the Schulwerk is by now probably one of the most celebrated as well as severely critiqued music education practices—or methods—in the modern history of music education. In a fairly recent anthology on reflections and directions for the Schulwerk, Carlos Abril (2013) provides an overview of the Orff critique from an insider's perspective. His summary of the more recent critiques includes allegations about Orff methodology as a blind faith in a "technicist" method (Regelski, 2002), an inappropriate use of recapitulation theory (Walker, 2007) and the Orff methodology as a system for control and coercion (Benedict, 2009). What is strange to me is that none of the critiques focus on Carl Orff's original practice in the Günther Schule and their pioneering focus on creativity and improvisation. Neither do they pay attention to Carl Orff's statements in 1963 about how his intentions and practice "had been misinterpreted and falsified to the point of caricature" (Orff, 1963, p. 69). What I find even more interesting, and to some point alarming, is the lack of critique in Abril's review on the *pedagogical essence* of the originally intended and experienced practice, namely, the pedagogic and didactic principles of the Orff teaching philosophy, such as the shape of lesson designs, the principle from text to instruments, the role of improvisation, the systematic sequencing from the simple to the complex, the skills and knowledge needed to be a good Orff teacher and more. It is tempting to suggest that the lack of focus on the Orff pedagogy could signal a *lack of interest* from the academic music education scientific community in the part of the Orff system which can be associated with the actual craft of teaching, and the everyday practice music teachers find themselves embedded in.[9] However, the critique of the post-Schulwerk reviewed by

---

[8] Basil Bernstein's (2000) analysis of knowledge differentiates between horizontal and vertical discourse. Whereas horizontal discourse will often be characterised as tacit, oral and local, vertical discourse "takes the form of a coherent, explicit and systematically principled structure…", p. 157. I have not focused on the role of politics in the development of music education in this chapter. For those who might be interested I refer to Espeland (1997, 1999), and Fautley and Murphy (2016).

[9] To me, the innovative work of Carl Orff and his colleagues is an impressive and pioneering example of a music education practice of high quality. They should neither be blamed nor praised

Abril suggests that the Orff movement by many scholars is regarded as an example of a craft guild in itself with specific recipes and codes protecting a specific practice to such an extent that the initial openness to change and adaptation to a changing world might be neglected. Any such evaluation, however, must always be balanced and include the pedagogical and didactic essence as well as the philosophical rationale for the practice and ideology in question. I would not hesitate therefore to recommend the continued use of the Orff methodology in schools and other institutions, as long as it reflects the overall goals for education in the contexts and society in question and contains space for a dynamic interplay between the traditional and the innovative.

The Significance of the Creative and the Improvisational

One evening in the early 1990s, I found myself seated in a comfortable chair in professor John Paynter's charming home outside York, England. I was not the first freshman in international music education in his chair. John Paynter, an established composer of music, and maybe the most important pioneer and proponent of the composition movement, was motivated both by his own and children's feeling of pride and personal growth as human beings when creating their own music to share. His belief in composing as a vital and creative part of the profession we call music education was rooted in a deep understanding of educational composing as comprising both the generative, in terms of inventing musical ideas in a wide sense; the productive, in terms of taking the creative process towards a product; and the communicative, in terms of performing, expressing and sharing their own meanings and sentiments through their own composed music.[10] Not only did John Paynter influence a whole generation of British music teachers, he also understood that for music education to be a vital force in education, it needed to be rooted in research and development and be built as an international craft guild of professionals who were able to demonstrate as well as document their innovative practices. His writings, international work and video documentation of composing practices in schools found its way to all continents during the late 1970s and 1980s[11] and contributed

---

for what their followers might have developed, allegedly in their name and spirit, but be judged on their own achievements in challenging contexts and times.

[10] John Paynter's publications are numerous, see Paynter, (1992; 1997; 2002); Paynter and Aston (1970). Our talk, however, focused for the most part on questions about creativity connected to my then, quite recently published article on responsive music listening in the *British Journal of Music Education*. Paynter liked the idea of linking children's creative expressions in the arts, music included, to responsive music listening, but he had many questions about my research project leading to the article, and what kind of music could trigger both expressive creativity and guided conversation about the music in question (Espeland, 1987).

[11] In 2005, I was deeply involved in a local Norwegian music education project connected to Guatemala. Together with the South American music education organisation, FLADEM, we organised an international conference in Antigua, Guatemala, where I took part as a clinician and

significantly to an international common description of international school music as a three-part construction consisting of listening, performance and composing.

Despite John Paynter's, and others', pioneering work, composing as an educational way into musical and personal education has not been adopted as a common practice in schools worldwide, and even less in teacher education and higher music education studies. The reasons are probably complex and seem to consist of a combination of a general accountability pressure in schools, deficiencies in teacher competence in schools and higher education, and perhaps also what I would describe as elitist attitudes in the profession of musicians and higher music education.[12] The social and political focus on *creativity* in education is much stronger these days than in the pioneering time of the composition movement. For the past 20 years or so, creativity and innovation have increasingly become buzzwords in educational policy documents and in political and research rhetoric. In schools as well as teacher education, however, creativity in the shape of music composition and improvisation still seems to play a minor role.

Even if this is the case, recent initiatives by the Organisation for Economic Co-operation and Development (OECD) might bring about a significant change to this situation.[13] Five years ago, the OECD Centre for Educational Research and Innovation (CERI) initiated a project on creativity in schools that was both theory and practice oriented. The project also included extensive fieldwork as well as practices in a number of school subjects, including music. The third draft report of the project titled, *Fostering Students' Creativity and Critical Thinking: What it Means in School*, was published in the late autumn of 2019 (Vincent-Lancrin et al., 2019). The music education profession has grown accustomed to many kinds of politically driven reports over the last decades. As a dedicated member of our music education "craft guild", as it were, I have been repeatedly frustrated by OECD initiatives such as the Programme for International Student Assessment (PISA) which has weakened the arts, including music, in schools as well as in higher education.[14] So, could

---

where we met with 250 teachers from Central America. One of the other clinicians was the Argentinian music education pioneer, Professor Violeta Hemsy de Gainza (then aged 75). During a long chat about international music education in an unforgettable atmosphere, she told me about her inspiration from and stay with John Paynter. She gave me her published teaching material for her piano students, which to my surprise only consisted of her pupils' own music compositions.

[12] There is little research-based evidence for this assertion. The few studies we have in Norway show that composition exists as an activity in schools to some degree, but that teachers find this part of school music more challenging than other parts. My impression of elitism stems first and foremost from my own experience as an advocate for composing in schools in discussion with colleagues in the University sector.

[13] Some years ago, I visited the OECD main office in Paris. Even though I was aware of the OECD's increasing role as an influencer of national school policies all over the world, I was still surprised to see their huge role in national evaluations of education as well as being an advisory service commissioned by governments, including my own.

[14] The Program for International Student Assessment (PISA) is probably the single most influential initiative with respect to school policies throughout the world. Its results and conclusions have been decisive for school policies at an unprecedented level, especially for the so-called basics, i.e. reading and writing programmes. Critics have pointed out its shortcomings as well as its negative

this be yet another attack on our precious craft of music education or is this OECD initiative different? The most conspicuous aspect of this very interesting OECD publication is perhaps the subtitle, *What it Means in School*. Seemingly a new approach, seeing *creativity* and *critical thinking* as two sides of the same coin, might be equally interesting. "The sub-skills", the OECD informs us, "that need to be deployed for each competence involve imagining, inquiring, doing and reflecting" (p. 63). The authors go on to say that:

> Creativity puts more emphasis on imagining (brainstorming, generating ideas and alternatives), while critical thinking puts more emphasis on inquiring, including its more analytical and systematic dimension (understanding and decomposing the problem, etc.). Critical thinking is mainly inquisitive, a detective way of thinking: creative thinking is imaginative, the artist way of thinking. (p. 63)

Tempting as it can be, I will not go into a deeper analysis of this quote, but would like to mention that the report's focus on cognition and thinking, and a suggested divide between how artists and the rest of us work, resembles something I would like to call "myths". Instead, I will focus on OECD's somewhat inconspicuous intention of introducing "creativity" as a new major element of the PISA testing system by 2021. This could mean a new day—but certainly not a less complicated day—for creativity in our schools, and therefore also for music education. The report claims to build on a vast repertoire of theoretical as well as experiential knowledge from creative practices in several school subjects. Music is represented as well, surprisingly maybe, by an Orff inspired school music fieldwork and practice. The report presents a rubric demonstrating quite concretely what this could mean for educational activity in schools concerning creativity and connected critical thinking in music. Major overall concepts for the structuring the OECD rubric are inquiring "imagining", "doing" and "reflecting", and they are all organised in a matrix with "creativity" and "critical thinking", respectively. The music rubric, for example, exemplifies the concept of creative "doing" as pupils' being able to "perform, compose, or analyse music with expressive qualities or relating to personally meaningful subject matter", whereas the "critical thinking" aspect of "doing" is described as pupils being able to "explain both strengths and limitations of a performance, a composition or an analysis of a music piece" (p. 27). The rubric is clearly designed to describe pupil educational activities in the tradition of attainment targets claiming to reflect recent creativity theories and theories of critical thinking.

It might be possible to connect the Paynter-inspired tradition of *composing* in music education to the major concepts in the OECD rubric, for example, in the description of creativity as coming up with new ideas and solutions and the verbs chosen to categorise activities and processes. But, and this is a huge and critical but, do we as a music education craft guild really believe—or want—creativities (Burnard, 2012) to be embedded in musical schooling because of the significance for schools ostensibly driven by a politicised PISA tradition? And what about

---

effects on other parts of curricula, e.g. the Arts. In Norway, the PISA results for 2019 are lower than when it all started in 2002.

testing and measuring the creativity as well as the critical thinking of young people in school music?

By now, my readers will probably already understand my enthusiasm for creativity as a major pillar when discussing the rationale for music education as craft.[15] If not, let me briefly encourage the reader to consider what music as an artform would be—through craftsmanship of many kinds—without human generation of musical ideas, their expression and production and their communication and impact since the birth of humanity. How can any member of the profession of music education *not* be enthusiastic about creativity in music education, but at any cost? For now, let us turn briefly to improvisation, sometimes described as "creativity's little sister" (Holdhus, 2019).

Actor John Cleese, famous for his creative part in the Monty Python adventure, defines "improvisation" as "a way of operating" in situations where one has to respond to something or someone in the spur of the moment.[16] I think this is a very simple, as well as sophisticated, way of explaining improvisation as a phenomenon fits very well with my conception of improvisation as a specific aspect of creative music making as well as in creative teaching, i.e. when operating as an open-minded, attentive and responsive music teacher. John Cleese's definition can also be applied to our improvisation in everyday life situations. To me however, improvisation is also an artistic, scientific and educational concept deeply embedded in the profession of music and music education, not only because it is a natural part of musical and artistic creation but also because I think it should be used and applied to a much greater extent than hitherto as *pedagogical* improvisation.

Recently, I had the privilege of acting as principal researcher in a comprehensive research study on improvisation in teaching together with a number of colleagues from music, other curriculum subjects and educational theory.[17] One of our first comprehensive discussions was on whether improvisation in teaching could be taught and learned or whether it just happened naturally, so to speak, in teaching situations where one had to find a solution to some kind of challenge or problem. The music people in the research group took their arguments from musical improvisation and argued that improvisation in teaching could and should be prepared as

---

[15] In 1997, I co-published the first music education resource book in Norway on *Composing in the Music Classroom* with my colleagues. This was instrumental for the choice of the theme for my PhD with the title, *Compositional Process as Discourse and Interaction*. My PhD is an open access publication as Espeland, M. (2007). *Compositional process as discourse and interaction: A study of small group music composition processes in a school context*, and can be accessed at hvlopen. brage.unit.no

[16] John Cleese has given a number on talks on creativity based on his acting and comedy experience for university students in education as well as business. Some of them are available on YouTube. My quote from him here is taken from https://www.youtube.com/watch?v=Gg-6LtfB5JA, accessed 20.01.20.

[17] The project, *Improvisation in Teacher Education* (2013–2017), was funded by the Norwegian Research Council and has produced a number of results described in articles, e.g. Holdhus et al. (2016); Mæland and Espeland (2017); Aadland, Espeland, and Arnesen (2017); Holdhus (2019); Espeland and Stige (2017); Espeland, Kvile, and Holdhus (2019).

well as rehearsed in much the same way as musical improvisation had to be rehearsed and prepared. Others in the research group used their experience from everyday life and argued that improvisation was only used when no other solution to a challenge was available and that the ability to improvise was rooted in personalities. Important findings in the project concluded that professional improvisation in education and teaching had four major characteristics:

- Professional improvisation in education and teaching involves interactive communication and dialogues;
- Structure and design dimensions are important in improvisational practices;
- Professional improvisation relies on learnable repertoires and the spontaneous use of ideas and examples;
- Professional improvisational practices are context dependent and domain specific to a great extent. (Holdhus et al., 2016).

To me, improvisation is one of several music concepts that can operate meaningfully far beyond music making. Just as in music making, it is a way of operating as a craftsperson, which is highly relevant for any kind of teaching. Improvisation should therefore be systematically embedded in our thinking about teaching in music, as well as in other subjects.

Characteristics of pedagogical improvisation, such as the ones researched and described above, make the concept of improvisation operational. It *is* possible to focus on interactive communication and dialogue, structure and design with space for improvisation and spontaneity in the use of ideas and examples in music teaching, and it *is* possible to prepare and train music teacher students in these skills. In the art of teaching, any teacher who wants to meet the student where she/he *is* needs to prepare professionally for the unexpected. Education and being a teacher *is* to be part of uncertainty, but in a constructive way where the teacher's way of operating as a listener, partner and adviser is crucial. Few have coined this uncertainty better than Gert Biesta (2015) in his book and phrase, *The Beautiful Risk of Education*. To be involved in education then should be a process, which at the start as well as during the process is partly hidden to us. How boring would it not be if children, students or teachers at a certain point in time would know everything that we at the beginning of a learning or teaching process did not know? Two years ago, I put myself in a position of educational and social uncertainty. I have been trying to learn a new instrument, the violin (or rather, fiddle) with my young grandson as my teacher.

The Significance of the Material and the Embodied

My motivation for starting to play the fiddle at my age is surprisingly (at least to me) similar to Eva Sæther's theme and research question in her article in this volume: *How is meaningful aging connected to musical learning?* I have never played the fiddle, but possess an old violin bought at a flea market in Budapest some 25 years ago. My grandson, now 17, is an able fiddle player and why not, I thought at the time, engage this 15-year-old young boy as my teacher. It would add another dimension to a sort of combined family and learning quasi-experiment. After 2 years of activity, our weekly sessions have become really fun and my repertoire is increasing week by week. The teacher seems to enjoy the situation too even if unskilled as a music teacher. The most surprising outcome of this meaningful ageing with regard to learning, however, is the extent to which I increasingly have familiarised myself with the physicality of the instrument and playing on or with it—its wood, curves, the relationship between my arms and shoulders and the moving of the bow, etc. Even if I am familiar with this kind of embodied experience as a flute player, the materiality of the fiddle has become embedded in my whole body in a very different way from my flute experience. Tiny bodily adjustments all over the place seem to mean a lot for the sound and my musical expression. Even as an aging musician, I seem to be able to fall in love with the materiality and personality of the instrument, wondering what kind of life this instrument has lived, and whether it has an agenda of its own, especially when the sounds coming from my playing, approach something that is musically acceptable.

Along with my new fiddle experience, I have been reading post-humanist and new materialist theory. It might be possible of course that my reading has influenced my self-observation as a learner of a new instrument and certainly my relationship to it. What this combination of reading and playing a new instrument at my age has fuelled, however, is my thinking about the role and significance of materiality and embodiment when considering "music education as craft". It would be a gross exaggeration to suggest that focusing on the material and the body are new considerations to the profession of music education. In the teaching of the violin, methods books since Geminiani's (1751) treatise on *The Art of Playing the Violin*, demonstrate continuously discussions about the relationship between expressive music making and the material characteristics of the best way to play expressively and meaningfully—including considerations about bowing, arm, grip and finger movement (Weiss & Taruskin, 2007, p. 222). Newer and well-known examples are the focus on embodiment and specially designed musical instruments as a basis for learning of music, e.g. in the Dalcroze, Orff and Suzuki music methods. The antidualist philosophy of Merleau-Ponty has also profoundly influenced music education as a profession over the last decades, even to such a degree that American professor, Liora Bresler, in her 2013 edited book, *Knowing Bodies, Moving Minds*, addresses the relevance of this topic for education as a "paradigm of embodiment". According to Bresler, embodiment can be described as "integration of the physical or biological body and phenomenal or experiential body suggesting a seamless though often-elusive matrix of body/mind worlds, a web that integrates thinking, being, doing and interacting within worlds" (p. 7).[18]

---

[18] In Liora Bresler's (2007) *International Handbook of Research in Arts Education*, Wayne Bowman and Kimberly Powell (2007) argue convincingly that "music is distinctively, perhaps uniquely, a form of embodied agency; the unity of the body-mind is a fact that musical experience demonstrates vividly, compellingly, irrefutably" (p. 1101).

Both before and after the publication of Bresler's handbook, numerous writers have added to our knowledge about the importance of an embodied understanding and practice of educational practices. Mark Johnson (2007), for example, drawing on contemporary sciences of mind in biology, cognitive neuroscience and cognitive linguistics, argues that "meaning is exclusively grounded in our bodily experience", that "reason is an embodied process", that "imagination is tied to our bodily process…" and that "reason and emotion are inextricably intertwined" (pp. 11–14). Meaning, reason, imagination and emotion are key aspects of any shape and form of *musical* education and have been so for a long time. So, what does post-humanist theory and new materialism philosophy bring to our discussion of music education as craft?

Post-humanist theory and, in particular, new materialist and socio-materialist theory raise a number of issues which to me seem to be very relevant for the understanding and practices of music education conceived of as craft. In their edited book, *Posthuman Research Practices in Education* (2016), Carol A. Taylor and Christina Hughes, observe that what they call "…the post-qualitative turn, new empiricisms, and new feminist materialism with the interest in ecological perspectives, are all manifestations of a rapidly growing engagement with post-humanism" (p. 1). This movement, if that is what it may be called, consists of, to put it mildly, a great variety of theoretical approaches and directions, including new materialism (Braidotti, 2010), actor network theory (Latour, 1993), posthuman performativity and agential realism (Barad, 2003), assemblage theory (Deleuze & Guattari, 1988) and concepts such as thing power, intra-action, rhizome, apparatus, diffraction, vibrant matter and materialisation, plus "others I don't know about" as Taylor puts it. However, they all agree about the necessity of *the de-centring of human beings* in all we do and understand. With regard to educational research as well as practice, Taylor and Hughes argue that putting posthuman theory to work in research and practice "…is both exciting and daunting. Post-humanism invites us (humans) to undo the current ways of doing – and then imagine, invent and do the doing differently" (p. 6).

Viewing music education as craft, we are all aware of the centrality of "doing", not only in various forms of musicking, to use Small's (1998) famous concept, but also in the way we carry out and focus our attention in research enterprises. For some time, we have been observing the increasing technological materialisation of music and music education brought about by all sort of new "things" available to us and to young people, creating new environments for music learning and appreciation and new conceptions of concerting and communicating. However, the centrality of matter and our relationship to "things" and "bodies in action" is not a new or strange idea to music lovers, performers, teachers and researchers.[19] But it is possible, that we have focused too much on the human-to-human actions and interactions, and on cultural and social aspects of learning and education, and not enough

---

[19] True, it can be argued that music education has, to some extent, focused too much on music theory, chord progression, notation and analysis. I have previously referred to such a focus as the "rationalification" of music and music education (Espeland, 2011, p. 165).

on the significance for musical learning and understanding of the intra-action and interaction of things, physical environments and human beings.

Advocating a social-materialist approach to learning, Tara Fenwick and Monica Nerland adopt what I will call "an additive approach" to post-humanist and new materialist theories. In their edited book, *Reconceptualising Learning: Sociomaterial knowledges, practices and responsibilities* (2014), they argue that "professional learning itself has conventionally been treated as an individual and person-centred process, related to personal experience as well as acquisition of disciplinary and problem-solving competencies in knowing what to do, how and why" (p. 3). And they continue:

> Countering this individualist 'acquisitional' metaphor, situated and sociocultural views introduced some time ago a 'participational' metaphor for learning. These views emphasised the importance of environment, rules, tools and social relations; they showed that knowing is always situated in activity and therefore is particular to settings and communities…Pushing this line of enquiry still further, a critical dynamic is materiality itself. Material forces—flesh and blood, forms and checklists, diagnostic machines and databases, furniture and passcodes, snowstorms and dead cellphone zones—are integral in shaping professional practice as a repertoire of routines as well as the particular knowing, decisions and actions that are enacted in any local instantiation of practice. Yet materiality is often overlooked or dismissed in analyses of professional practice and knowing….Human activity, of course, also comprises the 'social': symbols and meanings, desires and fears, politics and cultural discourses. Both material and social forces are mutually implicated in bringing forth everyday activities. (Fenwick & Nerland, 2014, p. 3)

Adopting a critical, but also open minded, additive approach to new waves of theory, which, by the way, hit music education regularly, is exactly what music education needs to do in order to survive, develop and prosper as a craft. What post-humanist and socio-material theory will mean for teaching as well as for the research practices of music education remains, for a great part, to be seen. Even if so, few other disciplines or crafts should be better equipped to focus on matter, materialisation, and embodied practices. To me, an additive approach to new sets of theories means that we should not throw away the useful insights and beliefs, established theories of ontology and epistemology in the way socio-culturalism and phenomenology have given us. However, opening up to the inclusion of post-humanist and socio-material theories, we might need to shift our focus and reconsider the rationale for music education teaching as well as research practices quite a bit. Such a shift could imply a number of new initiatives and trajectories, such as (i) studying musicians' or children's bodily interactions not only with or on the apparatus we call musical instruments, but within a much broader scope and physical and material environment; (ii) a renewed research focus on how musical works are materialised by artist and/or young people, and how such activity may affect their environments; (iii) a renewed and broader focus on the significance and role of physical learning environments and how such learning environments relate to sustainability challenges; and (iv) a much stronger focus on material teaching resources, including technological resources, how they shape, or challenge a doxa of existing beliefs or how they might undermine quality music education, and how the dynamism and effects of these units, including human beings, to use Fenwick and Nerland's words are "performed into existence in webs of relations" (p. 3).[20]

The Significance of the Democratic and the Relational

Early in 2020, I attended a music education research conference in Copenhagen. One of the days, I gave myself a break and visited the Copenhagen Glyptotek, an art museum which—with its world class collection of sculptures, art and antiquities— claims to offer new perspectives on human existence, craftsmanship, culture and civilisation as seen through 6000 years of art. In the museum shop I came across a fairly recent book by Thomas N. Mitchell (2019) titled, *Athens: A History of the World's First Democracy*, which became my reading companion on my return flight to Norway. Mitchell makes a point about the fact that global democracy as a way of organising and operating national states seems to be on the decline globally and that the prime issue about democracy is not whether people have the right to vote or elect their leaders. Rather, he claims, democracy, as it developed in ancient Athens, is:

> … an ideology, a set of political ideals derived from a particular view of the nature, dignity and social needs of human beings. The procedures and institutions of democracy are dictated by these ideals, designed to make them a reality. It is these ideals that form the defining character of democracy. Their realization is the end, the procedures and institutions are their means. (Mitchell, 2019, p. 3)

To a dedicated Deweyan like me, this does not come as a surprise. However, Mitchell's warning has a direct and very relevant significance for our discussion about music education as craft and the extent to which this craft of ours can be an institution in society and education, contributing as a means to uphold democracy as an ideology. John Dewey's ideas about democracy and education are now more than 100 years old. His basic tenet is that the small world of schools should be equal to the big world of society with responsibilities for its citizens, and both should therefore be democratic, securing the sustainability of nature, and the dignity and social needs of human beings. Dewey's book *Democracy and Education* was published in 1916, and it is hardly a coincidence that David Elliott, Marissa Silverman and Wayne Bowman published their newest edited book on *Artistic Citizenship. Artistry, Social Responsibility and Ethical Praxis* in 2016, probably conceived of as a 100-year celebration and continuation of Dewey's worldwide contribution to democracy in education. Elliott, Silverman and Bowman introduce readers to the concept of "artistic citizenship" which they hope will "…encapsulate our belief that

---

[20] In 2003, I published a chapter related to my ongoing PhD study in a book previously referred to in this chapter and edited by Maud Hickey: *How and why to teach Music Composition: New Horizons for Music Education* (Hickey, 2003). The title of my chapter opened with "The African Drum…" and was written as a reflection on a young pupil's interaction with a djembe. I knew nothing about new materialist theory at that time but realise in hindsight the importance of materiality in what I then researched with socio-constructivist lenses (Espeland, M. 2003).

artistry involves civic-social-humanistic-emancipatory responsibilities, obligations to engage in art making that advances social 'goods'" (p. 7).

In their introduction, the authors also pay homage to Dewey's work referring to his life-long commitment of arguing for the *"need to integrate art making and art taking* (whether by amateurs, professionals, or teachers) *with personal and community life"* (p. 5 [emphasis in original]). Referring to Dewey's *Art as Experience* (1934), the authors argue that "Art's importance stems from the effectiveness with which it is 'put to work' in the realisation of a variety of overlapping and interwoven human values or 'goods'" (p. 6). They go on to say that "the notion of resident or intrinsic value is not just misguided, but seriously misleading" (p. 6).

Wandering among the ancient sculptures in the Copenhagen Glyptotek, my experience shifted between two modes, so to speak. On the one hand, I could admire the excellent craftsmanship being displayed in works of art throughout human history, wondering about the craftsmen, processes, organisation and environments of their creation, and on the other hand I could feel that the objects of art surrounding me spoke to me irrespective of time and contexts. In *Art as Experience*, Dewey does not *only* argue for the integration of arts into community life: he also celebrates the intrinsic quality of art works, and I think this explains my feeling of communicating with the art pieces at the Glyptotek:

> Because the objects of arts are expressive, they communicate. I do not say that communication to others is the intent of an artist. But it is the consequence of his work—which indeed lives only in communication when it operates in the experience of others. (Dewey, 1934. p. 104)

So what would Dewey's response be to the idea of "artistic citizenship" as a major aspect of a democratic music education worthy of occupying a space in my selected topos of significance in our discussion about a re-framed rationale for music education seen as craft? I am pretty sure he would have appreciated such an initiative, but on certain conditions. In his 1910 book, *How we think*, (Dewey, 1910), he writes:

> That teaching is an art and the true teacher an artist is a familiar saying. Now the teacher's own claim to rank as an artist is measured by his ability to foster the attitude of the artist in those who study with him, whether they be youth or little children. Some succeed in arousing enthusiasm, in communicating large ideas, in evoking energy. So far, well; but the final test is whether the stimulus thus given to wider aims succeeds in transforming itself into power, that is to say, into the attention to detail that ensures mastery over means of execution" (p. 220)

What Dewey suggests here, I think, is that an artistic teacher responding to the concept of "artistic citizenship" needs to find a proper balance between "the wider aims" and the "details that ensures mastery over the means of execution". Such a balance is crucial in our thinking about music education as craft, because at the same time, it honours craftsmanship as well as an alert awareness of the bigger questions concerning our future as a civilisation built on the ideals of democracy—sustainability, dignity and the social needs of human beings.

I have argued elsewhere that music education, and particularly general school music, to a greater extent than hitherto, needs to adopt what is often called a relational pedagogy (Holdhus & Espeland, 2018). The relational turn in education and in the arts fits well with democracy as an overall ideology and the call to adopt "artistic citizenship" as a guiding principle in our teaching approaches as well as in our care for a sound development of our society (Dewey 1916). Togetherness, and the power to act together in democratic and ethical ways, is crucial for music education as craft if we aim to contribute to sustainable solutions to our common challenges in our time. As I see it, if anything has been and is destructive to craft guilds—such as music education—it is the development of these guilds into hierarchical systems with unhealthy relations between its members, often developed in the name of protection and preservation, and not very conducive to innovation and the ideals of democracy.[21]

Concluding Remarks

In the opening invitation to this book, the editorial group quoted my call to respond to some basic questions about the future of music education, considered as craft in a changing world. The questions I pose are introduced by question words such as, How? What kind of? For what reasons? And to what ends? Such questions may be regarded as a belief in ready-made universal educational and organisational solutions to very complex challenges. This has in no way been my intention, because universal and ready-made solutions will cease to be solutions if they do not adapt to human as well as non-human developments and contexts. But this does not mean that the solutions—educational, organisational, and/or political—to music education challenges, which we have seen and/or advocated over a long period of time, have not added to our repertoire and reservoir of horizontal and vertical knowledge structures. Our common efforts and achievements are a knowledge base we can critique, modify, use, copy, discard, praise or add to. As a music education craft and possibly "craft guild", we should never belittle or disregard such a knowledge base because it is the very basis of our *kraptr*. This knowledge, then, positions music educators as members of a *common* craft, hopefully with a vision of being a dynamic, well grounded, innovative as well as critical and self-critical craft *guild*. I

---

[21] New research on the history of craft guilds shows that they were very influential in society and "not just as European phenomenon, but were prominent all over northern Africa and the Middle East, as well as in many parts of Asia, including China and Japan. They existed in Latin America too" (Lucassen, De Moor, & Van Zanden, 2008, p. 8). Guilds, however, offer numerous examples of societies which failed to foster democratic ideals and which suffered breakdowns. The hierarchical relationship between master masons, apprentices and journeymen was probably well designed to uphold the quality of craftsmanship, but vulnerable to political and industrial changes and challenges.

hope and believe—maybe I could even say know—that this book will be one of many contributions to keep this vision alive.

In this closing chapter of this book, my contribution has been to focus on a what I have called "common topos of significance" when considering music education as craft. I have been given the privilege of bringing to the rationale table aspects of music education for a number of different reasons, including my 50 years of practical and theoretical experience in the field. I have described these aspects as (i) the significance of a dynamic interplay between the traditional and the innovative in our approach to music education practices; (ii) the significance of the creative and the improvisational in teaching as well as in learning processes; (iii) the significance of the material, and embodied practices in teaching as well as in learning environments; and finally, (iv) the significance of the relational and the democratic in our dealings with learners and colleagues. I have argued that it is of the utmost significance to foster, develop, discuss and critique these aspects of music education in order to maintain, develop, and perhaps even to reframe, a sustainable rationale for music education in a changing world.

References

Åadland, H., Espeland, M., & Arnesen, T. E. (2017). Towards a typology of improvisation as a professional teaching skill: Implications for pre-service teacher education programmes. *Cogent Education, 4*(1), 1295835. Hong Kong

Abril, C. (2013). Critical issues in Orff Schulwerk. In C. Wang & D. G. Springer (Eds.), *Orff Schulwerk: Reflections and directions* (pp. 11–24). GIA.

Barad, K. (2003). Posthumanist performativity: Toward an understanding of how matter comes to matter. *Signs: Journal of Women in Culture and Society, 28*(3), 801–831.

Barrett, M. (1998). Researching children's compositional processes and products. In B. Sundin, G. E. McPherson, & G. Folkestad (Eds.), *Children composing* (pp. 10–34). Malmö Academy of Music, Lund University, Sweden.

Benedict, C. (2009). Processes of alienation: Marx, Orff and Kodály. *British Journal of Music Education, 26*(2), 213–224.

Bernstein, B. (2000). *Pedagogy, symbolic control, and identity: Theory, research, critique.* Lanham, Maryland: Rowman & Littlefield.

Biesta, G. J. (2015). *The beautiful risk of education.* New York: Routledge.

Bowman, W., & Powell, K. (2007). The body in a state of music. In L. Bresler (Ed.), *International handbook of research in arts education* (pp. 1087–1108). Dordrecht, NL: Springer.

Braidotti, R. (2010). The politics of 'life itself' and new ways of dying. *New materialisms: Ontology, agency, and politics, 201*–220.

Bresler, L. (2007). *International handbook of research in arts education.* Dordrecht, NL: Springer.

Bresler, L. (2013). *Knowing bodies, moving minds: Towards embodied teaching and learning.* Dordrecht, NL: Springer.

Burnard, P. (2012). *Musical creativities in practice.* Oxford: Oxford University Press.

Colwell, R. (1992). *The new handbook of research on music teaching and learning.* Oxford: MENC/OUP.

Cox, G., & Stevens, R. (2017). *The origins and foundations of music education: International perspectives.* New York: Bloomsbury Publishing.

Deleuze, E. G., & Guattari, F. (1988). *A thousand plateaus: Capitalism and schizophrenia* (B. Masumi, Trans., Minneapolis. 1987). London: Continuum.

Dewey, J. (1910). *How we think*. Lexington, Massachusetts: DC Heath.

Dewey, J. (1916). *Democracy and education: An introduction to the philosophy of education*. New York: Macmillan.

Dewey, J. (1934/2005). *Art as experience*. New York: Penguin.

Elliott, D., Silverman, M., & Bowman, W. (Eds.). (2016). *Artistic citizenship: Artistry, social responsibility, and ethical praxis*. Oxford: Oxford University Press.

Espeland, Å., Kvile, S., & Holdhus, K. (2019). Teacher agency and teacher improvisation: A study of experienced teachers and student teachers in music classrooms. *Research Studies in Music Education*, 1321103X19861003.

Espeland, Å., & Stige, B. (2017). The teacher as co-musician: Exploring practices in music teaching. *International Journal of Education & the Arts, 18*(22).

Espeland, M. (1987). Music in use: Responsive music listening in the primary school. *British Journal of Music Education, 4*(3), 283–297.

Espeland, M. (1997). Once upon a time there was a minister: An unfinished story about reform in Norwegian arts education. *Arts Education Policy Review, 99*(1), 11–16.

Espeland, M. (1999). Curriculum reforms in Norway: An insider's perspective. *Arts and Learning Research, 15*(1), 172–187.

Espeland, M. (2003). The African drum: Compositional process as discourse and interaction in a school context. In M. Hickey (Ed.), *How and why to teach music composition: New horizons for music education*. MENC.

Espeland, M. (2007). Compositional process as discourse and interaction: A study of small group music composition processes in a school context. Doctoral Thesis: Danish University of Education.

Espeland, M. (2011). A century of music listening in schools: Towards practices resonating with cultural psychology. In M. Barrett (Eds.), *A cultural psychology of music education* (pp. 144–178). Oxford University Press

Fautley, M., & Murphy, R. (2016). Music education in a time of austerity. *British Journal of Music Education, 33*(1), 1–3.

Fenwick, T., & Nerland, M. (Eds.). (2014). *Reconceptualising professional learning: Sociomaterial knowledges, practices and responsibilities*. London: Routledge.

Geminiani, F. (1751). *Treatise on the art of playing the violin*. Author.

Hickey, M. (Ed.). (2003). *How and why to teach music composition: New horizons for music education*. Reston, Virginia: MENC, US.

Holdhus, K. (2019). Pedagogical improvisation: Musical improvisation's little sister? In G. G. Johansen, K. Holdhus, C. Larsson, & U. MacGlone (Eds.), *Expanding the space for improvisation pedagogy in music: A transdisciplinary approach* (pp. 195–210). Routledge.

Holdhus, K., & Espeland, M. (2018). Music in future Nordic schooling. *European Journal of Philosophy in Arts Education (EJPAE), 2*(2), 85–118.

Holdhus, K., Høisæter, S., Mæland, K., Vangsnes, V., Engelsen, K. S., Espeland, M., et al. (2016). Improvisation in teaching and education: Roots and implications. *Cogent Education, 3*, 1204142.

Johnson, M. (2007). *The meaning of the body*. Hove, East Sussex: Psychology Press.

Jorgensen, E. R. (2003). *Transforming music education*. Bloomington, Indiana: Indiana University Press.

Kaipayil, J. (2009). *Relationalism: A theory of being*. Bangalore, India: JIP Publications.

Latour, B. (1993/2012). *We have never been modern*. Cambridge, Massachusetts: Harvard University Press.

Lucassen, J., De Moor, T., & Van Zanden, J. L. (2008). *The return of the guilds: Towards a global history of the guilds in preindustrial times*. https://www.researchgate.net/publication/46711032. Accessed 13 July 2020.

MacPherson, S. (1910). *The appreciative aspects of music-study: Some thoughts and suggestions.* London: Joseph Williams.

MacPherson, S. (1912). *Modern ideas in the teaching of harmony.* London: Joseph Williams.

Macpherson, S. (1915). *The musical education of the child: Some thoughts and suggestions for teachers, parents and schools.* London: Joseph Williams.

Mæland, K., & Espeland, M. (2017). Teachers' conceptions of improvisation in teaching: Inherent human quality or a professional teaching skill? *Education Inquiry, 8*(3), 192–208.

Mitchell, T. N. (2019). *Athens: A history of the world's first democracy.* London: Yale University Press.

Orff, C. (1963). The Schulwerk: Its origin and aims. *Music Educators Journal, 49*(5), 69–74.

Paynter, J. (1992). *Sound & structure.* Cambridge, UK: Cambridge University Press.

Paynter, J. (1997). The form of finality: A context for musical education. *British Journal of Music Education, 14*(1), 5–21.

Paynter, J. (2002). Music in the school curriculum: Why bother? *British Journal of Music Education, 19*(3), 215–226.

Paynter, J., & Aston, P. (1970). *Sound and silence: Classroom projects in creative music.* Cambridge: Cambridge University Press.

Regelski, T. (2002). On "methodolatry" and music teaching as critical and reflective praxis. *Philosophy of Music Education Review, 10*(2), 102–123.

Schafer, R. M. (1965). *The composer in the classroom.* Scarborough, Ontario: Berandol Music.

Schafer, R. M. (1969). *The new soundscape: A handbook for the modern music teacher.* Scarborough, Ontario: Berandol Music.

Small, C. (1998). *Musicking: The meanings of performing and listening.* Middletown, CT: Wesleyan University Press.

Taylor, C. A. (2016). Edu-crafting a cacophonous ecology: Posthumanist research practices for education. In C. A. Taylor & C. Hughes (Eds.), *Posthuman research practices in education* (pp. 5–24). London: Palgrave Macmillan.

Vincent-Lancrin, S., Gonalez-Sancho, C., Bouckaert, M., de Luca, F., Fernández-Barrerra, M., Jacotin, G., et al. (2019). *Fostering students' creativity and critical thinking: What it means in school.* Educational Research and Innovation, OECD Publishing. https://doi.org/10.1787/62212c37-en

Walker, R. (2007). *Music education: Cultural values, social change and innovation.* Springfield, IL: Charles C Thomas Publisher.

Weiss, P., & Taruskin, R. (2007). *Music in the western world.* Boston, Mass: Cengage Learning.

Wikipedia. (2020, July). *Anthropocene.* https://en.wikipedia.org/wiki/Anthropocene

Lightning Source UK Ltd.
Milton Keynes UK
UKHW020728110522
402816UK00006B/558